Fractal
Repair

Fractal

Perverse
Modernities

A series edited by
Jack Halberstam
+ Lisa Lowe

Repair

Queer Histories of
Modern Jamaica
Matthew Chin

Duke
University
Press

*Durham +
London*
2024

Project Editor: Erin Davis
Designed by Aimee C. Harrison
Typeset in Minion Pro and Avara (by Raphaël Bastide) by
Westchester Publishing Services

Library of Congress Cataloging-in-Publication Data
Names: Chin, Matthew, [date] author.
Title: Fractal repair : queer histories of modern Jamaica /
Matthew Chin.
Other titles: Perverse modernities.
Description: Durham : Duke University Press, 2024. | Series: Perverse
modernities | Includes bibliographical references and index.
Identifiers: LCCN 2023033372 (print)
LCCN 2023033373 (ebook)
ISBN 9781478030225 (paperback)
ISBN 9781478025986 (hardcover)
ISBN 9781478059233 (ebook)
Subjects: LCSH: Gay Freedom Movement (Jamaica) | Sexual
minorities—Jamaica—Historiography. | Homosexuality—
Jamaica—Historiography. | Homophobia—Jamaica. | Gays—
Violence against—Jamaica. | Human rights—Jamaica.
Classification: LCC HQ76.45.J25 C45 2024 (print) | LCC HQ76.45.J25
(ebook) | DDC 306.76097292—dc23/eng/20230911
LC record available at https://lccn.loc.gov/2023033372
LC ebook record available at https://lccn.loc.gov/2023033373

Cover art by Aimee C. Harrison.

Publication of this book is supported by Duke University Press's
Scholars of Color First Book Fund.

Contents

Acknowledgments

In the seven years of its making, this project has incurred debts that I cannot hope to repay. The book would not exist without Donette Francis, Faith Smith, and Deborah Thomas, whose support for this project has been steadfast and unfailing. Their feedback, advice, suggestions, and introductions to other scholars were pivotal in shaping this project as it changed over many years. Thank you to Faith and Deborah as well as Anjali Arondekar and Jafari Allen for workshopping the manuscript with me prior to its submission to Duke. The insights that this gathering generated were invaluable in clarifying and focusing the book's main interventions. Charles (Val) Carnegie, Timothy Chin, Kanika Batra, and Jeff Albanese generously reviewed and offered comments on previous drafts of different book chapters. Conversations with Tracy Robinson, Moji Anderson, Geeta Patel, Kath Weston, Honor Ford-Smith, and Matthew Smith were also indispensable to this book's formation. The intellectual fellowship and support of the Caribbean-as-Method Working Group (Kelly Baker Josephs, Tzarina Prater, Janelle Rodriques, and Ronald Cummings) and the Jamaica Cultural Political Modern Project (convened by David Scott, Donette Francis, Deborah Thomas, and Don Robotham) inspired and helped me to find joy and camaraderie in the research and writing process.

I am grateful to those who shared and trusted me with their life stories, analytical perspectives, and personal contacts. The kindness and generosity they showed me was central to the project's success. Given the different kinds of violences that can accompany the revelation of identities around gender and sexual difference broadly conceived, the choice that some of these people made to remain anonymous in this project is understandable. I hope that this work contributes to conditions that allow them to receive the acknowledgment that they deserve in the future. Thank you to the former participants of Jamaica's Gay Freedom Movement (GFM) who spoke with me, including

Laurence (Larry) Chang and Donna Smith as well as those who chose not to be named. Thank you also to Marjorie Whylie, Bridget Spaulding, Judith Wedderburn, and Tony Wilson, who shared their experiences of living and working with Jamaica's National Dance Theatre Company (NDTC) during its early years. I am honored and humbled to have interviewed three other NDTC members from this period before their recent passing—Barry Moncrieffe, Bert Rose, and Barbara Requa. Finally, thank you to those named and un-named individuals who discussed their experiences of the initial period of Jamaica's HIV/AIDS epidemic. These individuals included health care work-ers, such as Dr. Peter Figueroa, Dr. Tina Hylton-Kong, and Dr. Peter Weller; activists, such as Ian McKnight and Christine English—and those infected and affected by HIV/AIDS. Whether participating in the first gay activist organization, the formation of a local dance-theater tradition, or respond-ing to a new deadly disease, all the people that I spoke to in this study were part of important transformations in Jamaican society in ways that I came to deeply respect.

This project was made possible by the support of administrators and staff at various library and archival institutions in Jamaica, the United States, and Canada. I am grateful to Tricia Lawrence Powell and the incredible staff at the National Library of Jamaica for their help over the many years of this proj-ect. Thank you to Marlon Simms, who allowed me to access NDTC's archive and to participate in the company's dance classes. I am especially grateful to NDTC's archivist Mark Phinn for his assistance in navigating the company's voluminous materials. Thank you to Dr. Tina Hylton-Kong, who arranged for me to have access to the historical materials of the Epidemiological Research and Training Unit; Lois Hue, who allowed me to review the Jamaican Red Cross materials addressing HIV/AIDS in the 1980s and 1990s; Ian McKnight, who facilitated my access to the library of Jamaica AIDS Support; and Maxine Wedderburn, who graciously let me look at some of the earlier HIV/AIDS research reports from Hope Enterprises. Larry Chang's permission to view his personal archive was essential to the book's last chapter on the GFM. The support of the Caribbean International Resource Network (IRN) and espe-cially Vidya Kissoon made it possible to digitize and post items from Chang's GFM archive on the Digital Library of the Caribbean. Staff at the following organizations also provided invaluable research support to this project: the Schomburg Center for Research on Black Culture (Cheryl Beredo), the New York Library of the Performing Arts, the Jamaica National Family Planning Board Library, the Jamaica Ministry of Health Library, the Special Collec-tions of the Library of the University of the West Indies, the Kingston and

St. Andrew Public Library, the ArQuives, the Toronto Reference Library, and the IHLIA LGBT Heritage Archives.

This project has benefited from extensive intellectual exchange. Many thanks to my colleagues for their generous feedback on earlier versions of parts of this book in the Department of Women Gender and Sexuality and the Caribbean Studies Network at the University of Virginia, as well as in the Graduate School of Social Service and the Interdisciplinary African and African American Studies Faculty Seminar at Fordham University. The Black, Brown, and Queer Studies fellowship and several invitations to present my work were also key to the project's formation. These included talks organized by Faith Smith in the Department of African and African American Studies at Brandeis University; Shamus Khan and Wallace Best in the Program in Gender and Sexuality Studies at Princeton University; Kareem Khubchandani in the Department for Studies in Race, Colonialism and Diaspora at Tufts University; and Hugo Benavides, Vivian Lu, and Julius Bowditch in the Department of Anthropology at Fordham University. I am grateful for invitations to share earlier parts of this work at gatherings coordinated by Anthony Bogues, Ronald Cummings, and Honor Ford-Smith at York University; Jallicia Jolly and Watufani Poe at Amherst College, and the Jamaica Cultural Political Modern Project at the University of Pennsylvania; in addition to online symposiums hosted by the Caribbean Digital, and the Caribbean IRN. The book's progress was also aided by supportive listeners at meetings of the Caribbean Studies Association, the Association of Caribbean Historians, the Center for the Study of Africa and the African Diaspora, and the Beyond Homophobia and Pride Jamaica Conferences.

Ken Wissoker, thank you for your enthusiastic support for the project. My deepest appreciation goes to Faith Smith, who graciously identified herself as one of the manuscript reviewers. Her extraordinary contributions to this book at different stages of its development are immeasurable. Thank you also to the other anonymous reviewer for their engagement and helpful comments. Any errors, omissions, or mistakes in the book are entirely my own.

Research support from the College of Arts and Sciences and the Department of Women Gender and Sexuality Studies at the University of Virginia, as well as from Fordham University and the Graduate School of Social Services at Fordham University funded and resourced this study. Earlier versions of sections of what follows were previously published as "Constructing 'Gaydren': The Transnational Politics of Same Sex Desire in 1970s and 1980s Jamaica," *Small Axe* 23, no. 2 (2019): 17–33; "Antihomosexuality and Nationalist Critique in Late Colonial Jamaica: Revisiting the 1951 Police Enquiry," *Small Axe* 24, no. 3 (2020): 81–96; "Tracing Gay Liberation through Post Independence Jamaica," *Public Culture* 31, no. 2 (2019): 323–42; and "Queering Chinese Crossings in Late Twentieth Century Jamaica: Larry Chang and the Gay Freedom Movement," *Interventions* 24, no. 8 (2022): 1309–27.

Lastly, I want to thank my family and friends. I am especially grateful to my mother, who instilled in me the kind of discipline necessary to complete a project like this one. I would not have written this book if Izumi Sakamoto had not insisted that I apply to do my PhD, and if Damani Partridge had not provided me with the support to complete it. Auntie Bibi and Uncle Ian Kerr, thank you for letting me stay with you during my summer research trips to Jamaica. You and the whole family—Amy, Kiran, Winsome and Viv, Tippy, and Morris—always made it difficult for me to go back! Matthew McGann for having to share a roof with me for much of the time that I researched and wrote this book, my apologies and deepest gratitude. Jasmine Thomas-Girvan, Justine Williams, Laura Waites, Ryan Blake, Clinton McBean, Lloyd Grant, and Neish McLean: spending time with you helped keep me sane with the intense pace of research during my summers in Jamaica. Thanks are also due to Shamus Khan, Laura Wernick, Rinaldo Walcott, Kris Hernández, Hugo Benavides, Aseel Sawalha, Desmond Patton, Shani Roper, Danielle Roper, Dwyane Lyttle, Moji Anderson, Jallicia Jolly, Carla Moore, Nikoli Attai, Cole Rizki, Laurie Lambert, Yuko Mik, Tyler Carter, Sony Coráñez Bolton, Kareem Khubchandani, Ian Shin, James Zarsadiaz, and Tom Saramiento. Your caring friendship helped me feel a much-needed sense of community as I worked on this project.

Introduction

Queer Fractals

Making Histories of Repair

Growing up in Kingston, Jamaica's capital city, in the late 1980s and early 1990s, I could not help but learn that violating expectations of gendered and erotic behavior was both wrong and potentially dangerous. As a young child, I quickly learned that my feminine behaviors and expressions, preference for quiet indoor play, and desire to socialize with girls were not acceptable for a boy. These ways of being elicited intense bullying from other boys, who did not hesitate to call me "battyman." Though I did not develop attractions to other boys until much later, these early experiences taught me that "battyman" was a derogatory term that marked not only sex between men but also the failure of boys to conform to codes of masculine behavior. As I became a teenager, Jamaica's popular music genre of dancehall became fixated on regulating gender and sexual behavior, with songs like Harry Todder's "Bad Man Nuh Dress Like Girl" and Buju Banton's infamous "Boom Bye Bye." The invocation of violence in the lyrics of some of these songs compelled me to hide my "softness" and filled me with terror at my burgeoning feelings for other boys. I was a sheltered, upper-class teenager, and only after I left Jamaica to attend university in Canada did I learn of Jamaica's gay human rights organization J-FLAG and that several of my friends also experienced same-gender desires. At the time, however, I felt intense isolation in my queerness and knew of no others "like me." In my last year of high school, before I would leave Jamaica for Canada, I found myself sitting beside a fellow classmate, unable to believe the ramifications of his surreptitious question, "You know there were two battyman here last year?" I turned to face him, flabbergasted. I had always admired the elegant angularity of his eyes and, as a Chinese boy, I wished that mine had the same shape. But in that moment, I looked at his eyes in a different way, searching for some sign that he was joking. His face, so much darker than mine, was dead serious. The gravity of his question forced me to consider what was previously unthinkable. In my world, "battyman" was so "other," that even as I reluctantly began to recognize myself in that term, I could not imagine that such a vilified figure (much less two!) could have a past so close to home. All I could manage in response was a stunned, "Yuh too lie," a characteristic Jamaican expression of disbelief. Even as it stared me in the face, I was unable to accept this opening to queer history.

Fractal Repair emerges as an attempt to re-engage this conversation. Anthropologists open their monographs as narratives of arrival; mine is a story of return.[1] I could not take on my schoolmate's question in the moment; I needed space and time to come back to it. This process of "turning back" characterizes my relationship not only to Jamaica's queer history but also to the theoretical and methodological approach that I use to construct it. It is a fractal relationship. Fractals refer to patterns that repeat, but never exactly in the same way. There is always a site of rupture, a space of difference in what might otherwise appear to be exact repetition. This ruptural difference animates the practice of queer history making that is my central concern in this book. What does it mean to return to explore a space of previously unrecognized difference? What kinds of theoretical investments are required to support this form of inquiry? And what sorts of historical narratives are forthcoming from this endeavor?

My return is motivated by the reparative capacity of history making in response to queer violence. I focus on Jamaica not only out of a commitment to redressing my own psychic harms but also because the island's contemporary reputation for supposedly being "the most homophobic place on earth" demands critical response.[2] Though *Time* magazine first attributed this moniker to Jamaica in 2006, the island continues to grapple with its association with homophobic exceptionalism almost two decades later. The supposed intimacy between Jamaica and queer violence operates as a blueprint for regional and global imaginaries. The island stands in for anti-queer sentiment across the Caribbean writ large, and the notion of a globally recognizable homophobia that famously calcified around Jamaica has become a durable framework through which to interpret and hierarchize queer violence across the world.[3] It is impossible to ignore the violations that queer people experience across multiple domains of contemporary Jamaican life. But the relationship of this violence to ongoing legacies of empire that pathologize racialized difference and gender and sexual impropriety is also unavoidable. These legacies are apparent in colonial epistemologies that animate racialized narratives of Jamaica in terms of sexed and gendered deviance and in the ways Jamaicans themselves struggle with how we have been conscripted into these narratives.[4] In this book I bring to bear the power of history making on the troubled/troubling space of queerness in contemporary Jamaica. I wager on the capacity of evoking the past to perform the cultural and political work of repair.

My approach to repair is indebted to the work of Deborah Thomas, who advocates "thinking about reparations as a framework for producing knowledge"; and Eve Sedgwick, who proposes reparative reading practices that "assemble and confer plentitude on an object that will then have resources to offer to an inchoate self."[5] In this book I thus explore how historical knowledge production can "confer plentitude" on the embattled site of queerness in Jamaica.[6] I am not undertaking a search for queer heroes in Jamaica's past in the hopes of offering a narrative of redemption. Nor am I tracing the origins of queer violence on the island to the racialized workings of colonial power as a way of externalizing contemporary regimes of gender and sexuality. Instead, I lean on the power that coheres in the practice of history making itself. Stuart Hall notes that "far from being grounded in a mere 'recovery' of the past, which is waiting to be found, and which, when found will secure our sense of ourselves into eternity, identities are the names we give to the different ways we are positioned by and position ourselves within narratives of the past."[7] Taking my cue from Hall, I wager that the practice of positioning in relationship to the past may be generative of reparative effects. This approach suggests that the potential for historical repair lies less in the content of historical accounts than in the process of constructing them.

In *Fractal Repair* I propose a theory and method of reparative history making by attending to the way that mathematics structures historical thought. The mathematics I am referring to is less about numbers that have come to represent objective, universal, modern facts, and more about the way mathematical argumentation entails a form of storytelling.[8] Brian Rotman contends that doing mathematics involves "reading and writing highly specific and internally organized sequences of mathematical sentences— sequences intended to validate, test, prove, demonstrate, show that some particular assertion holds or is 'true' or is 'the case.'"[9] Mathematics thus operates as a mode of representation with rhetorical force and epistemological effects. Different kinds of mathematics perform this (representational) work in different ways. The grammar of arithmetic is especially prominent in practices of history making. *Arithmetic* is derived from the Latin or Greek term for "art of counting" and is the branch of mathematics concerned with the computation of numbers: addition, subtraction, multiplication, and division. Arithmetic practices shape historical consciousness and often set the terms of debate over how representations of historical subjects are constructed. These practices are constitutive of the materials that historians often use as sources to create narratives of the past, such as census documents. They also influence the crafting of these narratives through structuring metaphors around "adding" subjects considered to be missing (perhaps "subtracted") from existing historical records.[10] Yet arithmetic practices can have intensely violent effects. The inscription of these practices performs discursive violence by erasing or monstrously objectifying subaltern subjects. They materialize technologies such as ledgers and surveys that facilitate the disappearance of Native women, the commodification of enslaved Black women, and the construction of Indian women in terms of sexual deviance.[11] In so doing, arithmetic operations enable the regulation of subaltern life according to broader political economic exigencies.[12] The numerical calculations that eliminate, commercialize, and fetishize racial, gender, and sexual alterity underwrite racial capitalism and colonial governance. Approaches to history making that take on arithmetic form thus run the risk of reinscribing these modes of violence. Scholars working at the intersection of digital humanities, critical race and ethnic studies, history, and science and technology studies are thus skeptical of the liberatory claims that often accompany the enactment of digital technologies. Rather than freeing minoritized subjects from the obscurity of history, the computational practices that undergird these technologies create new conditions of subjectification that reconfigure hierarchies of race, gender, and sexuality in the production of archival knowledge.[13]

In this book I follow Katherine McKittrick to ask what it might look like to make reparative histories that "count it out differently."[14] Evelyn Hammonds inspires this move with her suggestion that any inquiry centering Black lesbian sexualities requires "that we must think in terms of a different geometry."[15] The etymology of the term "arithmetic" indexes the act of counting. The term "geometry" derives from the Greek or Latin word "geometria," the root "geo" meaning "earth," and the root "metria" meaning "measurement." While arithmetic is concerned with the computation of numbers, geometry seeks to describe the properties of bodies in space via distance, shape, size, or position. A turn to geometry thus facilitates the kind of positioning in relationship to the past that Hall advocates. And even if arithmetic is the basis on which geometric operations are performed—it is not possible to practice geometry without the computation of numbers that constitutes arithmetic—making geometry the ground on which to conceive of history making opens up different avenues of inquiry. Rather than asking about figures that go missing in narratives of the past, a focus on geometry reorients reparative histories to questions of form and geopolitics. What are the appropriate forms through which to conduct and narrate historical research? How might relations of power structure the form of historical narratives across differentiated space? What kinds of approaches to history making would be useful in confronting the problem space of queerness in contemporary Jamaica?

I begin to answer these questions through the generative field of fractal geometry. While Ron Eglash illustrates how fractal formations permeated the knowledge systems of various African societies for centuries, the term "fractal" was first coined by the Polish-born French-American mathematician Benoit Mandelbrot in 1975 from the Latin verb "frangere" meaning "to break," or the Latin adjective "fractus" meaning "broken."[16] Fractals describe patterns that repeat at different scales. Mandelbrot used the concept of fractals to account for the supposedly irregular structures of nature that classical mathematics considered to be "pathological" or "monstrous" because they failed to conform to the logics of Euclid and Newton. He insisted that ocean currents, hurricane gales, and earthquake tremors were not haphazard. Instead, they were characterized by a kind of regularity as patterns that occur at various scales of repetition.[17] Fractal geometry is a fitting approach to Jamaican queer inquiry because the recursive properties of fractals bring together theories of queer formation and Caribbean subjectivity.[18] It encompasses Antonio Benítez-Rojo's understanding of the Caribbean as "a repeating island" while also making space for Judith Butler's notion of gender as constituted through repetition.[19] It aligns with the circularity of Édouard Glissant's poetics of relation that characterize Caribbean consciousness and the recursivity of Gilles Deleuze's theorization of history writing through eroticism.[20]

Nothing's Mat, the novel by Jamaican feminist theorist Erna Brodber, serves as a model for the kind of fractal history making that this book explores. Set in the twenty-first century, *Nothing's Mat* centers the efforts of Princess—the text's young, Black, female protagonist—to learn about her family history. Fractals function as the means through which Princess constructs her family's past and also as a structuring principle of the novel itself. Princess undertakes this quest as part of a high school assignment and quickly finds that she must leave England for Jamaica when her parents are unable to answer her questions about present and past family members. In the company of her Cousin Nothing (or Conut, for short), Princess soon discovers that the linear template she had initially planned to use is unable to account for the various relationships in her family. With Conut's help, she ends up fabricating a sisal mat made up of repeating circles encompassing family in England, Jamaica, Panama, and the United States that she submits as her assignment. In the end, Princess notes:

> My presentation did not use the straight lines and arrows that one normally sees in family trees. I used the circles as in Conut's mat, . . . I got an A for my paper and learned two new words—"iteration" and "recursion." I was not sure I knew what they meant then, but Miss had said that these were the principles we used in making the mat. "Your end is your beginning" she quoted from Conut and smiled "In what odd places does wisdom reside," she added. "The literature speaks of the West Indian family as 'fractured'; you might be able to prove that it is a fractal."[21]

Brodber's fractal history making highlights the fact that no return is identical. This space of difference that prevents exact repetition constitutes a potential site of repair. In the language of fractal geometry, the lines that change with each iteration are called active lines. (The lines that remain the same are called passive lines.) Though the characters in *Nothing's Mat* recognize the repetition of historical patterns, they also acknowledge the possibility of change. Princess thus notes a similarity between the relationship she has with her cousin Joy and the relationship that Conut has with her cousin Pearl in the generation above her. In Princess's words, "The structures were there and all we would be doing through our lives was replicating them: the two women so close you'd think they were sisters. She [Joy] and I were just a repeat of Nothing and Pearl."[22] Yet Princess is also determined not to let history repeat itself. She names her daughter after a deceased relative, vowing to give her a "second chance to live a normal and happy life *this time*."[23] At the completion of each circle of the fractal family mat there is always a string left hanging that can be taken up and woven in a different way. The difference in repetition that the hanging string implies is inherent in the recursive process.[24]

The gender and sexual politics of *Nothing's Mat* suggests that queerness marks the difference of repetition. The fractal structure of Princess's family mat incorporates queer subjects and relations in ways not possible within linear kinship systems. The mat thus includes Princess's relatives queered by transgressing expectations of female domesticity—such as Euphemia, who was so physically strong and economically self-sufficient in making a life for herself in Panama that her community members called her a "man woman." It also includes Conut herself, who planted sugarcane on her land in Jamaica and "got herself talked about" because women were not supposed to use the pitchfork. The mat also incorporates all manner of intimacies that exceed and unsettle relations of blood and marriage that not only prompt North Atlantic observers to use the label "fractured" but also puzzle many of the characters in Brodber's diasporic West Indian world. Some of these relationships include cousin-siblings, mother-sisters, fosterings, and adoptions as well as the return of deceased family members' spirits in other bodies, and interdependent sacred relationships with plant and animal life.[25] Conventional mappings of kinship are unable to render the fulsome family past that Princess seeks, because the queer kin and relations that she learns about are unthinkable within their structuring logics. It is her family's queerness that compels her engagement with fractal geometry as a way of narrating her family's past.

In this book I join the concept of fractals to the concept of queerness in order to propose queer fractals as a method and theory of history making. My use of the term "queer" draws on the late seventeenth-century English meaning of "queer" to refer to something "strange," "odd," or "peculiar."[26] Queer thus operates less as a fixed category and more as a relation to existing conditions.[27] In this capacity, *Fractal Repair* synthesizes two strands of critique. First, it considers the antiracist work of Afro-Trinidadian scholar J. J. Thomas. In his 1898 monograph *Froudacity*, he notes, "It sounds queer, not to say unnatural and scandalous, that Englishmen should in these days of light be the champions of injustice toward their fellow-subjects, not for any intellectual or moral disqualification, but on the simple account of the darker skin."[28] In his text, which critiques English knowledge production about the Caribbean, Thomas mobilizes queer to denounce colonial ideologies of racial inferiority.[29] Second, *Fractal Repair* engages the work of contemporary scholars in North Atlantic queer studies who use "queer" to refer to gender and sexual relations of power. Eve Sedgwick thus describes queer as "the open mesh of possibilities, gaps, overlaps, dissonances and resonances, lapses and excesses of meaning when the constituent elements of anyone's gender or anyone's sexuality aren't made (or *can't be* made) to signify monolithically."[30] Ron Eglash suggests that ruptures in cycles of repetition function as openings from which to examine relations of geography, race, gender, and sexuality; I contend that queer fractals involve looking at how these modes of alterity operate as sites of difference within the context of historical change.[31] *Fractal Repair* mobilizes these breaks with the past as an opportunity to produce counter histories, or representations of the past that are opposed "not only to dominant narratives but also to prevailing modes of historical thought and methods of research."[32]

Fractal Repair offers a way of thinking about how temporality and mathematics shape the relationship between history making and the work of repair. The language of reparations constitutes the globally dominant framework for situating the role of historical knowledge as a means of intervening in the present.[33] Within this framework, the practice of reparations often involves a juridical accounting of past harms as a means of repairing the effects of violence in the present.[34] For countries like Jamaica that struggled for centuries under the yoke of empire and are still reckoning with its legacies of violence, such an approach to repair holds out the promise of justice and accountability. And the fact that discussions of reparations often traffic in the language of finance—capital transfers to survivors of violence—is no small matter to impoverished nations who are grappling with structures of economic underdevelopment that colonial powers laid in their wake. Reparation discourses thus posit historical research as arithmetic inquiry in the service of a linear, progressive temporality. Only by quantifying the harms of the past that persist in the present can something like liberation be achieved for the future.[35] Yet Denise Ferreira da Silva notes that such an approach to redress constitutes "a failure to think colonial and racial violence in its full fractal complexity."[36] History does not proceed along the liberal coordinates of progress either in the Caribbean or for queer subjects.[37] The promises of revolution, emancipation, independence, and development remain unfulfilled in a region that continues to be plagued by social, cultural, economic, and political ills, and dependency on imperial powers.[38] And the fruits of liberation do not fully belong to those who fall under the sign of queer, for even those who have gained the most from the advances of LGBTQ activism continue to experience the psychic legacies of queer violence and stigma.[39]

How would practices of history making unfold if they took on the recursive shape of Caribbean and queer temporalities? And what are the implications of constructing fractal representations of the past for conceptions of redress and repair? *Fractal Repair* displaces arithmetic and centers geometry as the structuring logic of history making. While this move does not necessarily carry ethical or moral implications, it nevertheless compels a different approach to creating historical narratives.[40] *Fractal Repair* thus attends to the way the past, present, and future take shape through patterns that repeat but never exactly in the same way. This kind of history making shifts the mode of repair away from narratives of overcoming history and toward living with the recursive effects of the past in the present by holding on to the moments of rupture: those sites where exact replication fails.[41] The potential of repair in the future resides in these queer moments of contingency, "the unpredictable and the unknowable in time that governs errant, eccentric, promiscuous, and unexpected organizations of social life."[42]

History, Mathematics, Jamaica

Jamaica is a key site in the history of modern mathematical imaginaries because gender and sexual relations on the island have posed a problem for the racialized workings of colonial capital since at least the seventeenth century. Indeed, the conscription of Jamaica into calculations of empire around race, gender, and sexuality would later prove to have global implications for the demographic regulation of peoples across the Atlantic. My use of fractal geometry as a point of entry into the problem space of queerness in contemporary Jamaica is thus not new. Instead, it draws from and reconfigures the ways that the language of mathematics has already been used to produce colonial knowledge about the island. In so doing, *Fractal Repair* counters the notion that mathematics is somehow an objective practice; it takes for granted that mathematics is co-constitutive with the subjects who practice it and the contexts in which it takes place.[43] Jamaica is central—not incidental—to the formation of modern mathematical logics of race, gender, and sexuality.

In the aftermath of England's successful military campaign to wrest Jamaica from Spanish control in 1655, a major concern of the new imperial power was to populate the colony to provide adequate labor power for its economic purposes as well as military forces to defend England's new possession in the Americas. Yet England's Lord Protector, Oliver Cromwell, was troubled by the demographics of the island's population, with more than four men for every woman, a situation that he interpreted as stymying natural increase in the colony. Having conquered Ireland in 1649, Cromwell proposed to resolve what he interpreted as a gender imbalance through the forced migration of Irish women to Jamaica.[44] Though Cromwell's immigration scheme was never implemented, it was nevertheless pivotal to the development of modern mathematical thought because of its influence on Cromwell's secretary, William Petty. Petty was an English physician, economist, and natural philosopher who coined the term "political arithmetic," a new approach to statecraft using innovative quantitative techniques in ways that anticipated the modern social sciences of the Enlightenment.[45] He developed the principles of political arithmetic through policy proposals that exhibited a structural similarity to Cromwell's Jamaica immigration scheme. In Ireland, he advocated an exchange with women in Britain so that Irish women would be civilized by British society, while British women would marry Irish men and reshape Ireland to be more productive from within.[46] To prevent English "degeneration" overseas, he proposed that English men in the New World buy Native girls and marry them only after they had been raised to be English women.[47] Across the Atlantic, Petty applied a method of reasoning rooted in "number, weight, and measure" to manipulate demography as a means of maximizing British military and commercial strength.[48] His political arithmetic enacted a biospatial rationalism by manipulating race, gender, and sexual relations to support the workings of empire.[49] First conceived in relationship to Jamaica, Petty's political arithmetic constitutes an early example of what Michel Foucault refers to as biopower, or the regulation of bodies and populations as an exercise in the politics of life.[50]

If the demographics of colonial Jamaica warranted a particular kind of numerical intervention in the seventeenth century, the stakes became much higher in the period between the world wars. In 1926 Charles Benedict Davenport, American biologist and founder of the International Federation of Eugenics Organizations, seized upon Jamaica to carry out research on "race mixing." Funded by the Carnegie Foundation, this project was intended to be the first step of a larger effort to identify mixed-race people around the world and subject them to eugenic measures.[51] North Atlantic eugenics discourses held that racial mixing posed a threat to humanity because interracial reproduction not only jeopardized the advancement of the supposedly "superior" races but also produced pathological offspring.[52] Petty and Davenport both problematized the coexistence of "superior" and "inferior" people, but differences in the discourses of race under which they operated led them to approach this problem in different ways. Petty advocated a policy of race mixing that Davenport, in the promotion of racial purity, would later condemn. This is because prior to the seventeenth century, ideas of blood, civilization, nation, culture, and race were used interchangeably, as there was no clear line between cultural and physical elements or between social and biological hereditary.[53] Petty's demographic interventions thus sought to enact a flexible kind of racial alchemy that would later become untenable within the framework of race-as-biology that would come to underpin Davenport's work.[54] But if Petty and Davenport differed in their evaluation of interracial intimacies, they both nevertheless maintained an investment in white superiority through racial enumeration.

For Davenport, Jamaica proved to be an ideal research site. Davenport noted, "There still exists a fair proportion of pure blooded representatives of both the white and Negro races, as well as a large number of hybrids between these races."[55] This was far from the first of such studies and was certainly not the first attempt to quantify race since British statistician Francis Galton first coined the word "eugenics" in 1883.[56] The significance of the Jamaica race-crossing study lay in the mechanization of racialized enumerative practices in support of the kind of demographic intervention that Petty envisioned three centuries earlier. To deal with the sheer volume of quantitative information collected, Davenport partnered with IBM, whose machines could organize data by "reading" the holes in the columns and rows of Hollerith punch cards.

Davenport's eugenic researchers worked with IBM to adapt the punch-card system, which had originally been created to collect data for the US census, to collect and quantitatively analyze information that was thought to index racial difference, including a plethora of bodily measurements such as height, head length, nose breadth, mouth width, fingerprints, and so on.[57] With the ability to process 25,000 cards per hour, punch-card-based sorting machines could rapidly cross-tabulate human measurements against both eugenic standards and geographic markers to locate individuals for eugenic action. This was the first time that IBM created a system to track and report racialized characteristics. The system would later become significant for the practice of eugenics across the Atlantic. Five years later the company developed the punch-card systems used in Nazi Germany to automate racial warfare in the identification and location of European Jews and other undesirable peoples. Colonial Jamaica was the training ground for the mathematical technology of the Holocaust.[58]

Today, Jamaica—which has been formally independent from England since 1962—continues to occupy a prominent place in Atlantic imaginaries around race, gender, and sexual deviance, but for a different reason. Rather than indexing the colonial predicament of settler reproduction or the global problem of race crossing, Jamaica now stands in as "the most homophobic place on earth." As the island became even more firmly enmeshed in the structures of global capital at the end of the twentieth century, Jamaica began to garner a reputation for homophobia in American and European contexts where Jamaican same-gender-desiring and gender-nonconforming subjects were often represented in terms of violence.[59] While the lyrics of dancehall artists such as Buju Banton and Shaba Ranks were perhaps the most recognized of these representational forms, nuanced themes of queer violence also pervaded the creative works of Jamaicans living in the diaspora, such as writers Michelle Cliff and Patricia Powell in the United States, and Makeda Silvera in Canada.[60] In the next decade, North Atlantic human rights

organizations began paying greater attention to Jamaica, producing knowledge about queerness on the island for global audiences using inflammatory
rhetoric such as "hated to death."[61] But it was Tim Padgett's 2006 article for
Time magazine describing Jamaica as "the most homophobic place on earth"
that has proven to be the most enduring shorthand for associating Jamaica
with violence toward same-gender-desiring and gender-variant persons.[62]
Such narratives not only highlight how queerness operates as a site of systemic discrimination and violence across multiple domains of contemporary
Jamaican life; they also rehearse colonial epistemologies that mobilize the
attribution of racialized difference and gender and sexual impropriety as
markers of deviance and inferiority.[63]

My use of fractal geometry as an approach to history making to confront
the contemporary problem space of queerness in Jamaica is not unrelated to
the ways that the quantification of race, gender, and sexuality was mobilized
to address the challenges that the island posed to the workings of eugenics
and colonial capital. If the recursive nature of queer fractals refuses the positioning of reparations as a means of liberation from the past, the troubling
history of fractal geometry forecloses a heroic construction of queer fractals
as an approach to history making. Mandelbrot, the "father of fractal geometry," began working at IBM in 1958, and his access to the company's computer
and punch-card systems was indispensable to his thinking on this new field.[64]
The same company and the same technology that produced racialized knowledge about Jamaicans for transatlantic eugenics research served as the fertile
breeding ground for the formation of Mandelbrot's fractal thinking. There are
two implications of the fact that fractal geometry owes its existence (at least
partly) to IBM's punch-card system. First, the study of Jamaican queer history
cannot be separated from gendered and sexualized discourses of racial deviance within transnational projects of capital accumulation. Second, because
arithmetic is the basis on which geometric operations are performed, constructing fractal histories of queerness in Jamaica cannot escape the patholo-
gizing racialized arithmetic on which such mathematical procedures occur.

Rather than trying to avoid or minimize fractal geometry's troubled/trou-
bling history, I explore what it would mean to acknowledge and move with
its difficult legacies. In so doing, I take my lead from the way that Brodber's
protagonist, Princess in *Nothing's Mat*, navigates relationships of violence
in fabricating her family's history. While Princess's expansive fractal mat
accounts for queer kin that otherwise fall outside of linear kinship charts, it
also incorporates all forms of violations that characterize family formations
in the afterlife of the plantation.[65] The mat thus includes Mass Eustace, who

begat Nothing through rape, as well as Everard Turnbury, who, upon marrying Nothing after Mass Eustace's death, physically and sexually assaults her. It materializes repetitive patterns not only of love, intimacy, and solidarity, but also of hardship, suffering, and violence.[66] Nothing's sexual violation is a reiteration of what her own mother experienced. As a genre of history making, fractal geometry cannot evade the violent conditions and legacies that gave rise to its creation. But while *Fractal Repair* is not an innocent knowledge project, its capacity for producing representations of the past with reparative effects lies in the certainty that even if history seems to repeat, it never does so exactly.

History Making and Repair: Between Caribbean and Queer

Fractal Repair reconfigures the ways that Caribbean and queer subjects have long mobilized history making as a mode of repair. The very notion that queerness and the Caribbean have histories and that these histories should be created (or "discovered") and known is premised on the assumption that they are in fact valid historical subjects. The existence of something like "Caribbean history" or "queer history" is therefore not self-evident. Instead, they are claims produced through struggles to redress the racialized violence of empire and injurious regimes of gender and sexuality. The act of making Caribbean and queer histories takes shape in response to colonial ideologies that posit the possession of a triumphant history as an index of humanity proper, while also insisting on the pastlessness of subjects marked by racial, gender, and sexual alterity. Claiming queerness and the Caribbean as legitimate subjects of historical inquiry works to repair the damage imposed by this association of subalterity with history-lessness.

Yet histories of repair performed in the name of "Caribbean" and "queer" often do not overlap. Caribbean people have used the claim of historical specificity as an assertion of self-determination and a critique of European and American imperialisms. By insisting that the region exists as an autonomous entity whose past needed to be considered on its own terms, they broke with the prevailing notion that Caribbean pasts were simply an extension of North Atlantic history.[67] In so doing, they laid the foundation for contemporary projects of history making oriented toward demands for reparations from (former) colonial powers. Mimi Sheller notes that "one of the greatest silences in Caribbean historiography is the invisibility of queer subjectivities"; queerness escapes this anticolonial and (later) reparative investment in making

Caribbean histories.[68] On the other hand, queer subjects have relied on the power of invoking the past to destigmatize non-normative gender and sexual relations, by using history making to unsettle discourses of a "natural" gender and sexuality that enabled the pathologization of queer individuals and communities. Yet given the interrelationship between knowledge production and geopolitics the de-pathologizing effects of these history-making projects largely remain confined to the North Atlantic.[69] David Eng and Jasbir Puar thus critique "the institutionalization of queer studies as its own particular brand of US area studies," leading Kadji Amin to call for more queer genealogical approaches that "center racialized people and/or geographical locations outside Europe and North America."[70]

Fractal geometry provides a method that can bring together the reparative potential of Caribbean and queer history making. This approach insists on the relevance of mathematics for thinking about how relations of race, gender, sexuality, and geography shape the production of historical knowledge. Such geometry is the basis of my intervention into these two fields—space ("geo") structures my engagement with queer history, and form ("metria") structures my engagement with Caribbean history. *Fractal Repair* orients studies of queer history toward the Caribbean while locating queerness within the existing shapes of Caribbean thought.

In writing about the development of historical disciplines in the Caribbean, Barry Higman notes that "subjects which have become important in European and North American history-writing have sometimes been neglected or ignored by Caribbean historians. Gay and lesbian history, and the history of science, for instance, have found few practitioners in the Caribbean."[71] Extending Higman's observations, it is not only that North American and European historians produce accounts of gay, lesbian, and scientific pasts in ways that Caribbean scholars do not, but also that these historical narratives spatialize "gay," "lesbian," and "science" and construct them as distinctly North Atlantic phenomena. If spaces are not naturally discontinuous but instead are *made* to be separate through practices of place making, one of the many ways that spatial distinction is achieved is through the production of historical narratives.[72] Theories of queer formation that rely on the trope of modernity are prime examples of this process. Though the sense of novelty associated with modernity is produced through the calcification of *global* networks of exchange and production, the modernity that is foundational to historians' conception of queer emergence is often confined to the North Atlantic.[73] For Michel Foucault, the consolidation of a regime of power that regulates populations and individual bodies through sexuality becomes "an indispensable element in the development of capitalism," and the marker of "the threshold of our modernity."[74] In this model, the homosexual as a durable category of personhood eclipses—even if it never fully replaces—the more ephemeral classification of sodomite. Gaytri Spivak critique's Foucault's claim that the capacity to understand oneself (and be understood) in terms of sexuality indexes one's modernity. She points to the Eurocentricity of Foucault's writing and argues that "the topographical reinscription of imperialism does not inform his presuppositions."[75]

To the extent that modernity becomes axiomatic to theories of queer formation, the centrality of the Caribbean to conceiving modernity makes the region indispensable for queer historical inquiry. Michel-Rolph Trouillot maintains that the Caribbean's modernity lies less with any particular characteristic of the region itself and more with its insertion into a regime of history and sociopolitical regulation.[76] The systematic arrival of Europeans in the Americas at the end of the fifteenth century not only marked the first moment of globality and the making of the Atlantic World but also the production of the Caribbean as a modern region through colonization. Through European arrival, Indigenous genocide, and the importation of enslaved African and indentured Asian labor, the Caribbean became the site of a new international system of agro-industrial capitalism that joined colony and metropole, field and factory, producer and consumer, European and Other. Though these developments could only be interpreted as a break with the past, Sidney Mintz argues that the Caribbean functions as "an instance of precocious modernity, an unanticipated (indeed unnoticed) modernity—unnoticed especially, perhaps, because it was happening in the colonies before it happened in the metropolises, and happening to people most of whom were forcibly stolen from the worlds outside the West."[77] It is through this "unanticipated modernity" that this book explores the question of queer history.

Fractal Repair brings together this concern about the geopolitics of queer historicization with a preoccupation with how queerness figures into existing forms of Caribbean historical thought. For Caribbean historians, the concept "creole" marks the specificity of a history-writing tradition from within the region; it indexes a shift from an imperial to a decolonial approach to writing about Caribbean pasts.[78] In its initial formulation, the term was used to describe arrivals in the New World who differed from the Old World societies of their ancestry and the Indigenous people they encountered.[79] "Creole" condenses notions of sameness and difference as well as those of time and space. Although creole subjects may be the offspring of Old World parents, their distance from the Old World and their time in the New World marks them as different from their lineage.[80] While creolization, or the process of making creoles, may elicit romantic images of cultural formation through consensual interaction among equals, creolization instead occurs through dynamics of conflict (as well as accommodation) and always through unequal relations of power.[81] Creolization has become the master symbol of the Caribbean.[82] Caribbean creolization is a product of the region's fundamental modernity forged through relationships among various kinds of ethnoracial difference.[83] In a region made anew through European conquest, Indigenous depopulation, and the introduction of enslaved African and later indentured Asian laborers to create and maintain an international system of agro-industrial capitalism, the relations that developed within and between these various ethnoracialized groups could not be anything but modern.

Insofar as Caribbean people understand themselves as (and are understood as) historical subjects through creolization, this creolization takes on a queer, recursive shape. Kamau Brathwaite argues that "it was in the intimate area of sexual relationships . . . where the most significant—and lasting—interculturation took place"; and Sidney Mintz suggests that it was the social organization of these patterns of "mating" across ethnoracial lines that shaped the specific nature of creolization across Caribbean societies.[84] To the extent that queerness indexes gender and sexual peculiarity, the forms of intimacy that Brathwaite and Mintz discuss taking root among Caribbean people were intrinsically queer/peculiar to the systems of gender and sexual propriety that existed in Old World and the New.[85] This is because neither the region's Indigenous inhabitants nor its later arrivals, who came under diverse conditions of unfreedom, were able to faithfully reproduce the logics of intimacy with which they were familiar (I discuss this point in greater detail in chapter 2). I maintain that as Caribbean people mobilized discourses of creolization to position themselves as legitimate historical subjects, queerness was key to their foundational logics.[86] Strange forms of gender and sexuality alchemize Indigenous, European, African, and Asian people, transforming them into modern New World subjects. Ultimately, in this book I bring together the reparative impulses of Caribbean and queer history making to theorize queer formation through Caribbean modernity and to conceptualize the shape of creolization through queerness.

Fractal Repair offers a theory and method of history making from the time space of late twentieth-century Jamaica. This is a critical period in the country's cultural political formation across colonial, post-independence, and neoliberal eras that occurred immediately before the emergence of the island's global reputation as "the most homophobic place on earth." Chapter 2 illustrates the workings of queer fractals as a mode of narrating the past by providing historical context for this book. It represents the history of Jamaica from the first arrival of the Spanish to the end of the twentieth century. Given the vast multiplicity of what could count as "queer" and "Jamaica" in the past, I do not seek to perform a historical inventory or accounting. Instead, this chapter gestures to the repetitive shape—in a necessarily partial and limited way—of Jamaican queerness over time. This tentative narration fleshes out the multiple dimensions of Jamaican gender and sexual peculiarity in the shape of transnational race relations, especially as they articulate with questions of labor and capital accumulation.

The next four chapters explore the question of repair through a queer turning to the past. Each chapter brings the method of queer fractals to an archive of repair. Where an archive is understood as being a "system that governs the appearance of statements as unique events," archives of repair index those systems that generate reparative statements as events.[87] *Fractal Repair* thus turns its attention to archives that materialize different moments in which Jamaican individuals, communities, and institutions sought to re-dress the injuries of history. In keeping with the figuration of the Caribbean as a porous region with permeable boundaries, the geographic reach of each archive extends beyond Jamaica's shores. The geometric approach of using queer fractals for history making facilitates this kind of inquiry because it confronts questions of both time and space. Yet far from being random or haphazard, the nature of these scalar moves runs parallel to the spatial imaginations that cohere within each historical moment under consideration.

The archives of repair that I assemble draw from a wide range of sources. While I detail the construction of each archive in the chapters that follow, it is worth noting that in this book I bring together Kamau Brathwaite's injunction to "develop a discipline of social arts to work along with (and sometimes run counter to) the social science" with Jack Halberstam's scavenger methodology that advocates combining methods that are often at odds with each other.[88] For this reason, *Fractal Repair* produces archives that weld together newspaper articles with photographs, oral history interviews with performance video footage, and government reports with novels. In this process of bricolage, conflict arises not only in comparing the content of these sources and the conditions under which they were produced and circulated, but also in the process of bringing together the diversity of their forms. For instance, newspapers and novels are different kinds of texts that perform differently in the world according to the conventions of their genre. Rather than flattening these differences, I seek to mobilize the productive tension that arises from holding them together in the same analytic frame. The archives that emerge from this far-reaching assemblage, much like the processes of repair that they index and seek to produce, are syncretic, heterogeneous, and internally contradictory.

The chapters are organized in two pairs. Chapters 3 and 4 attend to the question of historical continuity. If queerness takes shape as a site of rupture within patterns that repeat, it indexes not only iterations of difference but also the stable backdrop that makes this difference legible. Indeed, the very materialization of queerness as difference relies on the continuity/sameness of what surrounds it. These two chapters mobilize queerness to lay bare the durability of archival effects. Chapter 3 attends to the repair of knowledge within the framework of empire. The mid-twentieth century marked the institutionalization of a "native" tradition of social science inquiry in Jamaica and across the English-speaking Caribbean at least partly in response to colonial epistemologies that pathologized working-class Afro-Caribbean kinship patterns. By investigating intimate relations that departed from North Atlantic models of nuclear family, these academics produced knowledge that nationalists later mobilized in support of claims of Caribbean distinctiveness. In this chapter I construct an archive of this anticolonial response to consider how it narrated queerness. More specifically, I investigate how the workings of coloniality make distinctions among various gender and sexual peculiarities by analyzing the kinds of historical evidence (if any) they leave behind in their wake. I contend that interrelated workings of color, class, gender, and nation structure the ways that queerness is inscribed in, and as, Jamaica's past. Same gender intimacy and gender nonconformity within the Afro-Creole spiritual tradition of Pukumina persist in the margins of Jamaica's institutionalized archival collections that are overwhelmed by the omnipresent figure of the foreign white "homosexual."

Chapter 4 takes on bodily repair. Here I focus on the outbreak of HIV/AIDS in the Anglophone Caribbean, which was first reported in Jamaica in 1982. Very quickly this illness was understood to be transmitted through sex, which compelled Jamaicans to publicly grapple with sexuality in new ways. In this chapter I examine how HIV/AIDS comes to be an occasion to produce knowledge about sexuality and especially about same-gender-desiring subjects, who are most associated with the illness. In contrast to the social scientists discussed in chapter 3 that operated within the framework of empire, the public health workers that take center stage in this chapter are oriented toward the well-being of the national body. These workers found themselves navigating the epidemic through the dual imperatives of surveillance (producing knowledge for institutions to combat the epidemic) and care (seeing to the needs of those infected and affected by HIV/AIDS). The decisions they made about what, how, and among whom they shared the intimate knowledge they generated through their relationships with their patients were consequential, not only for the well-being of individuals and the general population, but also for how the archives of sexual health take shape. Hierarchies of color, class, and gender shaped Jamaican frontline health workers' knowledge-making practices, such that the same-gender-desiring subjects they most associated with HIV/AIDS were poor and working-class Black men.

Chapters 5 and 6 focus on the potential for historical rupture. In chapters 3 and 4, queerness showed up as a way of highlighting the persistence of archival infrastructures; in chapters 5 and 6, it materializes to construct narratives of the past that depart from existing historical accounts. Chapter 5 explores the repair of performance in response to the debasement of Caribbean cultural practices that contravened racialized colonial codes of gender and sexual propriety. It focuses on Jamaica's National Dance Theatre Company (NDTC), which became one of the country's most prominent cultural ambassadors after its founding in 1962—the year of the island's formal independence from Britain. Whereas Caribbean social scientists of the 1950s operated in the discursive space of empire, and Jamaican health workers of the 1990s directed their attention to the national body, Jamaican and Caribbean cultural workers of the 1960s functioned within the problem space at the juncture between region and nation. The dance company sought to create a distinctively Jamaican and Caribbean dance form by combining the movement vocabularies of Jamaican and Caribbean folk traditions with North Atlantic and African dance forms. In this chapter I present a close reading of NDTC's early performances and their reception on the island, within the region, and across the North Atlantic. I argue that the company's performances and how they were interpreted highlight the pervasive but covert way that same-gender intimacy and gender nonconformity were foundational to how Jamaicans sought to understand themselves in the wake of independence. This narrative unsettles existing historical accounts of Jamaica's immediate post-independence period, which emphasize the twinning of overpopulation and national development discourses in the promotion of Euro-American forms of kinship.

Chapter 6 turns to the question of political repair. With the election of Michael Manley as Jamaica's prime minister in 1972, Jamaicans experienced a sense of political possibility in which they could challenge various forms of national and international inequality. The island occupied a position of leadership in challenging unequal arrangements of power on the global stage while the flourishing of Black Power, feminist, and labor movements in Jamaica indexed an intensive participation in local public life. In this chapter I take up the work of Jamaica's Gay Freedom Movement (GFM)—the first self-proclaimed gay activist organization of the English-speaking Caribbean, which came into existence in 1977. In chapters 3, 4, and 5, respectively, empire, region/nation, and nation marked the discursive terrain for social scientists, health workers, and performers; for the activists in chapter 6, the discursive frame is nation/transnation. Closely attending to GFM's work, I argue that this small grassroots organization positioned same-gender erotic autonomy as a defining feature of Jamaican cultural identity and situated the island as a key node of international gay activism. In this chapter I offer a narrative that expands existing accounts of the period in which heterosexuality marked the limits of Jamaican struggles to transform national and international relations around gender and sexual inequality.

In the epilogue I conclude *Fractal Repair* with a brief meditation on the implications of queer fractals for thinking about futurity. What conceptions of the future are forthcoming from nonlinear approaches to temporality that spurn the illusions of liberation? I engage this question by revisiting the first moment of modern globality—the European conquest of the New World. I focus on the letter Diego Álvarez Chanca wrote to the Municipal Council of Seville as physician to Christopher Columbus on his second voyage to the Americas. Written in 1494, this letter's account is often considered to be the first written natural history and ethnography of the Americas. Chanca's representations of Caribbean Indigenous gender and sexual relations as "beastly" inaugurates racialized discourses of deviancy that justified conquest in the nascent workings of transatlantic capital. A queer reading of this text unsettles discourses of progress that envision the future as a clean break with this past by moving with the recursive temporalities that characterize Caribbean and queer realities. The future takes shape, not through a linear departure from the past, but instead as a ruptural space of indeterminacy that accompanies patterns of history that seem to repeat. The future will not yield an end to the modernity of racial capitalism that has simultaneously violated and shaped Caribbean subjects. If this is the case, futurity may lie in the practice of moving with the loops of history while holding fast to the (queer) promise that each iteration can never be the same.

1

Queer Jamaica, 1494-1998

What would it mean to use queer fractals as a way of narrating Jamaica's past? What kinds of historical accounts about the island would be forthcoming if we attend to the ways queerness operates as a site of rupture within patterns that repeat? The difficulty in answering these questions lies in the fact that queerness and Jamaica exist, not as immutable objects, but as relations that change over time. In the language of mathematics, queerness and Jamaica are both independent variables. The gender and sexual relations of actions, events, and people considered to be unremarkable in one space-time may be rendered peculiar, strange, and queer in another.[1] And if the case of Hispaniola—the island divided into Haiti and the Dominican Republic—is any example of the contingency with which national boundaries map onto supposedly natural formations, what counts as "Jamaica" is not necessarily confined to the geographic borders of the island itself. This contingency indexes not only the workings of diaspora and how Jamaicans (re)construct themselves, their relationships, and their communities offshore, but also how the political singularity of Jamaica is a recent phenomenon. Prior to the island's independence, Jamaica was part of the British Empire, with British Honduras (now known as Belize) and the

Cayman Islands as its dependencies.[2] While it now makes sense to speak of Jamaica as an independent nation, the desirability of this political singularity was hotly debated during its membership in the regional West Indian Federation in the years 1958–62. Given the vast multiplicity of what *could* count as queer and Jamaica in the past, my goal here is not to perform an inventory, calculation, or accounting, but instead to gesture to the recursive shape—in a necessarily partial and limited way—of Jamaican queerness over time.

In this tentative narration, I flesh out the dimensions of gender and sexual peculiarity that emerge as sites of rupture in the repetitive patterns of Jamaica's conscription into mutations of racial capital. Somewhat analogously to Cedric Robinson's definition racial capitalism as the way that race relations saturate the social structures emergent from capitalism and its subsequent architecture as historical agency, I draw on the insights of feminist and queer scholars such as Kamala Kempadoo, Roderick Ferguson, Grace Hong, and Shannon Speed to consider how gender and sexual relations figure into the conjoined workings of racial and capitalist technologies.[3] I focus on how economic exigencies of empire—whether enacted before or after the island's nominal independence from Britain—unfold through the idiom of race in ways that give rise to novel configurations of intimacy, femaleness, and maleness. In so doing, I mobilize standard frames in the fields of Jamaican and Caribbean history: European conquest; Indigenous genocide; African enslavement and emancipation; Asian indentureship; and other racialized labor migration regimes, as well as domestic responses to global designs of political and economic disenfranchisement. I use these frames to illustrate how the workings of capital, the materialization of racial difference, and the enactment of gender and sexual peculiarity across space are mutually constitutive.

But this queerness is not isomorphic. Just as the conjoined processes of racialization and capital accumulation contort and twist back on themselves, the forms of gender and sexual peculiarity that they materialize also shapeshift. The range in the kinds of queerness that I discuss (including formations of kinship, patterns of reproduction, gender roles, and [erotic] intimacies) and the diversity of racialized groups within and across which I explore them (including Indigenous, white/European, Black/African, brown, Indian, and Chinese) challenge any easy attempt to generalize about the ways queerness persists or changes over time. Rather than delineate a set of organizing principles, I offer an illustrative example. Though colonial authorities opposed sexual relations between English men and enslaved African women in eighteenth-century Jamaica as well as sexual relations between Jamaican soldiers and English women during World War I in England, they considered these interracial intimacies to be disturbing and dangerous—that is, queer—in different ways. I discuss these scenarios separately later in this chapter, but for now it is sufficient to note that while English men crossing the color line in the colony besmirched the integrity of the national body overseas, English women crossing the color line in the metropole profoundly imperiled the integrity of the national body at home. Even as the British Empire employed differently racialized men to perform different kinds of labor in different spaces at different times, the queerness of their interracial sexual liaisons signified differently. This is a fractal queerness; it repeats, but not exactly in the same way.

I begin this narration with Europe's first sustained contact with Jamaica with the arrival of the Spanish in 1494 in the search for mineral wealth.[4] As I suggested in the introduction, the modernization of the Caribbean region produced relations that differed from the forms of gender and sexuality that previously existed in both the Old World and the New. Jamaica was not immune to the queer formations produced through these violent forces of modernity. The Spanish framed their accounts of the New World through the language of sexual conquest and constructed the indigenous people they encountered in terms of raced (savage) and gendered (female) difference.[5] Spaniards considered the Native people they encountered to be "abominations," demonizing what they interpreted as a lack of adherence to binary gender norms and stigmatizing practices of sodomy among Native men and "immodesty" among Native women.[6] By the time England conquered Jamaica in 1655, the Spanish had decimated the island's Indigenous peoples through warfare, enslavement, and disease.

Jamaica under the English transformed dramatically with the intensification of plantation agriculture, the meteoric rise in the importation of enslaved Africans, the increase in severity of enslaved labor and punishment regimes, and the hardening of ideologies of racial difference. Yet for all the power they wielded to shape the New World, the English were unable to fully transplant Old World expectations of intimacy. For instance, Barry Burg explores practices of eroticism among male communities of English sea rovers to the Caribbean that contravened legal statutes criminalizing sodomy in the seventeenth century.[7] As Jamaican creole society began to solidify at the end of the eighteenth century, white residents found themselves unwilling and/or unable to adhere to middle-class expectations of nuclear family that were firmly taking root in Victorian England.[8] Plantation overseers saw marriage as a deterrent to their plans to accumulate wealth and return to Europe as quickly as possible, and the elite families that employed them struggled to maintain a sense of kinship among its members, who often were scattered across the

Atlantic.[9] English women in Jamaica were excluded from new gender ideologies that emphasized chaste and passive domesticity, as their metropolitan counterparts considered them to be lustful, unruly, and passionate—more in line with late seventeenth-century European discourses of womanhood.[10]

Enslaved Africans were also unable to fully re-create the patterns of intimacy expected in their home societies, because their subjectivities and forms of social organization took shape in relationship to the exigencies of Atlantic agro-industrial capitalism. Omise'eke Natasha Tinsley creatively imagines the journey of enslaved Africans across the Atlantic Ocean as a site not only of horrific violence and suffering but also of intimate same-gender bonds that work against the debasement and commodification of African bodies.[11] In opposition to gendered systems of labor division that existed in Ibo, Ashanti, Dahomean, and other West African societies, enslaved women and men were assigned the same intensity of physical labor and punishments in Jamaica, because African women were considered to possess the strength and physical musculature of men.[12] It was only in their relationship to reproduction and sexuality that Europeans differentiated enslaved women and men.[13] Planters only very grudgingly and in the smallest ways possible adjusted plantation work regimes to allow for the labor of pregnancy, childbirth, and nursing.

Unlike slaveholders on the American mainland, Jamaica was unable to maintain its enslaved labor force through natural reproduction.[14] When both planters and metropolitan authorities sought to address these low levels of natural increase at the end of the slave trade in 1807, the policies they created—extra time off, additional food allowances, awards for childbirth, and so on—did not fundamentally transform the harsh labor regime of the plantation that made reproduction so difficult.[15] Even those who took flight from the plantation to join the Maroons in the island's hinterland could not escape the forces of modernization that structured the social organization of gender and sexual relations. Maroon communities were compelled to devise new systems of kinship to address changing demographic realities. Men not only outnumbered women as a consequence of the preference for enslaved male labor, but they also were more likely than the women to have the opportunity to flee the plantation.[16] Windward and Leeward Maroon communities addressed this "shortage of women" differently: Leeward Maroons developed systems of "wife sharing" among men, whereas Windward Maroons created rules around men's access to women that were strictly and violently enforced.[17]

New forms of gender and sex took shape not only within but also across increasingly hardened racial lines. Charles Davenport became fixated on Jamaica as a site of race mixing in the early twentieth century, but the spatialization of this racial-sexual dynamic is connected to a longer history of what Faith Smith refers to as a "taboo of miscegenation" in the Caribbean.[18] While interracial unions were threaded into the social fabric of West African societies in the seventeenth century, the institutionalization of interracial sex in Jamaica unsettled metropolitan English sensibilities. During her stay in Jamaica in 1801–5, Lady Nugent was compelled to put aside her disapproval of the island's multiracial families, because, as the wife of Jamaica's governor, she was obliged to respect local customs regardless of her personal sentiments.[19] Eroticism between enslaved laborers and their masters in the New World was based on fundamental asymmetries of race and gender. The enslaved were reduced to mere flesh and made into objects of sexual and violent impulses, or what Hortense Spillers refers to as "pornotropping."[20] This is evident in the unrestrained sexual violence of English overseer Thomas Thistlewood toward enslaved Black women in eighteenth-century Jamaica.[21]

The offspring of such unions introduced a new set of racialized subjects into Jamaican colonial society. Unlike the American mainland, where the ratio of Africans to Europeans was not as high, Jamaican authorities addressed the "problem" of mixed-race people through integration.[22] In contrast to the United States, which sought to prohibit "mulattos" through statutes prohibiting mixed unions, Jamaica passed legislation granting persons of mixed race certain rights in order to win their support in the context of white depopulation and the threat of Black revolt.[23] Not only did mixed-race subjects further stratify racialized hierarchies of free and enslaved labor, but they also modified existing regimes of gender and sexuality. For instance, the desirability of brown women in the eyes of white men produced the "concubine" as a new racialized subject of kinship in white families. Brown women mobilized these intimacies with white men for economic security, freedom, and status for themselves and their children, while white family members came to resent the claims that these women made on family resources. The desire for brown mistresses (but not wives) marked European men's acculturation to the Caribbean. Indeed, white Jamaican women sought to marry English men as soon as they arrived on the island and before they could acquire this racial-sexual proclivity. The possibility of emancipation as well as social and economic advancement for themselves and their children positioned brown women to eschew marriage with brown or Black men for the opportunities that came with being a white man's mistress—even if this made their fate more precarious, dependent as it was on white men's individual whims.[24]

In the aftermath of slave emancipation in 1834 (followed by an "apprenticeship" period of four years), race, gender, and sexual relations became key sites of contestation in the struggle to shape a new "free" society. Despite colonial authorities' attempt to restrict freed people from acquiring land, in Jamaica the support of Baptist missionaries helped formerly enslaved people in Jamaica be more successful in establishing peasant communities than were freed people in other British Caribbean territories. Yet freed people on the island still could not fully escape the grasp of the plantation, which they continued to rely on— however sporadically—for waged work. Less than a radical break with the past, manumission facilitated new avenues of regulating formerly enslaved people: to be properly free required certain moral and economic sensibilities.[25] Freed subjects were to establish families according to Christian values of monogamous marriage and Victorian expectations of female domesticity, which in turn would require formerly enslaved men to continue working on plantations as wage laborers.[26] Some freed women and men were able to lay claim to the positions of wife or mother and wage-earning family provider made available by these hegemonic discourses of propriety in a strategic bid for safety and economic security.[27] But the price could be quite high for subjects who were either incapable or unwilling to align of themselves with these expectations of respectability.[28] Jamaican elite anxieties about Black freedom took shape through a massive increase in the prosecution of sexual offenses (rape, sodomy, bestiality): manumission was accompanied by a stringent demand for sexual propriety and the severe punishment for sexual deviance.[29] In this period, the island's planter class may have demeaned the masculinity of newly freed women such as those who took part in the Morant Bay Rebellion of 1865, but even they could not entirely escape the intense scrutiny around gender and sexuality that pervaded post-emancipation society.[30] Formerly enslaved men used colonial ideologies that constructed their masculinity in terms of labor to critique wealthy white and brown Jamaican men. Freed men interpreted their nonlaboring status as an index of inferior manhood.[31] Yet the racialized arrangements of power in newly emancipated Jamaica blunted the effectiveness of these charges from below. For instance, despite extensive incriminating evidence, Jamaican plantation attorney Alexander Grant was cleared of allegations of sexual assault against formerly enslaved men.[32]

To avoid paying higher wages to formerly enslaved people in the context of the loss of protections for sugar exports on the British market, Jamaican planters sought to import new sources of labor in ways that further transformed race, gender, and sexual relations on the island. In the British Caribbean, post-emancipation systems of indentured labor differed from earlier contract labor schemes in two ways: first, they attempted to procure not only European and African but also Asian workers (coolies); and second, these labor arrangements were not disparate private endeavors but central-ized through state regulation.[33] Though these workers came from both China and India, Indian coolies far outnumbered those from China, at least partly because the trade in Chinese workers officially ended in 1866, whereas Indian coolies continued to arrive in the region until 1917.[34] Coolies were consid-ered to be units of labor and not settlers or future citizens. Jamaican planters thus exhibited a preference for men because of their assumed capacity for physical labor in ways that skewed the gendered ratio of indentured work-ers heavily against women.[35] These demographic realities facilitated new relations, such as the formation of same-gender intimacies among Indians, as they crossed the Atlantic, that persisted into their new Caribbean lives.[36] Indian experiences in Jamaica also transformed the social organization of intimacy "back home." Plantation managers unsettled extended/joint In-dian family formations by insisting on household distribution according to nuclear family ideologies. Given their small numbers in Jamaica, Indians also found it difficult to marry among themselves—much less maintain caste proscriptions. And even with the passage of the 1896 Immigrant Marriage Divorce and Succession Law, which was meant to facilitate religious ac-commodations, they encountered challenges to their attempts to adhere to Hindu and Muslim marriage conventions. Further, the overabundance of Indian men in Jamaica meant that wedding dowries, typically given by the bride's family to the groom's, reversed directions.[37] The unequal gender ratios among coolie arrivals to Jamaica facilitated greater social and sexual freedom for Indian women, to which their male counterparts responded with increasing levels of surveillance and control.[38] British colonial authorities responded to incidences of Indian spousal murders by passing legislation to protect immigrant women from intimate partner violence while also issuing punishments for the seduction of immigrant wives.[39] Such intimacies and violence did not occur only among Indians. White plantation managers took Indian mistresses, and Indian workers entered into intimate partnerships with Black (rare) and Chinese (even more rare) partners.[40] For the majority of Indians who opted against repatriation, the recognition that they would be unable to continue their intercaste, interreligious, interracial relationships in India may have played some role in their decision.[41] Colonial authorities were particularly concerned about relationships between coolies and ex-slave populations, fearing that intimacies between these groups would lead to cross-racial solidarities. Such exchanges interrupted the positioning of coolies as a buffer zone between white and Black groups, and threatened both the colonial political order and plantation profits.[42] This was particularly the case with the Chinese, at least partly because, unlike the Indians, the Chinese were not guaranteed passage back to their home country and therefore were more likely to leave the plantation and find other ways of making a living.[43] The Chinese also did not face the same kind of caste and religious marriage restrictions as Indians and thus were more likely to engage in intimacies with Black Jamaicans. Incomes permitting, Chinese men pursued polygamy, continuing a Chinese tradition of having secondary wives: maintaining a wife in China and a Black mistress in Jamaica.[44]

Jamaica's post-emancipation period was marked not only by the entry of Asian indentured workers but also by the exit of Black labor.[45] Given the intense economic hardship on the island toward the end of the nineteenth century and the fact that formerly enslaved people now had the capacity to travel, many opted to leave the island in search of better economic opportunities elsewhere.[46] Many migrants departed for the United States, Mexico, Cuba, and Costa Rica, but most Jamaicans went to Panama, to work first on the Panama Railroad and then on the Panama Canal.[47] This large-scale, predominantly male migration impacted gender and sexual relations both in Jamaica and in the territories the migrants traveled to work. Some migrants regularly returned to Jamaica and sent remittances to financially support their families; others abandoned their kin, leaving them to fend for themselves. In the context of extreme poverty, women found themselves returning to the plantations they had left upon manumission to take on forms of waged work that men had earlier fought to claim as exclusively theirs.[48] Laboring overseas alongside other Caribbean and Asian migrant workers, Jamaican men and women engaged in new practices of gender and intimacy. In places like Costa Rica, Jamaican men found themselves taking on tasks that women typically practiced, such as cooking and laundering, or more frequently entering into new intimate and/or economic arrangements with local women to perform this domestic work.[49] In Panama, the greater occupational flexibility of Jamaican migrant women—compared to their male counterparts who ostensibly traveled to engage in specific forms of manual work—elicited various forms of scrutiny and social control.[50] The "Caribbean immigrant woman as prostitute" became a site of contestation among US authorities who feared that this figure would lead to the degeneration of their military personnel, Panamanian officials who imagined this figure to protect the virtue of local women, and Caribbean immigrant men who mobilized this figure to make claims for higher wages to protect and support "their" women.[51] Jamaican migration in the nineteenth century was a largely regional phenomenon, but the way that these movement practices reconfigured gender and sexual relations would recur as Jamaican migration increasingly took on a North Atlantic character in the twentieth century, especially when the United States established an immigrant agricultural worker program in 1943 and Britain granted colonial subjects the right to settle in the metropole in 1948.

Jamaica's involvement in World Wars I and II altered gender and sexual relations not only on the island but also in the spaces where Jamaicans engaged in war work. Jamaican men who served overseas created new forms of intimacy with other men from all corners of the British Empire.[52] In England they were confronted by colonial anxieties around white male inadequacy in the face of Black men's supposedly heightened masculinity and metropolitan fears of interracial intimacies with white women that were thought to threaten national integrity.[53] The masculinization effects of war were visible in Jamaica as World War I provided opportunities for women, particularly wealthy white women, to unsettle colonial policies that otherwise encouraged women's private domestic labor by engaging in civic acts of service.[54] These women mobilized tropes of military manhood to encourage Jamaican men to enlist and resorted to accusations of femininity to shame those who refused. Later, these women successfully capitalized on their contribution to the war effort to push for the right for elite women to vote in 1919.[55] In World War II, the participation of largely middle-class Jamaican women as members of the Auxiliary Territorial Service (ATS) unsettled the gendered expectations of military service in Jamaica and elicited heated debate in England about the desirability of Black women in uniform.[56] Jamaican women's involvement in the ATS would later pave the way for women's entry into the previously exclusive masculine domains of police and army work on the island.[57] Yet not all of Jamaican women's war work was equally valued. Though colonial authorities condoned sex with prostitutes as a prerogative of foreign soldiers stationed in Jamaica, they pathologized and criminalized working-class Jamaican women for engaging in this form of labor.[58]

Between World Wars I and II Jamaica witnessed a burgeoning race, class, and nationalist consciousness. The persistence of economic hardship worsened by the Great Depression, combined with the widespread sentiment of colonial oppression and the establishment of Marcus Garvey's United Negro Improvement Association (UNIA) and Rastafari set the stage for significant change in Jamaican society.[59] Jamaican contests over the configurations of nationhood, Blackness, and economic security played out on the terrain of gender and sexual relations. Though Jamaica's anti-Chinese riots in 1918 erupted long-standing animus toward the Chinese as an increasingly prosperous group in the context of systemic Black deprivation, it is significant that the widespread unrest was sparked by the conflict that occurred when a Chinese grocer stumbled upon his brown paramour in the intimate embrace of a brown police officer.[60] The rise in race and class consciousness of Jamaicans, many of whom returned to a faltering economy—either as soldiers stung by racism in World War I or as migrant laborers for whom national borders overseas had been closed—produced a critical stance toward Asian "aliens."[61] This was especially the case for Chinese, who ascended into the middle class as grocers and merchants.[62] Colonial authorities were pleased that most Chinese migration to Jamaica in the 1920s and 1930s consisted of the wives and fiancées of existing settlers, because this reduced the threat of interracial intimacies.[63] Yet the arrival of Chinese wives produced tension, friction, and conflict with their husbands' Black and brown mistresses.[64] Further, this show of intraracial prosperity—because only wealthy men could afford this practice—was difficult to take for the island's struggling masses who already viewed the Chinese as "clannish" and looked askance at the funds they sent to their families overseas.

For Black middle-class Jamaicans, the process of configuring racial pride in the early twentieth century entailed grappling with the proper parameters of gender and sexual relations. Working against the ways racism denied the application of bourgeois notions of masculinity and femininity to Black people, Garvey structured the UNIA so that men's and women's leadership roles were separate and hierarchical, with men taking on public roles of authority and power and women taking on private roles of cooperation and uplift.[65] Yet women within the UNIA challenged these institutional norms, and the organization served as the training ground for Black middle-class feminists such as Amy Bailey and Una Marson, who in 1936 would form the Women's Liberal Club, which fought against race and gender discrimination in Jamaica's public sphere. The efforts of these and other Jamaican women were crucial to passing Jamaica's Sex Disqualification (Removal) Law of 1944 that permitted women's entry into areas of public life from which they were previously excluded.[66] Further, the popular variety shows that UNIA hosted contravened the emphasis it otherwise placed on middle-class sexual respectability by celebrating working-class subjectivities and welcoming openly same-gender-desiring actors and cross-gender performances.[67]

Gender and sexual relations became a key terrain on which to grapple with the process of refashioning Jamaica in the aftermath of the massive labor riots of 1938. This unrest—as part of a broader labor agitation movement across the Caribbean—illustrated working-class power, challenged British colonialism, and provided an opportunity for Jamaicans to imagine their society anew. The West Indian Royal Commission that the British government set up to investigate the riots sidestepped questions of economic inequality, identified "disorganized" Black lower-class family life as the root cause of social disorder, and promoted the formation of bourgeois nuclear families.[68] The commission allowed England to exercise an authority that the labor unrest brought into question while also displacing responsibility for the riots from the colonial order that it commanded and unto the colonial people it subjugated. It also allowed upper-class and, increasingly, middle-class Jamaicans who contributed to the commission's investigation to both distance themselves from working-class Black Jamaicans and to carve out a space for themselves in the increasingly strident calls for nation building.[69] If the supposed inadequacy of lower-class Black families produced anxieties about Jamaica's "readiness" for nationhood, then respectable upper- and middle-class Jamaicans were best positioned to address these problems of unruly intimacies.[70] Gender ideologies structured the project of reforming lower-class Black family life: the construction of mothers as hypervisible and fathers as marginal centered masculinity in the project of nation building.[71]

Foregrounding Black working-class kinship as pathology would be crucial to the management and production of knowledge of Caribbean societies. This problematization of intimacy played a key role in the formation of emerging Caribbean social science disciplines, such as sociology and demography, that took up questions of family as foundational to their remit (I discuss this point further in chapter 3).[72] It also prompted changes to Jamaica's 1943 census by, for instance, transforming the definition of work in ways that occluded women's labor to align Jamaican realities with the ideal family unit of breadwinning husbands and domesticated wives.[73] Yet the process of tying together nation building with respectable family life through a gendered configuration of work failed to consider how male employment could undo the proper intimacies it was intended to cultivate. For instance, the preeminent Jamaican newspaper the *Daily Gleaner* praised Patrick Nelson for migrating to Wales in 1937 to take up the position of gentleman's valet to "Lord Stanley." But in early twentieth-century England, this kind of labor was often performed by queer men and frequently functioned as a "cover" for intimate relationships between employer and employee.[74] Indeed, it is likely that Nelson's swift dismissal from his position was due to the discovery of his intimate relationship with his employer.[75]

Colonial authorities and Jamaican elites used allegations of sexual deviancy among the island's poor Black masses to explain various economic problems in the aftermath of emancipation in 1834 and in the wake of the labor riots one hundred years later. In keeping with a pronatalist approach in which population size indexed the strength and wealth of empire, they constructed the shortage of plantation labor upon manumission as the dilemma and Black sexual depravity as its cause.[76] In the late 1930s, drawing from global eugenics, neo-Malthusian and tropical medicine movements that posited non-white reproduction in the colonies as pathological, they turned to Black sexual depravity to account for the overpopulation—and subsequent high unemployment rates and economic hardships—that precipitated the widespread labor unrest.[77] If Black reproduction rates were insufficient to meet the demands of colonial capital in 1834, they were excessive in 1938. Jamaica in the 1930s was marked by a period of intensified nationalism in which birth control became a contested site through which to articulate what Jamaica should look like. The return of Jamaican migrant labor as host societies closed their borders, combined with a drop in mortality rates, produced an increase in the island's population between 1921 and 1943. This growth exacerbated the economic hardships of the Great Depression, which were made even worse by the devastation of the fruit industry, the sector that employed many rural Jamaicans.[78] Jamaican upper- and middle-class advocates for birth control interpreted this state of affairs as a problem of overpopulation that threatened both economic and social stability as well as maternal health and family life.[79] They focused their attention on, and received the most involvement from, working-class women who sought support in gaining autonomy over their reproductive lives as they faced health concerns and economic precarity.[80] Yet many Jamaicans opposed birth control on race, class, and religious grounds. They argued that it contravened the Christian edict to "go forth and multiply," appeared to be a coercive ploy to reduce the numbers (and therefore political power) of poor and Black people, and detracted attention from the root causes of economic inequality.[81] Over time, the work of Jamaica's Birth Control League, the Beth Jacobs Clinic, and the Jamaica Family Planning Association—established in 1939, 1953, and 1957, respectively—were successful in wresting birth control into the mainstream.[82]

If Jamaica's independence in 1962 did not carry with it the same revolutionary fervor as earlier interregna, the election of Michael Manley of the People's National Party (PNP) as prime minister in 1972 marked a moment in which Jamaicans envisioned the possibility of change.[83] During Manley's leadership, the PNP sought to align Jamaica more closely to democratic socialism; and the island witnessed a flourishing of Black Power, feminist, and labor movements. It was also in this period that the Gay Freedom Movement, Jamaica's first self-proclaimed gay activist organization, was formed in 1977 (this is the subject of chapter 6). In contrast to earlier eras of women's struggle in the late nineteenth and early twentieth centuries, Jamaican women's change-making efforts in the immediate post-independence period were wider-reaching in both scope and scale as part of a larger regional women's movement.[84] Though the rise of Jamaica's industrial and service industries (especially tourism) produced employment opportunities for some lower- and middle-class women in the island's growing cities, firms systematically positioned women in lower-status positions and paid them less than men.[85] Grassroots feminist groups such as Sistren pushed public dialogue around women's experiences of employment discrimination, state neglect, and domestic violence, and women's advocacy within Jamaica's political institutions began to yield significant changes.[86] During the PNP administration, Jamaica established a Women's Bureau in the Prime Minister's Office and passed the Equal Pay for Men and Women Act, the Status of Children Act, and the Maternity Leave Act. These three pieces of legislation formally altered women's position in the workforce and how the state recognized and regulated family intimacies: they effected a legal re-evaluation of kinship categories and women's labor (including reproductive labor).[87] Yet even as the Status of Children's Act sought to legally remove the distinction between children born in and outside of wedlock, the system of family courts created to administer this and other newly established family laws had the effect of eroding mothers' relationships to their children while providing a way for men to exercise control over family relations and resources.[88]

This period also witnessed the burgeoning of Black Power. This movement was perhaps most evident in the riots protesting Jamaica's decision to refuse entry to Walter Rodney, a Guyanese history lecturer at the University of the West Indies (UWI), upon his return from a Black Power conference in Montreal, and in the increasingly sympathetic stance taken toward Rastafari upon the release of the findings of a study carried out by UWI researchers.[89] In the 1970s, Jamaicans thus developed a new relationship to Blackness.[90] The PNP rose to power with the campaign slogan "Black man time now," and the island's middle and upper classes—especially young people—began to embrace reggae and other cultural practices associated with Rastafari.[91] These shifts in Jamaican race relations had important consequences for elite practices of intimacy and kinship. Wealthy white Jamaicans always had casual erotic relationships with Black and lower-class persons, but they typically entertained the possibility of marriage only with those of the same color and class background.[92] The practice of engaging in both marital and extramarital intimacies occurred in relation to the workings of power and hierarchy in Jamaican society. Elite married men could thus participate in affairs in ways that were much more difficult for elite married women.[93] To the extent that affairs were expressions of classed and gendered power, elite men could engage in "outside relations" with women across Jamaica's color spectrum. In contrast, the expectation that women engage in intimacies with men of a higher standing constrained elite women's options; they were compelled to seek out those of at least a similar class and/or complexion.[94] The social liberalism of the Manley years unsettled this state of affairs, such that "some [elite] men and women married brown or Black Jamaicans of the upper middle class, that is . . . partners who were 'one notch down.'"[95]

In 1980 the turbulent transition in power from the PNP to its rival, the Jamaica Labor Party (JLP), continued a shift in Jamaica's political economic landscape occasioned by the transformation of its relationship to global capital. In the context of an international recession, the skyrocketing price of oil, and the flight of both domestic and foreign capital, the PNP was compelled to borrow funds from international financial institutions in support of its development projects under conditions that were at odds with its democratic socialist agenda. When the JLP took office, it continued the debt-constrained, export-led approach that the PNP initiated but more openly embraced the principles of free trade.[96] The structural adjustment policies that the JLP implemented in support of this development path facilitated untrammeled access of global capital to Jamaica's resources and people in ways that deteriorated social conditions and exacerbated economic inequality and levels of poverty.[97] Women, especially lower-class women, bore the brunt of these policies that unsettled the terrain of feminist struggle and transformed the island's gender and sexual relations.[98] This is perhaps most evident in the rise of sex work in Jamaica, especially in the tourism sector that came to life after World War II and surpassed sugar and banana exports as the island's main earner of foreign exchange.[99] Race, gender, and class dynamics shaped the patterns of Jamaican sex work. Although both women and men came to this line of work, given the difficulty of making a living through other means, the economic challenges facing lower-class women were particularly dire because these women were less likely to be formally employed, more likely to be hired into jobs that paid lower wages than "male" occupations, and more likely to be the main income earner of their families as head of household. Gender also influenced the way that Jamaican women and men engaged with their clients. In their interactions with tourist women, Jamaican men were more likely to participate in longer-term, romance-type relationships where they acted as cultural brokers and hosts to their clients, whereas Jamaican women were more likely to engage in transactional intimacies with male

tourists.[100] Jamaican men capitalized on the island's global popularity for reggae, wearing dreadlocks to play into tourists' racialized desires in ways that
were less available to Jamaican women seeking male clients because of the
gendered nature of this raced exoticism.[101] Finally, gender and class relations
patterned the criminalization of sex work. Predominantly working-class Jamaican women were arrested for soliciting clients in public. This was because,
even if Jamaican men were accused of subverting patriarchal expectations
through their economic dependence on their female clients, they were less
visible than women as sex workers.[102] And even though middle-class women
also practiced sex work, the more private way that they were able to conduct
their business shielded them from the eyes of the state.[103]

In the last two decades of the twentieth century, the arrival of HIV/AIDS
and the rise of dancehall music brought queerness to the forefront of Jamaican public life. Here I focus on dancehall, given the extensive discussion of
HIV/AIDS in chapter 4. In its current form, dancehall emerged in the late
1970s as a music of protest from Jamaica's poor Black urban communities.
In dancehall settings, DJs delivered oral performances over sonic rhythms
amplified through loudspeaker sound systems.[104] Its sexually explicit lyrics
and performances facilitated spaces for Black working-class women to reconfigure race, class, and gender ideologies that positioned them as inferior to
upper-class white/brown respectable "ladies."[105] Debates over dancehall most
visibly illustrate the shift that Deborah Thomas identifies, from a British-
inflected middle-class creole multiracialism to "modern Blackness," a vision
of citizenship premised on urban Black expressions of popular culture influenced by American forms of neoliberal subjectivity.[106] Conservative upper-
class Jamaicans may have condemned dancehall as "vulgar" or "slack," but
its glorification of Black lower-class women's bodies and sexualities unsettled
the politics of class and color that historically valorized proximity to whiteness as the ideal of femininity and beauty.[107]

In the 1980s and 1990s, dancehall foregrounded women's bodies through
provocative dances and revealing clothing, whereas it emphasized male
status through lyrical artistry whereby male DJs boasted of their sexual
prowess with women and their capacity for violence.[108] Dancehall "gun"
lyrics emerged in the context of Jamaica's increasing prominence in the international drug and gun trade as working-class men in Kingston turned to
this informal domain of work as a consequence of the failure of Jamaica's
formal economy to provide a feasible way of making a living.[109] As Black
urban working-class masculinity took shape through the practice of com-
pulsory heterosexuality and the exercise of violence, it came to articulate

itself through aggressive expressions of homophobia.[110] Unlike girls, boys in economically disenfranchised Kingston communities were pressured to prove their manhood and heterosexual orientation and often faced violent reprisals if they did not (for instance, if they exhibited "softness" associated with women or amorous interest in other men). The work of anthropologists from this period suggests that these pressures did not resonate in the same way with middle-class expectations of masculinity and that they were directed most forcefully toward those perceived as outsiders within tight-knit poor, working-class, and rural communities.[111] Nevertheless, Jamaican dancehall artists in the 1980s and 1990s lyrically regulated the boundaries of appropriate gender and sexual behaviors in ways that forcefully excluded homosexual men writ large.[112] This is most evident in Buju Banton's song "Boom Bye Bye," which became a lightning rod for dialogue across the North Atlantic around Jamaica's supposed penchant for homophobic violence. Though Banton has since removed the song from his discography, the way that Jamaican dancehall artists were drawn into international debates about gay rights at the time prompted Jamaicans on the island and in the diaspora to offer defensive arguments in support of cultural sovereignty in the face of what they interpreted as the imposition of Euro-American cultural imperialism.[113] Jamaica's Forum for All-Sexuals Lesbians and Gays—now known as Equality JA—established itself in 1998 in the context of this fervent transnational debate over sexual citizenship as a human rights organization in support of gender and sexual minorities in Jamaica.[114] This is yet another moment in which global economic transformations unfold in lockstep with the emergence of racialized discourses of gender and sexuality in and about Jamaica. This period marks the consolidation of the contemporary problem space of queerness in Jamaica and brackets the historical narrative that this book offers.

Part I   Archival Continuities

2

Knowledge

A "Native"
Social Science

In 1938, England established the West India Royal Commission—more popularly known as the Moyne Commission after its chair, Lord Moyne—to investigate the causes of massive labor unrest across British Caribbean colonies during the Great Depression. Instead of examining the uneven effects of global capital, the commission identified the Black family as a source of weakness in the social fabric of British West Indian societies and financed social science research to study and make policy recommendations around Caribbean kinship.[1] This racialized preoccupation with improper intimacies exceeded the purview of formal government discourse in the metropole to pervade public discussion in the colonies. On January 10, 1952, Florence Sylvia Foot, the wife of the island's governor, addressed the annual general meeting of the Women Workers Federation in Kingston, Jamaica. In her talk she launched into a scathing critique of children born to unmarried parents on the island:

> Our church has been here in Jamaica for over three hundred years and in that time, what have we produced? A completely amoral community on a whole.... Our country churches are filled with little old ladies who look

respectable, yet if you visit them at their homes, what do you find . . . three illegitimate children—each having nine illegitimate children.

And yet there is no shame, no stigma attached to it. . . . All roads we start on end up [in] this smelly alley. I need a new broom to sweep it clean.[2]

Published on the first page of the *Daily Gleaner*, Jamaica's most widely circulated newspaper, Foot's remarks—particularly her use of the term "smelly alley"—set off a heated public debate across the island in the decade before Jamaica was to be granted independence from England in 1962. The debasement of Black intimacies in state and public discourses was part of a broader hemispheric concern about the "Negro problem" across the Americas that associated the alleged deviancy and criminality of African diasporic people with their purportedly loose, disorganized, and even perverse sexual practices.[3]

The formation of a "native" social sciences in the Anglophone Caribbean took shape in relationship to these colonial discourses of Black sexual depravity and had the reparative effect of countering the epistemic violence that they performed. The founding of the University College of the West Indies (UCWI) in 1948 marked the institutionalization of local knowledge production in the region. Many of UCWI's first generation of social scientists sought to study kinship, which meant that early academic iterations of Caribbean self-understanding took shape through the study of intimate relatedness. Tracy Robinson thus notes that in the mid-twentieth century, "participant observation, the lens of anthropological scrutiny, and Caribbean family studies quickly became the most legitimate means of 'knowing' the West Indian subject."[4] In this period, local scholars unsettled colonial narratives of Black sexual deviancy by illustrating that phenomena such as illegitimacy were rooted in the sociocultural and economic conditions of West Indian societies.[5] Far from being pathological, children born out of wedlock and other queer iterations of kinship, such as female-headed households and "visiting unions," were legitimate forms of intimate relatedness. These studies were not just academic exercises. Anglophone Caribbean citizens came to understand themselves through this process of reclaiming kinship forms rendered deviant under colonial epistemologies. The rise of nationalism in the region also meant that emerging Caribbean nations used the knowledge that these scholars produced to articulate a sense of distinctiveness.[6] The move to recalibrate colonial forms of morality played out within the scholarly realm of social scientific study as well as within public forums of debate. Jamaican feminist, activist, and writer Una Marson penned a letter to the *Daily Gleaner* in response to Lady Foot in which she stated:

I do not know how well our first lady is informed on the history and custom of illegitimacy in Jamaica . . . let it not be forgotten that the Jamaican peasant is reaping today, not what his ancestors sowed witlessly and willfully, but the fruit of the way of life into which they were driven during the dark days of slavery. . . . [Illegitimacy] is a fact in our life and unfortunately our history. . . . It is hardly fair to call it a "smelly alley" and be surprised at old ladies who look respectable yet have illegitimate children and grandchildren. They are, in fact respectable and some of them truer ladies than may often be found in "high society" cliques in our midst.[7]

In this chapter I assemble an archive of repair by drawing together forms of knowledge that redress the violences enacted by colonial discourses of Black sexual depravity. It comprises three sources. The first is the mid-twentieth-century social scientific studies of kinship, including Edith Clarke's *My Mother Who Fathered Me: A Study of the Families in Three Selected Communities of Jamaica*; Judith Blake's *Family Structure in Jamaica: The Social Context of Reproduction*; Madeline Kerr's *Personality and Conflict in Jamaica*; Michael G. Smith's *Kinship and Community in Carriacou* and *West Indian Family Structure*; and several of Fernando Henriques's works, including *Family and Colour in Jamaica, Jamaica Land of Wood and Water*, and *Love in Action: The Sociology of Sex*. The second and third sources contextualize these academic studies and include newspaper articles from the *Daily Gleaner*, the *Jamaica Daily Express*, and the *Jamaica Times*, as well as novels from the period such as *Black Lightning* by Roger Mais, *The Hills of Hebron: A Jamaican Novel* by Sylvia Wynter, and *Escape to an Autumn Pavement* by Andrew Salkey.

A queer reading of these materials illustrates the passive lines of fractal formations at the level of archive. Fractals materialize through repetition with difference, and passive lines are the ones that remain the same; they index continuity with the past. Even as the materials assembled to construct this archive had the effect of redressing discourses of Black sexual deviancy, they continued to reproduce the raced, classed, gendered, and national asymmetries embedded in existing archival arrangements. In this chapter I use queerness to surface these asymmetries and highlight the persistence of archival inequities. I consider how same-gender intimacy as a specific form of queerness comes to be inscribed in and as Jamaica's past. The problem space of illegitimacy centers poor and working-class Black women in ways that make it difficult to discern how this practice takes shape among other subjects, and in this chapter I explore how a similar kind of archival imperative functions for same-gender intimacy. I investigate how the workings of coloniality hierarchize different kinds of queerness by attending to the kinds of historical "evidence" left behind in their wake. While the figure of the white male homosexual foreigner emerges prominently across Jamaican social science studies, news media, and literature, Pukumina, the working-class Afro-Creole religion, emerges only in the margins of these sources as a site of queerness. Traces of queerness among the island's brown middle classes are even more difficult to identify according to positivistic conventions of historical inquiry, occurring largely in the imaginative realm of the island's literary works. The reparative effects of knowledge production in late colonial Jamaica may have revalorized certain previously debased gender and sexual relations, but the colonial logics that animated these regimes of debasement persist. These logics are the passive lines of fractal formations. They are what remain the same in cycles of repetition and difference and shape how knowledge formations archive queerness in the present. Destigmatizing illegitimacy did not prevent the raced, classed, gendered, and national valuations that gave life to illegitimacy's debasement from shaping who and what counts as queer in the historical record.

"Alleys in England That Smell Much Worse"

The cultural imaginaries of late colonial Jamaica positioned illegitimacy and same-gender intimacy differently across the uneven landscape of archival infrastructures. The fact that illegitimacy became a site of anticolonial struggle in a way that same-gender intimacy did not means that they were materialized as traces in different ways. Discourses of illegitimacy and same-gender intimacy of the period thus differently distributed archival visibility across raced, classed, gendered, and national formations. Using queerness to trace this visibility vis-à-vis illegitimacy brings into focus the contours of archival arrangements and the persistence of their effects in producing historical subjects in the present. Poor and working-class Black women emerge as the presumed historical subject of illegitimacy, but an altogether different historical subject takes shape from hegemonic discourses of queerness: white male foreigners. This is perhaps most evident in the words of Jamaica's House of Representative member Will O. Isaacs, who, in his contribution to the debate between Marson and Foot, notes:

> No one will seek to defend or be proud of the high rate of illegitimacy in Jamaica. But I am tired of the way non-Jamaicans living here make it a habit to speak contemptuously of the Jamaica[n] people.... Lady Foot,

however, should remember that there are Alleys in England that smell much worse than ours and they are to be found in an enormous amount of abortions or child murder that take place in England every year; not to mention the great social evils of homosexualism and hermaphroditism that are a foul blot on a large part of English society at the present time.

Reputable Englishmen whom I met at Mackinac last year told me with a sad heart of the spread of these evils in England and assured me that they were so widespread that the Foreign Office, the Colonial Office, and the Houses of Parliament have not escaped.

We know what are our faults and the evils of our country and English people are not going to correct them. We will correct them ourselves and believe me, bad as our Alley is, I prefer it to the Alleys in the country from which Lady Foot comes.[8]

Unlike Marson, Isaacs does not disagree with the undesirability of illegitimacy. Instead, he questions Foot's authority as a foreigner to comment on Jamaican society. His defense of Jamaica against foreign criticism is expressed in the idiom of queerness, alleging that England is home to even more deviant forms of sexuality and gender.

This was not the first time that Isaacs mobilized anti-homosexuality rhetoric as a form of anticolonial critique. In 1951 he successfully lobbied Jamaica's House of Representatives to carry out a Commission of Enquiry into the Police by drawing attention to several problems with the force, including mismanagement, corruption, and homosexuality among "imported" officers.[9] As the vice president of the People's National Party (PNP), Isaacs's call for a Commission of Enquiry aligned with the broader goals of the party, which began as a nationalist movement that sought to wrest control of state institutions from colonial authorities.[10] His insistence on homosexuality among foreign officers became a point of investigation in the inquiry as it sought to determine "whether there is reasonable cause to believe that any and, if any, what officers, sub-officers or constables of the Jamaica Constabulary Force are addicted to homosexual practices or have committed or attempted to commit any unnatural offence with any other officer, sub-officer or constable of the said Force or have attempted to induce any other officer, sub-officer or constable of the said Force to commit or to submit to any such unnatural practices."[11] Though the commission ultimately neither offered significant censure of the island's police force nor indicated the presence of homosexuality among its members, Jamaican newspapers nevertheless dutifully reported on the proceedings of the Enquiry and made visible the very frank talk about improper intimacies that surfaced in witness testimonies.[12]

Isaacs's mobilization of anti-homosexuality rhetoric to critique the workings of colonial power exhibited a structural similarity to the way sexuality became an idiom through which to articulate political anxieties across the North Atlantic.[13] Isaacs's criticism of homosexuality in Jamaica's police force resonated with the "Lavender Scare" that purged homosexuals from federal government employment during the anticommunist panic in the United States.[14] The United States pressured Cold War allies to exclude homosexuals from government positions, but it is not clear whether such pressure had reached Jamaica.[15] However, it is likely that Isaacs was familiar with this policy, given his involvement in leasing military bases in Jamaica to the United States.[16] Further, Isaacs's insistence that Jamaica's homosexual police officers were foreign—mostly English personnel of high rank—aligned with the Wolfenden Committee proceedings in England that discursively foregrounded elite white men in calling for the decriminalization of homosexuality.[17] Both Isaacs and the Jamaican public were well aware of these proceedings across the Atlantic. Isaacs suggested as much in his letter where he discussed "the spread of these evils in England." And when the chair of the Wolfenden Committee visited Jamaica in 1960, an interview with the Englishman revealed that "[his] name has run from one end of the island to the other because of the Wolfenden Report . . . every Jamaican has read about that."[18] In adopting an anticolonialist approach in his response to Foot and his call for the Police Enquiry, Isaacs's use of anti-homosexuality rhetoric resonated with discourses of homosexuality in England (metropole) and the United States (hegemon).

The relationship that Isaacs makes visible between queerness and foreign men emerges in different sites in mid-twentieth-century Jamaica, from the literary to the academic to news media.[19] In these sites, queerness was understood in terms of the behavioral consequence of external conditions. In her 1962 novel *The Hills of Hebron: A Jamaican Novel*, Sylvia Wynter offers a retelling of the story of Revival leader Alexander Bedward in which she alludes to male sexual exploitation in the context of enslavement. Gatha, the matriarch of Hebron, the community in which Wynter's novel is set, recalls her grandmother telling her the story of her great grandfather, Cato.

When he was born, his English master Randall, named him Cato. . . . And as for his not having a son, well, many people had hinted that that was because of Cato's closeness with his master, which had started when he was very young and the white man had first observed the smooth black of Cato's skin, the big gentle liquid eyes of a wild beast, the tiny pointed ears, the rows of perfect teeth, the delicate limbs molded by some ancient civilization that had refined itself out of existence. Cato Randall didn't have a son, many people said, not because of any curse, but because he had tried to be a man when it was already too late. Gatha nodded her head solemnly, but she did not understand her grandmother's veiled explanation.[20]

Wynter constructs the relationship between Cato and Randall in terms of the dichotomies of child/adult, enslaved/free, Black/white. In this context, the "closeness" of the relationship is occasioned by the English man's ownership of the boy. That this intimacy is imposed is suggested not only by the difference in power between them but also by the fact that Randall's agency is foregrounded in the relationship.[21] Indeed, when Cato finally actualizes his desires ("tried to be man"), it is in relationship with the woman he comes to marry. The fictional nature of Wynter's account offers a particular kind of engagement with the past. Indeed, Wynter suggests that the novel as a genre indexes the reality of plantation societies in ways that North Atlantic methods of history writing fundamentally distort.[22] It is therefore significant that critics in both Jamaica and the United States at the time when the novel was published maintained that *The Hills of Hebron* was "not so much of excellent artistic invention as of actuality, excellently reported," such that it's "characters are all real . . . [and] the situation very true to life."[23]

The association of queerness with male foreignness is also present in Jamaica's foundational kinship studies. It is important to note, however, that sexuality was not an object of analysis in its own right. Jamaican social scientists studied sexuality as a by-product of moral concerns about the proper organization of family life and economic preoccupations around levels of population growth that supposedly threatened social welfare and national development. Inspired by structural functional approaches to kinship, Caribbean scholars were largely concerned with reproduction ("mating") and the way that sexual practices between men and women were socially organized. Even though Caribbean subjects involved in these early studies were not always forthcoming about their intimate lives, queerness does appear in mid-twentieth-century Jamaican social science texts.[24] The best-known example is Jamaican anthropologist M. G. Smith's work in Carriacou among "lesbians" (known as "madeveine" or "zami" on the island).[25] Though Smith does not explicitly address queerness in his research on Jamaica, his colleague Fernando Henriques takes up this task. A lengthy excerpt from his chapter "Sexual Behavior" in the monograph *Jamaica, Land of Wood and Water* reads:

> Homosexuality as a social institution in a European context can be broadly defined as falling into two types. This division is roughly synonymous with urban and rural areas. The rural types can be regarded much more as a natural growth, as is beastiality, whereas the urban type is essentially an artificial growth fostered by the climate of opinion sophistication and the intellectual inequality of women. This division leaves aside the physiological factor which operates in both types. What is here considered is induced homosexuality.
>
> It is suggested that where access to the other sex is easy, the incidence of homosexuality will be found to be slight. This is the case in Jamaica. Its occurrence is mainly concentrated in the seaport towns. This is largely due to two factors: the transient population of sailors, and the tourist. On shore the sailor may seek the company of women or boys according to his fancy. The port exists, from the amusement point of view, to cater for his needs. The result is the existence of the professional homosexual youth.
>
> It is said in Jamaica that tourists are responsible for much of the homosexuality. Again, this is on a professional basis. It is difficult to ascertain how far this is so, but there is no doubt that many tourists are homosexual, and it is reasonable to conclude that they would seek sexual satisfaction of this kind. The highest incidence is found in the main tourist areas of the island. Some towns which were the center of the banana industry were, in their day, notorious for this type of sexuality. The reputation still lingers on.[26]

As Henriques was the only social scientist to write about homosexuality in mid-twentieth-century Jamaica at any length during the period, his discussion on the topic is worth critical scrutiny. The above passage raises four important points. First, he considers homosexuality to be a physiological condition that can be divided into "natural" and "artificial" types. Second, while he grants that "natural" homosexuality may exist in rural Europe, in Jamaica homosexuality is "induced." Unlike contemporary notions of "sexual orientation" rooted in individual identity and personhood, Henriques suggests that sex between men in Jamaica is the behavioral consequence of external conditions. Third, Henriques's reading of homosexuality is not neutral. Like Smith, he interprets homosexuality in structural functional terms whereby homosexuality constitutes a deviation from "normal" sexual practice that occurs as a result of (presumably abnormal) conditions. Fourth, in Jamaica, the primary conditions that "induce" homosexuality are the opportunities to make money occasioned by the sexual desires of foreign men such as sailors and tourists.

The association between homosexuality and tourism in mid-twentieth-century Jamaica is not surprising, given the full maturation of Jamaica's tourist industry with a shift from largely short-term to long-term visitors and the extension of tourism on the island from one season to all year round. Supported by state incentives such as the Hotels Aid Law (1944), which subsidized hotel construction, and the formation of the Jamaica Tourist Board in 1954, the number of visitors to the island grew from 34,370 in 1945 to 226,945 in 1960.[27] Though largely concentrated in the hands of hoteliers and travel agencies, the tourist industry generated significant profit on the island as the value of Jamaica's tourist industry jumped from £2.7 million in 1949 to £10 million in 1957.[28] In opposition to its positioning as a laid-back, casual beach holiday in contemporary Euro-American imaginaries, in the 1950s Jamaica garnered a reputation for being the posh vacation getaway for the rich and famous, attracting stars such as Errol Flynn, Katherine Hepburn, and Ian Fleming.[29] The transformations wrought by the tourist boom were most acutely felt in Montego Bay as it quickly eclipsed Port Antonio as the island's tourist capital in the post–World War II era with the increasing movement away from travel by ship to travel by airplane. Jamaicans greeted this rise in tourism with ambivalence. While some interpreted it as an economic necessity, others saw it as a new form of imperialism. Jamaica was now open to the rest of the world in a way it had not been during World War II. This openness, combined with the energies mobilized toward national self-determination, produced anxieties expressed in terms of sexuality around citizenship, identity, and belonging. Jamaicans thus located improper sex among the island's visitors, interpreting the tourist industry as "[a] prostitute's trade" and its patrons as idle whites who were "over rich, over sexed and over here."[30] In so doing, they reversed colonial epistemologies that associated the Caribbean and its people with sexual decadence.[31] In assuming the position of minister of trade and industry in 1955 to direct the growth of the island's tourism industry, Isaacs played a key role in fostering this connection between tourism and sexual deviance in Jamaican popular discourse.[32]

Foreign homosexuality exhibited a structural relationship to whiteness in late colonial Jamaica. African American gay Harlem Renaissance artist Richmond Barthé quickly became aware of how whiteness, homosexuality, and foreignness trafficked together on the island when he temporarily moved to Jamaica in 1947. At the time, Barthé was most known for his sculpture that explored the physicality and sensuality of the Black male figure. Though he

2.1. Excerpt, *Daily Gleaner,*
February 14, 1954, 13. Source: National
Library of Jamaica, Kingston.

ARCHDEACON

CONDEMNS

MONTEGO BAY

MORALS

Gleaner Western Bureau
MONTEGO BAY, S.J., Feb. 14:
In an outspoken sermon at the
St. James Parish Church today,
Archdeacon Fox condemned the
rise of homosexuality in Jamaica's Number One tourist resort, and pointed out that by
allowing it to grow unchallenged the district was becoming
the mecca of foreign pederasts
who were in turn corrupting the
local youth.

sought to integrate into the island society, Jamaicans largely rebuffed his efforts and labeled him as white.[33] Notwithstanding his skin color, his foreignness, ability to purchase a home on the island, and evident sexual inclinations
meant that Jamaicans associated him with "a burgeoning and highly visible
north coast homosexual community led by [Noel] Coward."[34]

This notion of homosexuality as a form of deviant sexuality induced by
external factors—primarily foreign white men—also circulated in the island's
news media, such as the *Daily Gleaner*'s story of the St. James Parish Church
archdeacon who "condemned the rise of homosexuality in Jamaica's number
one tourist resort and pointed out that by allowing it to grow unchallenged,
the district was becoming the mecca of foreign pederasts who were in turn
corrupting the local youth" (see figure 2.1).[35] Alongside these more sensa-
tional events, Jamaican news reporting of homosexuality typically took place
in relation to sex crimes between men under Jamaica's Offences Against the

Persons Act. The cases that indexed tourism elicited much more detailed reporting than the cases that did not, and tourist destination parishes prominently featured in newspaper coverage of gross indecency and sodomy cases. For instance, in the news report of a ruling on a charge of gross indecency in 1955, Justice Clare noted that the defendant was a thirty-five-year-old waiter employed at Round Hill Hotel and decided to give a more lenient sentence, noting to the defendant, "You probably are a victim of circumstances brought about by the type of work you do and the place where you are employed."[36]

The proceedings of such cases were confined not only to courtroom audiences and those who read about such cases the next day in the island's newspapers. Going to court was a source of entertainment, particularly for working-class Jamaicans, who would travel far distances to attend. And while they may have not been able to afford the proper attire required to enter the courtroom, they reveled in the company of their friends, sharing news about the court proceedings afterward.[37] Far from being a private issue, talk of sex between men in Jamaican courtrooms became both a topic of public interest and a matter of concern for the colonial state.

"Sodomy More Common among Pocomanians"

Identifying how the production of historical knowledge of same-gender desire can foreground subjects that are not wealthy white male foreigners highlights the salience of existing archival arrangements. Constructing queer figures in relationship to other raced, class, gendered, and national formations necessarily requires engaging with the constraints of these arrangements that constitute the passive lines of fractal formations; they are what persist in making queer histories of repair. Thus, the practice of constituting the history of same-gender intimacy in late colonial Jamaica in ways that decenter wealthy white male foreigners reveals less about "what happened in the past" than about the continuity of archival infrastructures that shape historical narratives. Figuring poor and working-class Black women as the historical subjects of same-gender intimacy requires working against these infrastructures that would otherwise discursively render them in terms of illegitimacy.

Sylvia Wynter's novel *The Hills of Hebron* offers a way into this counter archival imperative. The novel offers a searing critique of all forms of intimate relations—whether they be the forms of kinship that Caribbean social scientists reclaimed or the Eurocentric norms of nuclear family they sought to decenter. While the novel characterizes women's relationships to men in terms of violence, exploitation, and oppression, it also situates Pukumina as a site through which women experience a certain kind of freedom and pleasure.[38] At one point in the novel, Obadiah, the elder of the fictional community (Hebron) after which the novel is named, fervently searches for the man who slept with his wife. The urgency of this search prompts an onlooker to note, "At this moment, his [Obadiah's] face was that of his mother. . . . Of all Pocomania dancers Obadiah's mother became the most completely possessed. Perhaps because she fought the hardest against this exaltation, this wild release that sent her spinning, leaping, whirling, her body held stiffly, breasts erect and pointed, her nostrils flaring, her lips slightly parted and pressed against white teeth that glinted in the light of the torches."[39]

Building on the informal missionary work carried out by slaves who were Christianized in the United States and brought to the island by Empire Loyalists in the aftermath of the American Revolution, Pukumina as an Afro-Christian spiritual practice took root in Jamaica after a period of widespread intense religious upsurge in 1861–62 called the Great Revival.[40] Revivalism in mid-twentieth-century Jamaica was characterized by a belief in multiple spirits that influence the human world and the need to interact with these spirits through public or private rituals, sometimes with the intercession of Revival leaders, in order to solicit their support and/or avoid their wrath.[41] Revivalism was largely practiced by uneducated, poor, and working-class Black Jamaicans. Prerequisites to attending other churches included having the proper clothes and sufficient resources to contribute tithes, but Jamaicans did not experience such economic barriers with Revivalism.[42] Taking place on Sundays as well as two or three weekday nights, Revival meetings were often held outdoors and were boisterous, hours-long events characterized by drumming, singing, preaching, spirit possession, and healing. Jamaican Revivalism has two variants: Pukumina and Revival Zion. Though they are very similar, Pukumina differs from Revival Zion in several ways. Pukumina is considered to be the more African variant of Revivalism. It is characterized by more extreme healing practices, a greater willingness to engage in both healing and harmful spiritual work, and—as opposed to Revival Zion's stronger emphasis on preaching and the reading of scripture—Pukumina is more oriented toward singing, dancing, and emotional expressiveness.[43]

This freedom of expression is indexed in the *Daily Gleaner*'s account of Mrs. Isceylen Thompson's request to divorce her husband in 1954. According to the *Gleaner*, Thompson was upset with her husband's attempts to keep her from attending Pukumina meetings, stating that she "wanted to be free."[44] That Mrs. Thompson sought freedom, and Obadiah's mother experiences spiritual and erotic release in a religious context where women outnumber men by ratios as high as five to one, is significant.[45] It suggests that Pukumina may have operated as a site through which intimacies among women were socially organized.

The work of British psychologist Madeleine Kerr and American sociologist George Simpson appears to confirm this. Kerr notes that "there does seem to be a connection between Pocomania and homosexuality in some cases. One Kingston informant said that there had been a split in one group of Pocomania Shepards between those who were homosexual and those who were not. Another Kingston informant told of another Pocomania band the members of which were all homosexual, both male and female."[46] Simpson supports Kerr's claim and states that "in the case of some revivalist leaders, there can be little doubt that sexual irregularities, heterosexual or homosexual, characterize their relationships with some followers," and that, compared to Revival Zionism, West Kingstonians considered "sodomy more common among Pocomanians."[47]

A closer reading of mid-twentieth-century research into Pukumina reveals that the religious practice comes to be associated not only with same-gender intimacy but also with the subversion of gender norms. Contrary to other religious groups on the island at this time in which positions of leadership were reserved for men, women's leadership in Pukumina groups was institutionally inscribed in the position of "Mother." In this role, women were responsible for carrying out specific ritual ceremonies, and they received messages from Pukumina spirits that empowered them to act on the sect's behalf and to provide religious guidance to the sect's practitioners.[48] Pukumina not only permitted a more flexible configuration of gendered dynamics of power but also created space for more expansive practices of gender expression. In her field notes from a mourning ceremony, Madeleine Kerr was especially attentive to the unusual gender presentation of the men participants. She states,

> Shepherd Pappa was dressed in a long red robe which he held up as he danced. On his head was a white cloth and a white veil was hanging down his back giving a bridal effect. A loop of white in a different material also hung down his front. When he spun round holding his skirts up, silk knickers and a petticoat coat could be seen. He also had women's bangles on his wrists.... Another man now joined in.... He screamed and shouted in a feminine voice as he danced. He has quite a normal male voice at other times.[49]

In commenting about the otherwise unremarkable behavior of these men in this religious context, Kerr suggests that expectations of men that existed in other spaces of Jamaican society were not necessarily always applicable in Pukumina settings.

As we saw earlier regarding Henriques, these statements may index less about Jamaican sociocultural practice and more about the context of the research process and the biographies of the researchers themselves. The findings of North Atlantic scholars conducting social research in a British colony composed of largely African-descended subjects must be subject to careful and critical analysis. In 1955 M. G. Smith noted that research in the Caribbean had largely been "conducted by visiting social scientists from America or Britain . . . guided by theories and themes of interest developed in studies of societies and cultures outside the British Caribbean."[50] To what extent do the statements that Jamaicans relayed to Simpson and Kerr operate as forms of gossip that index the differences in race, class, and geography between interlocutors? How does Kerr become fixated on gender performance, and on what criteria does she attribute femaleness to clothing and voice? These questions suggest that what is at stake in Kerr's and Simpson's work is not their "truthfulness" but their discursive effects. Regardless of whether or not gender and sexual peculiarity "actually" took place within Pukumina communities, it is significant that statements about this association persist.[51] These statements function as a kind of inheritance that Jamaicans must grapple with regardless of their veracity.

This focus on Pukumina as a site of sexual and gender non-normativity aligns with more recent scholarship that identifies manifestations of queerness in Afro-Creole religions across the Americas. Gloria Wekker's work on the relationship between Winti and women-loving women in Suriname, Omise'eke Natasha Tinsley's consideration of how the queer Vodou figure of Ezili surfaces in the work of African diasporic artists, Khytie Brown's location of contemporary Jamaican Revival Zion as an "afroqueer ontological position," and Conner and Sparks's oral histories of queer practitioners of Santeria, Vodou, and Candomble all suggest the productivity of grappling with iterations of non-normative sexualities in the Caribbean through an attention to spiritual experience.[52] Jacqui Alexander maintains that spiritual practitioners engage with the sacred as a kind of embodied practice where the body becomes a site of memory.[53] What would it mean to extend Alexander's insights to consider how Pukumina exists as a site through which to work through and reconstruct a history of queerness in Jamaica? Such an endeavor would require not only analyzing where histories of queerness may be found, but also refusing to presume who their subjects may be. It would also require displacing hegemonic narratives that situate homosexuality as a foreign imposition in order to center studies of the sacred as legitimate sites of queerness in Jamaica. In this framework, Afro-Jamaican working-class women, as opposed to foreign white men, become key figures in Jamaican queer historiography.

Such an endeavor calls for an analysis of Pukumina's position in Jamaican society and how this predominantly Black, working-class women's religious practice comes to be inscribed in Jamaican history. In the long 1950s, Pukumina occupied an ambivalent space in Jamaica. On the one hand, within the context of a broader valorization of "the folk," Pukumina served as a source of inspiration in the construction of national culture. The religious practice manifested in literary representations such as Andrew Salkey's *A Quality of Violence* as well as dance, theater, and film—such as *Anancy and the Magic Mirror*, choreographed by Ivy Baxter; *Pocomania*, produced by Rannie Williams; and the British documentary *Jamaica Problem*. Pukumina also came to occupy a significant place in Jamaica's foreign relations, with tourists and social scientists coming to the island to witness Pukumina gatherings.[54] Elements of Pukumina cultural expression were even included in the festivities arranged to mark the Queen's visit in 1953.[55] Yet Pukumina's presence in the cultural sphere largely consisted of superficial appropriations that extracted Pukumina practices from their religious context and often reproduced them erroneously.[56] Most Jamaicans of this period did not have a solid grasp of this religious practice and tended to conflate it with Revivalism more generally.[57]

Though it was acceptable to use decontextualized Pukumina practices in the service of Jamaican culture, the religion itself generally was not taken seriously and certainly was not subject to the kinds of legitimizing projects around sexuality carried out by social scientists at the time. Given the widespread acceptance of the notion "that the European is ideal and the Negro inferior," Pukumina was heavily stigmatized in mid-twentieth-century Jamaica as the more African variant of the two kinds of Revivalism.[58] The *Daily Gleaner* prominently advertised cultural events drawing from Pukumina, while also vilifying this spiritual practice, describing it as a "bogus" religion characterized by "mass hysteria" and "sin and vice of every type."[59] Echoing missionary reports of "mysterious sexual doings" of the Great Revival, from which Pukumina emerged, these descriptions were also sexualized in their reference to Pukumina gatherings as "harems" and "orgies."[60] Edward Seaga suggested that government censuses greatly underestimated the number of Pukuminans on the island, given the religion's supposed widespread practice across Jamaica but its low status within the context of dominant Christian norms.[61] Unlike studies of kinship intended to address problems of underdevelopment and overpopulation or even research on Rastafari groups that sought to investigate their supposed danger to Jamaica's social order, studies of Pukumina held no such practically oriented appeal, especially when the religion's low status made it difficult to grasp why it would be important to understand this religious practice on its own terms.

Alongside Pukumina's contested location within the racial politics of pre-independence Jamaica, the elision of women's intimate lives outside of the heteronormative frameworks that colonial authorities and Jamaican social scientists prioritized meant that the kinds of intimacies that Black women shared among themselves through Pukumina did not register as noteworthy of official documentation. In recounting recollections of narratives about same-gender-desiring women in mid-twentieth-century Jamaica, Makeda Silvera and Carol Thames highlight how intimacies among women were not necessarily considered remarkable and rather formed the backdrop to social life on the island. This taken-for-granted-ness of closeness among women, and perhaps the chauvinistic notion that intimacies among women "don't count," may help to explain the relative absence of these gendered forms of erotic subjectivities and relationships in conventional traces of the past. Thames states,

> Growing up in Jamaica [late 1950s, early 1960s], I heard stories about lesbians. They didn't use the word lesbian, they used the word sodomite. . . . I thought I had never seen any of the women they were talking about—lesbian/sodomite. But looking back at my childhood, who is to say those women weren't talking about themselves. . . . [M]y culture, in an unspoken way, is a lesbian-based culture or a woman-based culture. The priority is not so much around male partners but around your children, having children, raising them, carrying on the generation. The intimacy is shared. More of an emotional compassion, touching, caressing, hugging, supporting each other—rather than based on sex.[62]

Silvera validates Thames's observation and suggests that compared to men who had sex with men, knowledge of and violence directed toward women who shared intimacies with each other were made to be private. In quoting from a discussion with her mother's friend, Silvera states,

> When I was growing up, we didn't hear much 'bout woman and woman. They weren't "suspect." There was much more talk about "batty man business" when I was a teenager in the 1950s . . . [but] sometimes crimes were committed against the women. Some very violent; some very subtle. Battery was common, especially in Kingston. A group of men would suspect a woman or have it out for her because she was a "sodomite" or because she

act "man royal" and so the men would organize and gang rape whichever woman was "suspect." Sometimes it was reported in the newspapers; other times it wasn't—but when you live in a little community, you don't need a newspaper to tell what's going on. You know by word of mouth and those stories were frequent.[63]

In contrast to the association of homosexuality with white male foreignness that prominently featured in newspapers, courtrooms, and churches in Jamaica's immediate pre-independence era, the prevailing social organization of racial and gender relations backgrounded intimacies among women from the conventions of archival practice. As Silvera illustrates, this was the case not only for Pukumina, but also for gender-based and sexual violence. It thus becomes possible to track queerness in the past through the incidences of violence marshaled against it. But these (heteropatriarchal) forms of violence leave traces that often do not show up in the materials of archival institutions. Even if they were "reported in the newspapers," this coverage would likely not indicate that such violences took place in response to intimacies among women. Instead, these traces materialize through oral narratives ("word of mouth") and inscriptions carved into the psyches and bodies of the survivors of violence. The differences between how white male foreigners and local Black women take shape as historical subjects of same-gender intimacy highlight the continuity of asymmetries in archival infrastructures that persist in shaping the practice of history writing in the present.

"We Are a Couple of Queer Ones, Eh, Pardner?"

If queer analyses surface the persistence of archival infrastructures in ways that foreground wealthy white male foreignness and sublimate local working-class Black womanhood, what kinds of narratives around middle-classed-ness might these analyses produce? What does the persistence of middle-classed-ness as archival structure entail, and how does mobilizing queerness make the passive lines of this fractal formation evident? A focus on middle-class iterations of queerness in Jamaica is significant because it facilitates a reconsideration of the politics of race and class at the nominal end of empire. Though race and class do not directly map onto each other in late colonial Jamaica, the category of colored or brown—designations that index the mixing of the island's European- and African-descended peoples— is associated with the island's middle class. Jamaica's 1960 census counted 72.07 percent of the island's population as "African" and 17.98 percent of the population as "Afro-European," "Afro-Chinese," and "Afro-East Indian."[64] Even though the island achieved universal suffrage in 1944, boosting the esteem of Jamaica's majority Black population, vestiges of racial discrimination continued to pervade Jamaican society where bias toward lighter skin color structured employment opportunities, social standing, and intimate partner selection.[65] Thus, while brown and Black people both occupied the island's lower and middle classes, brown individuals were more likely to be middle-class, given the social and economic advantages conferred upon them by virtue of their lighter complexion. The relationship between brownness and being middle-class is not only one of numbers but also one of ideology. Belinda Edmonson contends that "the actual population of mixed-race people who inhabit the middle class notwithstanding, brownness is a central category for a discussion of middle-class Caribbean identity because it speaks directly to the middle-class issue of quasi-elite status and humble origins."[66]

Jamaica's (brown) middle class occupied an ambivalent position in the politics of nationalism prior to the island's nominal independence in 1962. It vacillated between affirming the right to conduct their own affairs and a reluctance to directly oppose British rule, and between an opposition to the workings of white supremacy and class exploitation and an acceptance of the privileges conferred on those with lighter complexions and nonmanual occupations. Jamaica's middle-class strata ultimately developed nationalist ideologies that were vague and indeterminate in terms of racial and class oppression.[67] Even though they often advanced the claim that their mixed heritage indexed their belongingness to Jamaica more so than either their European- or African-descended counterparts, the way they navigated their intermediary positioning in mid-twentieth-century Jamaica often reproduced the colonial status quo.[68] By internally and externally branding Jamaica as a multiracial paradise, a rising middle-class intelligentsia sidelined Black nationalist articulations of the island that sought to address the intertwining of raced and classed hierarchies. Deborah Thomas describes these political maneuvers as a kind of creole multiracial nationalism that "ultimately emphasized self-help through moderate middle-class leadership and the transformation of (lower class) people's cultural practices, without substantial reform of the larger political and economic context."[69]

An attention to queerness may unsettle these received notions of political conservatism by highlighting the way Jamaica's brown middle classes contravened hegemonic forms of late colonial sexual regulation. Tracy Robinson argues that the island's pre-independence period was marked by nationalist anxieties that manifested in attempts to promote heteropatriarchal forms of family as the most appropriate unit of social reproduction.[70] Yet Fernando Henriques's ethnographic work suggests that even as middle-class Jamaicans promoted this ideal form of intimacy, they failed to practice it in their personal lives. He thus contends that even though brown (more so than Black) middle-class families paid lip service to the Euro-American ideal of the patriarchal nuclear family, "the usual pattern is for a man to have a legal wife and children and a separate establishment for his concubine and her children. Or he may indulge in promiscuous activity with the knowledge of his wife and neighbours."[71] Henriques's work is important because it allows for a consideration of the political potential of configurations of intimacy that exceed hegemonic expectations of monogamous coupling. Though Henriques ends up examining such alternate configurations between women and men, I am interested in attending to other forms of queerness.

Nadia Ellis and Gemma Romain have already begun this work in their exploration of how migration to England reconfigures middle-class Jamaican men's relationships to race, gender, and sexuality. I extend their work by turning from the metropole to the colony.[72] Roger Mais's 1955 novel *Black Lightning* is instructive in this regard. Mais's significance lies in his classed relationship to nationalism. Though he came from a brown middle-class background, his involvement in Jamaican political life reveals an allegiance with the island's Black working classes.[73] His 1944 *Public Opinion* article "Now We Know" presented a scathing critique of British colonialism that led to a charge of sedition for endangering England during World War II and a six-month prison sentence. His imprisonment aroused strong public sympathy and copies of his article circulated by the thousands across the island, becoming well known among the Jamaican populace. Mais was a prolific journalist, novelist, poet, and playwright.[74] Evelyn Hawthorne notes that he "attempted to foster the nationalists' agenda of building identity and unifying the society, and he achieved these goals: he raised national consciousness by "nativizing" the subjects and concerns of his writing; he supplied a corrective to colonialism in his overt criticism and by reclaiming, in his works, subverted or disregarded histories; he gave authority to the island's language and voice, in this way vindicating it against colonial discrediting."[75]

Intimacy, eroticism, and sexuality are dominant themes in Mais's work, which has led critics such as Hawthorne to note that the characters of his texts tend to exhibit a "disturbing ambivalence over sexuality."[76] Yet the scope of his interventions into Jamaican sexual politics through his novels is not fully appreciated, given the disparity in the recognition these novels are accorded. Unlike his first two works, *The Hills Were Joyful Together* and *Brother Man*, which were published to widespread acclaim for their attention to the suffering of island's urban poor, *Black Lightning* with its focus on Jamaica's rural middle class has received far less attention.[77] In contrast to wealthy white male foreigners to be found on the island's tourist resorts, or Black working-class female Pukumina practitioners located in poorest regions of Jamaica's most populous city, *Black Lightning* operates as a critical site through which to analyze how queerness may materialize among the island's rural brown middle classes.

Black Lightning chronicles the life of a rural household headed by Jake, a well-to-do blacksmith, his wife Estella, and their various servants and employees. Over the course of the novel, Jake becomes obsessed with completing a wooden sculpture of the biblical figure Samson. His relationship with the sculpture indexes his struggle to both create and exist independently of others. His abhorrence of his interdependent relationship with Estella leads to their separation, and his singular religious devotion to his sculpture causes him to absent himself from church, much to the concern of other community members.

In contrast to this tension arising from the process of individuation from his wife and community, Jake finds himself drawing closer to his physically disabled friend Amos. The relationship between these men is gendered as Jake treats Amos in much the same way other men in the novel exert their power over women in intimate relationships. In Jake's internal monologue, "he tried to figure out why it was that he encouraged the ugly little hunchback about him . . . he encouraged Amos not for Amos's sake, but because of the good that he got out of it. And then another thought came, and he put this one out of his mind. He thought the reason why he encouraged Amos about him was because he wanted to overlay the other's weakness with his own strength, as a man might put his own coat about another to shield him from the cold."[78] For Jake, it is the difference between Amos's physical impairment and Jake's stature as "a very big man, tall and powerfully built," that cements their relationship in ways that were not possible in his marriage with Estella.[79] This distinction between the two men, coupled with their fierce independence, draws them together. Sharing a smoke after dinner, Jake turns to Amos and says,

> "We are a couple of queer ones, eh pardner? You and me. I guess that's why we get along together. To most people you're poison, but to me. . . ." He laughed again, his lips curling a little: "It's just like we're kin."
>
> And Amos said, eagerly: "You think so, Jake? Really?"
>
> "Sure. Don't you? Look Amos, I'd like to ask you something. Why do you come here at all? I know you don't like people. You like being off some

place by yourself. You've run away from people all your life. What's the difference between me and—and everybody else, that you come and sit here afternoon upon afternoon? Tell me, eh?"

Amos said, gruffly: "You just said it yourself."

"And yet I treat you like dirt—When I'm in my black moods . . ." He broke off. Then: "Why don't you play something?"[80]

"You want to talk, that's why." "What is talk? Play."

But Amos didn't play. Of a sudden he had become very thoughtful.

He said slowly: "Just a couple of God's creatures, born out in the cold. You an' me. Kin. That's us."

"Don't know much about us being born that way, pardner. Maybe we did that ourselves." Amos spat contemplatively on the floor, then immediately erased it with his boot.

He said: "Maybe. After all what does it matter, Jake?"

He said: "We got something in common, ain't we? You think so?"

"You grew up all crooked like that," said Jake, staring at the floor just in front of him. "You grew that way from a boy. Maybe there is that difference. Some folk say your mind is twisted, the same. And sometimes I believe them."

But Amos only laughed.

He said: "Still an' all, we mix."[81]

The dynamic between Jake and Amos shifts after Jake is struck by lightning, rendering him blind. Jake is plunged into despair as a consequence of his impairment which makes it even more difficult for him to complete his sculpture. Amos's actions after this fateful event illustrate that, like Jake, he too is affectively invested in their relationship. He moves into Jake's home to help look after him, much to the relief of Bess, Jake's housekeeper, because "when he [Jake] was in one of those moods, there wasn't no one but Amos could do anything with him."[82] Amos also saves his salary from working as a store clerk to buy Jake a leather tobacco pouch—a gift so extravagant that the other man almost refuses to accept it. The intimacy that characterizes the men's relationship does not escape the attention of the novel's other characters, who openly describe the affective bond between Jake and Amos as love. For instance, Bess turns to Amos,

She looked at him closely. "You love him [Jake], don't you?"

He didn't reply, just sat scowling at her across the table. She looked down at her hands. And then he said, slowly: "He's been a powerful good friend to me, Bess."

"What he ever done for you?"

... "He's given me my life again as a man. Do you understand what I mean? Now I have something. I have him now, to lean on me."[83]

For Amos, it is through caring for Jake that he derives his manhood. Kamau Brathwaite interprets the relationship between Jake and Amos within the broader context of what he sees as Mais's attempt to reckon with the formation of creole culture in Jamaica. For Brathwaite, Mais attempts to reckon with Akan cosmology through Jake and Amos's relationship. He maintains that okra is "[the] symbol of interdependence, is the child who sits or walks in front of the ohene on state occasions and on whom he sometimes appears to lean. This child, for the Akan, is the ohene's symbolic ancestor and moral avatar ... in the 'real life' of the novel, Amos, after Jake's blindness, becomes his okra."[84]

In the context of Jamaican middle-class ambivalence toward the colonial social order, *Black Lightning* maps the imaginative space in which middle-class intimacies unsettle heteronormative logics of gender and sexual regulation. Far from being extraordinary or illicit, the closeness between Jake and Amos occasioned by physical debility is constructed as a mundane dimension of rural middle-class domestic life. Indeed, taking seriously their understanding of each other as "kin" expands the repertoire of Jamaican family practices identified by social scientists of this period, who were overwhelmingly concerned with heterosexual intimacies among the Black working class. If, following Carr, "his [Mais's] fiction is to be read as constituting an outraged yet compassionate sociology," *Black Lightning* offers an opportunity to seriously consider how brown queerness manifests in late colonial Jamaica.[85]

Such an investigation counters the workings of archival power that make traces of brown queerness more difficult to discern than traces of queerness among elite white male tourists or Black working-class female Pukumina practitioners. The fact that *Black Lightning* is one of the few sites through which to identify queerness among the island's middle classes highlights the way that class relations can structure archival arrangements. Part of the difficulty lies in determining what counts as middle-class at all. Edmonson maintains that in societies like Jamaica,

[where] there are only creoles and no natives, ... the very idea of a native cultural tradition inevitably begins and ends as a classed notion. As a consequence, much analysis of Caribbean culture starts from the presumption that society is divided into two discrete and exclusive camps: the derivative "highbrow" cultures of the elites and the authentic cultures of the working

class.... In this region, where the majority of people are poor and comparatively few are what in the United States would be called middle class, the Caribbean middle class is de facto elite. Yet it is still not *the* elite.[86]

This difficulty in distinguishing middle-class from elite and working-class formations produces vigorous efforts at ensuring that such distinctions are discernible. And because sexuality becomes a vector through which such class differences are articulated, forms of intimacy that fail to adhere to class expectations are interpreted as a liability in maintaining class status.

Peter Wilson's articulation of a politics of respectability is productive in conceptualizing how class relations structure whether and how certain kinds of intimacies come to be inscribed in Jamaican history. He identifies respectability as a female-oriented, middle-class approach to sexual morality that aligns with the formal procedures of the law. In contrast to masculinist, working-class orientations to sex that valorize sexual promiscuity and circulate in primarily community contexts, respectability politics prioritize marriage as a privileged form of intimacy that is legible by the state.[87] The Women Workers Federation response to Lady Foot's tirade about illegitimacy that started this chapter is perhaps a useful example of respectability politics at work. Unlike Marson or Isaacs, who dispute Foot's claims, Federation member Rose Van Cuylenburg rushed to Foot's defense in her letter to the editor of the *Gleaner*, noting that "as one of the women present, I can assure your readers that all the women listening, and concerned, in this problem of the complacent attitude of our people on the evil of sexual immorality which is making Jamaica notorious, were heartily in agreement with what Lady Foot said . . . we thank such a generous and loving-hearted woman, as Lady Foot undoubtedly is, for calling on us to help her, as our 'First Lady' in the Island to combat these evils."[88] The utility of Wilson's conceptualization of respectability lies in the way it highlights how middle-class ideologies about sexual propriety limit the ways that non-normative forms of intimacy enter conventional archival sources *as middle-class*. Thus, even as middle-class people's intimate practices exceed public declarations of respectability—particularly in the case of middle-class men's liaisons with working-class women, as seen earlier in the discussion of Henriques—these relationships are understood and documented in terms of working-class Blackness as opposed to middle-class brownness.

The period immediately preceding Jamaica's nominal independence marked the production of local forms of knowledge that unsettled colonial discourses of Black sexual deviance. Materializing queerness through the archives left in the wake of this reparative process reveals less about the kinds of subjects that existed in the past and more about the continuity of archival infrastructures. If fractals are about repetition with difference, queerness functions here in the service of repetition; that which persists over time. Constructing brown subjects in relationship to queerness entails identifying how ideologies of respectability shape the historical inscription of illicit middle-class intimacies. In a similar vein, it becomes possible to conceive of Pukumina as a site of queerness only by grappling with the ways that the debasement of Blackness and expectations of female heteronormativity condition the production of historical sources. In contrast, white male foreigners emerge as paradigmatic figures of homosexuality across a range of historical materials in early twentieth-century Jamaica, illustrating how anticolonial nationalist anxieties constitute the hegemonic queer archival affect of the period. Queer analyses surface the durability of archival arrangements that foreground some as historical subjects of same-gender intimacy while occluding others. Late colonial Jamaican knowledge projects revalorized some Black intimacies while also reinscribing hierarchies of race, gender, class, and nation within queer archival imaginaries. These hierarchies constitute the passive lines of fractal formation that shape historical narratives of Jamaican intimate life.

3

The Body

Responding to HIV/AIDS

On September 22, 1983, the front page of Jamaica's most widely circulated newspaper, the *Daily Gleaner*, proclaimed in bold red lettering "AIDS Is Here."[1] By the time of its printing, acquired immunodeficiency syndrome (AIDS) was not new to Jamaicans; they had already been hearing about this mysterious illness in news reports from the United States and Canada.[2] Yet this was the first time that they were learning that there was AIDS on the island. As was the case for many countries across the Caribbean and the world, within the first decade of AIDS emergence in Jamaica, the illness would become a major concern in terms of national public health as well as social and economic development. The island's first national plan for HIV in 1987 conservatively estimated that with 960 AIDS cases by 1992, the epidemic would cost the state some JMD $240 million.[3] While international medical experts initially outlined various routes of AIDS transmission—including blood transfusion and needle sharing during intravenous drug use—Jamaican health authorities were quick to identify AIDS as a predominantly sexually transmitted infection on the island.[4] The fact that this disease was both incurable and largely transmitted through sex meant that Jamaican efforts to address AIDS were structured around attempts to both understand and intervene in the island's sexual practices. The island was no stranger to regulating sex, given its experience addressing outbreaks of syphilis and gonorrhea as well as implementing family planning and population control initiatives, but the arrival of AIDS—and the human immunodeficiency virus (HIV) that caused AIDS—made Jamaicans take sexuality seriously in a way they had not before.[5]

In this chapter I explore how same-gender desire becomes an object of knowledge in the pursuit of repairing the national body. I focus on the period between 1983, when the virus was first identified in Jamaica, and 1998, when the gay rights organization J-FLAG was established. J-FLAG's formation is significant because it signals a change in the sexual politics of HIV/AIDS on the island, formed as it was to discursively separate the response to HIV/AIDS from attempts to advocate for the well-being of gender and sexual minorities.[6] Given Kemala Kempadoo's assertion that HIV/AIDS has "carefully raised the issue that homosexuality or gayness is not an uncommon feature of Caribbean societies," I am interested in analyzing how the arrival of HIV/AIDS becomes the occasion on which to know same-gender eroticism in Jamaica.[7] In this analysis, I examine the role of sexuality in the relationship between race and pathology in postcolonial contexts.[8] In contrast to studies that investigate how race and coloniality shape the pathologization of intimate relations, I focus on illness as a site through which discourses and social practices of racialized erotics are brought into being in postcolonial Jamaica.[9]

My approach of using HIV/AIDS as a starting point for producing knowledge around same-gender desire in the past adopts the forms of inquiry embedded in the historical materials that I consulted. It takes on the narrative structure of Patricia Powell's 1994 novel, *A Small Gathering of Bones*, which outlines the lives of three gay men, Dale, Ian, and Nevin, as Ian succumbs to AIDS in Jamaica's capital city of Kingston in 1978.[10] Dale is the narrator of the text, and his preoccupation with Ian's symptoms of poor health—coughing, shortness of breath, weight loss, and purple lesions on his skin—drives the plot. These embodied signs of AIDS repeatedly preface Dale's narration of various aspects of gay life in Jamaica's most populous city, including his on-again, off-again relationship with Nevin, cruising for sex, and socializing in gay bars. Thus, in this chapter I follow Powell's literary strategy of foregrounding HIV/AIDS as a starting point from which to narrate the history of same-gender eroticism in Jamaica. *A Small Gathering of Bones* provides the framework and direction of this chapter's inquiry, and the work of Jamaican contact investigators (CI's) provides its methodological template. CI's—also known as field epidemiologists—played a crucial role in Jamaica's response to HIV/AIDS. I discuss the work of CI's in greater detail below; for now it is sufficient to note that a major component of their work involved contact tracing. In this process, CI's sought to construct individual sexual histories by locating those who were infected with HIV and interviewing them with the aim of locating and testing their contacts for the illness.[11] Just as CI's used contact tracing to identify how HIV/AIDS took shape across Jamaica's social body, I utilize this practice as a method of historical inquiry to investigate how same-gender eroticism is archived in the early years of the epidemic.

Powell's novel and CI records constitute a small part of a more expansive archive of repair that I assembled from the materials that inscribe Jamaicans' attempts to make sense of and address HIV/AIDS. This process of assemblage required attending to prevailing protocols around where, how, among whom, and what kinds of sex can/should be discussed and/or documented. Rhoda Reddock and Dorothy Roberts's claim that HIV/AIDS occasioned greater public debate about sexuality and gender in the Caribbean was no less true for Jamaica, which witnessed not only greater talk about erotic relations among and between women and men but also a proliferation of this talk to new venues, audiences, and formats.[12] My archive-building efforts engage this expanded landscape of HIV/AIDS and sexuality by bringing together three kinds of sources. First, I conducted oral history interviews with the first generation of HIV/AIDS survivors and those who sought to support their well-being, including doctors, nurses, contact investigators, and community activists. Second, I carried out archival research at the National Library of Jamaica, the Kingston and St. Andrew Public Library, the University of the West Indies; and the libraries of the Ministry of Health, Jamaica AIDS Support, the National Family Planning Board, the Epidemiological Research and Training Unit, the Red Cross, and Hope Enterprises. In these venues, I consulted a wide cross section of newspaper coverage of HIV/AIDS in the Jamaican newspapers *Daily Gleaner, Jamaica Observer, Jamaica Star, Jamaica Herald,* and *XNews;* HIV/AIDS studies, policies, and reports created by state, academic, and nongovernmental organizations; and HIV/AIDS public awareness materials in radio, print, and television formats. Finally, I examined cultural texts of the period that dealt with HIV/AIDS and/or same-gender intimacies, including the Jamaican novels *A Small Gathering of Bones* by Patricia Powell and *No Telephone to Heaven* by Michelle Cliff; the Trinidadian play *One of Our Sons Is Missing,* by Godfrey Sealy, which toured across Jamaica to widespread acclaim in 1993; and the unpublished play *An Existence Mirrored* by Jamaica AIDS Support member Robert Cork.

A queer reading of these materials illustrates the persistence of archival arrangements in shaping historical narratives. Re-storying the history of HIV/AIDS in Jamaica through queerness does not transform these arrangements but functions to make them visible. Fractals materialize through repetition and difference; this chapter illustrates how queerness foregrounds what stays the same with each iteration. The efforts of frontline health workers are central to my argument. Frontline workers were highly protective of what they learned from their patients in a sociocultural context where even the suggestion that one has HIV and/or desires for the same gender could render one vulnerable to various forms of violence. The strategic decisions that they made about what, how, and with whom they shared the intimate knowledge that they cultivated through their work were consequential, not only for the well-being of their individual patients and for Jamaican public health, but also for constructing archives of sexuality. I maintain that hierarchies of color, class, and gender shaped how they crafted same-gender eroticism in Jamaica's historical imagination of HIV/AIDS. Early accounts of the epidemic specifically foreground sex between men. Yet this process of visibilization did not impact all men equally. Public health surveillance protocols and the Jamaican public were most likely to conscript poor and working-class Black men as the face of the epidemic. In contrast, expectations of sexual respectability shielded middle- and upper-class brown and white men from public scrutiny of their erotic relations with other men. The ways that Jamaican social hierarchies structure how archival practices incorporate same-gender-desiring subjects illustrate the difficulty of using queerness to narrate historical accounts that radically differ from those that have gone before. Fractals unfold through repetition and difference; queerness showcases the repetition of archival effects in structuring the process of historical subjectification around same-gender desire. Rather than offering a break with the past, queerness emphasizes the continuity of archival infrastructures and their consequences for history-making practices in the present.

The Politics of Intimate Knowledge:
Frontline Health Workers, HIV/AIDS, and Sex between Men

The emergence of HIV/AIDS brought homosexuality into the Jamaican public sphere in a direct and sustained way for the first time.[13] This is because HIV/AIDS became discursively associated with sex between men on the island. Though the first case of AIDS in Jamaica was reported in 1983, it was not until 1987 that the Ministry of Health formally established an STD/AIDS program within its Epidemiology Unit and launched the first STD/AIDS Awareness Week. In his 1987 address to the public, Jamaica's minister of health, Karl Samuda, stated, "In order for us to understand more about this dreaded disease, the time has come for us to give more assurances to these people with unusual sexual practices (homosexuals and bisexuals who are more susceptible to AIDS).... Jamaicans must accept that homosexuality and bisexuality is a reality of life."[14] The connection Samuda made between men who have sex with men and HIV/AIDS was shared with the general Jamaican population as a nationally representative survey carried out by the island's Ministry of Health in 1988 noted that 81 percent of Jamaicans agreed with the statement "AIDS is a homosexual disease."[15]

Men who have sex with men were constructed as an important "risk group" in the context of Jamaica's HIV/AIDS epidemic for two reasons. First, it was among these men that the disease was first recognized in Jamaica, and they were thought to bring the infection to the island through their sexual contact with foreign men, through either travel abroad or liaisons with visitors to the island.[16] Second, the rate of HIV/AIDS among this group was reported to be much higher than in the general population. In 1997 the rate of HIV/AIDS in Jamaica's general population was reported to be around 1 percent; among men who have sex with men, it was reported to be as high as 30 percent.[17] It was through HIV/AIDS that homosexuality became a legitimate subject of knowledge in Jamaica.[18]

Yet this discursive pairing of HIV/AIDS and homosexuality proved challenging in two ways for Jamaican authorities who sought to safeguard the health of the island's population. First, the widespread and erroneous assumption in the early days of the epidemic that HIV/AIDS was only a "homosexual disease" meant that many Jamaicans failed to perceive public health messaging about the illness as relevant to their lives. Part of the problem lay in the fact Jamaicans' understandings of both homosexuality and AIDS were in flux, especially at the beginning of the epidemic. Homosexuality and AIDS existed for them, not as objective facts, but instead as contested categories whose meanings were continually negotiated.[19] Focus groups conducted across various demographics (age, class, gender, rural/urban) indicated that Jamaicans in 1995 did not see themselves at risk for HIV/AIDS because it was a homosexual disease and many of the respondents felt that "nobody I deal with would be into that."[20] Even though men who have sex with men were thought to be an important risk group, within the first four years of identifying HIV/AIDS on the island, the Ministry of Health announced that HIV/AIDS on the island was predominantly transmitted through heterosexual sex.[21]

Thus, even if same-gender-desiring men were at greater risk of contracting HIV/AIDS, in 1997 only 5.8 percent of AIDS cases in Jamaica were transmitted through sex between men; 58.5 percent of AIDS cases were transmitted through heterosexual encounters.[22] The connection between HIV/AIDS and homosexuality proved to be so strong—despite extensive public awareness campaigns attesting to the contrary—that health workers, especially men, found themselves having to disabuse other Jamaicans of the notion that they were gay simply for working in the HIV/AIDS sector.[23]

Second, the stigma attached to HIV/AIDS and homosexuality made it difficult for health authorities to gather the information they needed to combat the epidemic, because Jamaicans simply did not want to be associated with either. Previously, young men had perceived contracting an STI as desirable because it served as an index of their sexual prowess and ability to procure sexual partners.[24] With the emergence of HIV/AIDS, rather than being proud to be seen in line at the sexual health clinic boasting of their gonorrhea, men were now worried that their presence at the clinic might suggest that they had contracted the deadly virus.[25] This was partly a consequence of the Ministry of Health's first public awareness-raising campaign around HIV/AIDS, which was carried out under the theme "AIDS Kills," and had the unintended effect of striking fear into the hearts of the island populace (see figure 3.1).[26] The prominence of violent public declarations against homosexuality also meant that Jamaicans were hesitant to identify as same-gender-desiring subjects. The proclaimed willingness to inflict harm on these individuals was evident in the lyrics of dancehall songs of the period—most notably Buju Banton's "Boom Bye Bye"—and the vociferous backlash against the proposal to decriminalize sodomy that manifested in a violent anti-gay rally in Kingston.[27] The intensity of the disavowal of HIV/AIDS and homosexuality was perhaps most clearly illustrated in Jamaica's 1997 prison riots. Inmates and warders opposed the mandate that condoms be distributed within the island's prison system. They interpreted this order, which was intended to prevent the spread of HIV/AIDS, as implicating them in homosexuality, thereby shaming them in the eyes of their families and communities.[28] The subsequent riots that broke out at the General Penitentiary and St. Catherine prisons forced the Jamaican government to issue a state of emergency and to call police and army personnel to quell the unrest that ultimately left sixteen dead and forty injured.[29]

The harm that was likely to befall those who were—or were simply suspected to be—HIV-positive and/or homosexual had important implications for how knowledge about HIV/AIDS and homosexuality was produced,

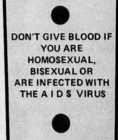

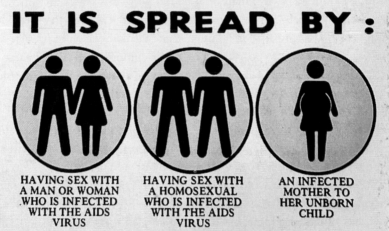

3.1. *AIDS Kills* pamphlet, Jamaica Ministry of Health, 1987. Source: National Library of Jamaica, Kingston.

circulated, consumed, and/or destroyed. The stakes were high if information about one's HIV/AIDS status and/or intimate relations became public knowledge. For example, Devon, though born in a rural area of St. Mary, had moved to Kingston to take up a job as a civil servant; there, in 1992, the young man was diagnosed with HIV.[30] Over several years, he struggled to maintain both his health and his job while keeping his HIV/AIDS status a secret from his employers. This became difficult when he started to exhibit severe weight loss and rashes on his skin that were recognizable as telltale signs of his illness. To make matters worse, a security guard at work tried to blackmail Devon, demanding money in exchange for his silence about the effeminate young man's sexual inclinations. When Devon refused to pay, the guard wasted no time in telling his co-workers that Devon "was fish." Devon subsequently was harassed by his colleagues, who would call him names, make teamwork difficult, and refuse to invite him to office social events. When his health took a turn for the worse in 1998, requiring him to use up his sick days and other forms of leave to visit his doctor and recuperate from his bouts of illness, Devon felt compelled to reveal his HIV status to Human Resources to obtain additional time off. Out of fear that he would transmit HIV to his co-workers, Devon was promptly fired. In his time of need, he was fortunate to have family members who were both aware of his health condition and supportive as he struggled to take care of himself without a job. Many others with the illness were not so fortunate, and instead were mistreated and thrown out of their homes by family members upon learning of their HIV-positive status.[31] In 1994 a woman, Terri-Ann, became the first person in Jamaica to publicly identify as HIV-positive. She did this on local television, giving a face to the epidemic and helping to humanize the disease for Jamaicans. But it was not enough to overcome the stigma against HIV/AIDS in the country.[32]

The impulse to shield knowledge of one's HIV/AIDS status and same-gender desires from the public had important implications for HIV/AIDS frontline workers. This category included doctors, nurses, and CI's who were responsible for taking care of HIV-positive individuals, as well as volunteers and staff at the National HIV/STD Helpline. It also included those who worked at AIDS service organizations, such as the Family Center based at the University of the West Indies at Mona, and Jamaica AIDS Support (JAS), the island's first HIV/AIDS community-based organization. In fact, it was at JAS that Devon and other same-gender-desiring men and women would take part in the organization's Gay Lesbian and Bisexual Community (GLABCOM) initiative. GLABCOM members gathered not only to discuss sexual health matters but also to socialize and develop a collective sense of being in a space that operated as a respite from the violence often directed toward them in other sectors of Jamaican society.[33] These meetings built on the focus groups conducted among men who have sex with men as part of HIV/AIDS research endeavors as well as the earlier community-based work of Jamaica's Gay Freedom Movement (1977–84) that took shape from within the informal networks of the island's illicit, though vibrant, post-independence gay social life.[34] Participants understood that the intimate knowledge generated in these various sites—health clinic, Helpline, JAS, and so on—had to be handled skillfully and delicately. An impulse of care informed this handling of information that worked both alongside and against the fear and violence directed toward HIV/AIDS and same-gender eroticism in many public spaces.

Those who worked at Jamaica's National HIV/STD Helpline were hyperaware of the need to navigate the calls that they received with discretion and sensitivity. The Helpline was established in September 1989 to provide counseling, education, support, and referrals on issues related to sexual health.[35] As an anonymous, toll-free telephone service available to Jamaicans across the island, the Helpline became a critical site for talk about sex. It started out as an entirely volunteer-run initiative that operated from 7 p.m. to 10 p.m. However, the combination of the high need for the service and the high turnover of volunteers prompted a restructuring of the Helpline, which came to be run by both staff and volunteers, from 10 a.m. to 10 p.m., weekdays.[36] Young women were the majority of those who worked at the Helpline, which was located at an undisclosed address in Kingston. Most callers were twenty to twenty-nine years old, and although the Helpline received calls from every parish, most of its calls came from Kingston and St. Andrew.[37] Helpline staff and volunteers fielded an average of 35 calls per day (totaling some 4,738 calls in 1993). Most callers were concerned about HIV/AIDS, but they also sought information on a wide range of topics related to sex and sexual health more broadly.[38]

Patricia Henry was instrumental in building the Helpline, and her years of experience with the initiative highlight the kind of open-ended and nonjudgmental approach required when talking to Jamaicans about sex health.[39] As a young middle-class woman, Henry had moved from her family home in Mandeville to Kingston, where she rented a studio apartment from her pastor and successfully secured a secretarial job with the Ministry of Health in 1988. Quickly recognizing her potential, ministry staff recruited her to be involved with the development of the Helpline, and Henry soon mastered not only taking calls but also training volunteers and taking on a leadership role. In the narrative below, she describes her early experiences of talking with men who have sex with men and the necessity of Helpline staff and volunteers mobilizing counter-hegemonic approaches to sex and gender through language.

I remember talking to a guy who is a homosexual one day. He began to say to me that he had sex. And I said, "So what kind of sex did you have?" He said [Patricia Henry (PH) animating an angry voice] "What type of sex you know people fi have miss? What kind of sex? Nuh mus one man and woman sex?" And I said, "That's what you think! But no. Man and man have sex." [He said (PH animating a shocked voice)] "Miss!" And I say, "Of course man and man have sex." [He said (PH animating an angry voice)] "Miss, dem deh people fi dead!" [PH responded] "Me seh, look here, why are you saying that people fi dead? You don't call about that. Let's talk about what you call about." He was there talking, and ramping, and I was there talking, talking, talking to him. Then he say, "Miss, you know me a go tell you the truth. Me like how you talk. Me like how you talk. You no sound like one of them wicked one deh. I'm a homosexual you know miss." I said, "A dat you afraid to tell me? You're a human being first. You're a human being." And they will call and behave like that. And when you ask them "What type of sex did you have? Because I have a list here [of questions] that I would like to ask, and you don't have to answer them. You can answer if you want. But these are just to help us to help you better and for educational purposes." And then when you reach to the question about anal sex. "Have you ever had anal sex?" [PH imitating male caller in an angry voice] "What kind of nastiness dat you ask me!" I say "Look here, that is not nasty." And you find ways to say, "Maybe you've never had it yet but some people would say it's the most enjoyable sex so I have to ask it." And then they would own up to say they are homosexual. They are afraid because they don't want to be identified as a homosexual. So they are afraid to say it. They are genuinely afraid to say it. . . . And that is why when you train on the line, if a man call you, or a woman call you and say they have sex, you don't assume that it's a male so it [the other sexual partner] must be a female. And if a male call, you don't assume that the person call himself a male. So you don't begin with "yes sir." Because some of the male will tell you that their name is Jane or their name is Mary and they are not a male. Although they have male physique, they act as the woman in the relationship. So you can't hear the voice and assume is a man talking to you. You can't assume gender because they will get offended and probably don't talk to you again, and you want to talk to them, so you have to be very open. So it take a lot out of you, you know! You have to be a very strong person to do that and nonjudgmental.

In order to interact with a broad range of Jamaicans who might call in to the Helpline, staff and volunteers could not make assumptions or moral valuations about the lives of their callers. In her narrative, Henry discusses the importance of unsettling expectations about the acceptability of certain sexual practices, about the appropriateness of specific gendered configurations of intimacy, and even about what "male" and "female" voices are supposed to sound like. These linguistic practices were necessary to fully engage with callers who sought out Helpline support but who nevertheless continued to be plagued by the stigma attached to HIV/AIDS and same-gender eroticism, even in the context of an anonymous conversation. Such practices therefore became important for Helpline volunteers and staff to provide appropriate counseling, education, and referrals to their calls. Yet as Henry notes, "it take a lot out of you" to continually dismantle normative expectations. Whether having to account for one's own emotions (Henry's surprise that her caller identified as homosexual), or how these emotions may be communicated to callers (regulating the affect in her voice to prevent her caller from identifying her surprise), or engaging with caller's heightened emotionality (his impassioned declaration that men who have sex with men "fi dead"), working on the Helpline involved intense, affective labor.

Unlike Helpline volunteers and staff who spoke with individuals who willingly sought their support, contact investigators (CI's) had the more difficult task of interacting with Jamaicans who might not want to engage with them at all. With the eradication of Yaws in Jamaica in the 1970s, the island's contact investigation program that was established in the 1930s to address this disease was reconfigured to focus solely on sexually transmitted infections.[40] By 1996 there were twenty-three CI's in Jamaica, and though they were responsible for the clinical treatment of patients, data reporting, and community outreach and education, contact tracing was the largest component of their work.[41] This involved locating and attending to the well-being of those who tested positive for a communicable disease as well as learning about the person's contacts, locating them, and bringing them in for testing.[42] This series of tasks could be quite difficult in the case of sexually transmitted infections. Jamaicans did not want to disclose the identities of their sexual partners to CI's—who were strangers to them—especially if such erotic interactions were considered illicit, as in the case of same-gender relationships. The situation was made even more difficult in the case of HIV/AIDS because of the intense stigma attached to the disease. HIV-positive individuals often feared that once a CI had reached out to their previous sexual partners, encouraging them to get tested, these partners would find out about their HIV status and make it public knowledge (even though CI's were bound to maintain confidentiality during this process).

Lacking the authority to "force" individuals to provide them with information, to get tested, or to even accept medical treatment, CI's had to rely on strong interpersonal and communication skills in working with Jamaicans who were HIV-positive or considered to be at risk of HIV. Eliciting sexual contacts from individuals who had tested positive for the virus was especially difficult in the case of sex workers, for whom knowledge of their HIV status would impact their livelihood, and men who had sex with men who were unwilling to reveal their sexual inclinations. Tony Samuels, who first became a CI in 1986 in the Jamaican parish of St. Catherine, revealed that when he talked with HIV-positive individuals who were unwilling to give him the names of their sexual partners, he often resorted to appealing to their care for others:[43]

> They are some [contacts] they won't open up and tell you. When you realize they are "closing shop on you," you leave it and you go and you talk about other things. You talk about how you can give your family member the virus without even actually having sex with the person by saying that, you could have sex with this man, and he is a bisexual and [he] eventually have sex with somebody who eventually have sex with your relative and pass it on to them. And when they think about that, they might give up another name and thing like that. That's how it is. Because when you realize that they nuh want to give you [a name], you leave and you talk and make it dawn on them that by them not doing this [sharing their sexual contacts], other things could really happen. You say "Look at it. You are going to be treated . . . but the persons you might be having sex with might not even know they have it and might not be showing signs and symptoms, and passing it on to other persons and they are getting worse. Wouldn't you want them to be treated and to be around also?" And you find that they might give up another one or two contacts.

But getting contacts was only half the battle. CI's like Samuels then had to track down these contacts, convince them to come in for HIV testing, and then obtain their sexual contacts if the tests came back positive. Samuels and other CI's indicated that it was often difficult to trace the contacts for men who have sex with men because of the frequently transient nature of these kinds of relationships. Unlike other patients who might have more information about their sexual partners, men who had sex with men often only knew their partner's first name (but not the last name) and perhaps a phone number (but not an address). In addition to having solid medical training to diagnose and treat illnesses as well as excellent skills in building rapport to talk with strangers about intimate matters they might be unwilling to discuss, CI's thus also had to have a strong standing in the communities to which they were assigned. This standing impacted their ability to locate individuals about whom they had little information and who often did not want to be found. Most importantly, however, they had to be able to maintain confidentiality to prevent the kind of treatment Devon experienced at his workplace. In their training, CI's were told that they "will always find it necessary to talk to many people on behalf of persons . . . [they are] required to investigate. However, in soliciting, locating, or obtaining other information about these individuals, it is always important to approach these situations with tact and caution so as to avoid causing any embarrassment to the suspect or a disturbance of the suspect's community status."[44] In mapping out sexual networks to address HIV/AIDS (and other sexually transmitted infections), CI's became sexual ethnographers in learning about Jamaican's erotic lives.[45]

As HIV/AIDS was a new disease whose emergence on the island brought previously tacit forms of intimacy into Jamaica's public sphere, health workers like CI's and Helpline volunteers and staff were entering new territory. The ground on which they interacted with HIV-positive individuals and those deemed vulnerable to HIV was still taking shape. The models that Jamaican health workers used to identify HIV/AIDS both in and outside the laboratory were modified international prototypes. For instance, to avoid the high cost of the Western Blot test—which was considered to be the gold standard in HIV testing in the early days of the epidemic—Jamaica's Ministry of Health constructed its own testing strategy. After two years and many false starts, the Ministry successfully developed, field tested, and evaluated a Jamaica-specific HIV testing strategy with technical assistance from Germany and the United Nations in collaboration with the Caribbean Epidemiology Center.[46]

Frontline HIV/AIDS workers also repurposed knowledge from international bodies, synthesizing newly acquired foreign training with medical education they had already received on the island and adapting it to the specific communities and circumstances in which they worked. For instance, CI's often had previous professional experience in other health care roles in their communities—as public health inspectors, midwives, nurses, and so on—which made them uniquely qualified to take on the CI role.[47] In the early days of the HIV/AIDS epidemic, CI's were provided with training on the island—drawn from the local work already being done through organizations like the Association for the Control of Sexually Transmitted Diseases established in 1970—and also sent to the United States for additional training at institutions like the University of North Carolina.[48] The United States continued to feature prominently in the ongoing development of Jamaica's CI program, providing both funding through the United States Agency for International Development (USAID) and technical support through the Centers for Disease Control and Prevention (CDC), whose staff visited the island to assist with CI training as well as the development of a local CI training model.[49] The formation of Jamaica's Helpline similarly drew from knowledge and expertise within and beyond the island's shores. Though Jamaican health authorities consulted with the National HIV/AIDS Helpline that Trinidad had already established in developing its own model, the initial cadre of Helpline volunteers received technical training from Jamaican doctors as well as training in communication skills from Jamaican radio broadcasters and staff at Jamaica's Women's Crisis Center.[50] In the early days of the epidemic, scientific knowledge of the virus was still in its infancy and was not widespread among the Jamaican medical community. Those who worked in the HIV/AIDS sector found themselves not only critically appraising the latest HIV/AIDS research and models of care from around the world to determine if and how they might be applicable to Jamaican realities, but also educating health professionals on the island who were not immune to neglecting and mistreating HIV-positive patients.[51]

Jamaican health professionals started to notice changes in themselves as they participated in this new line of work to combat HIV/AIDS. This was not only a cognitive process that, for instance, required understanding the mechanisms of virus transmission, but also an affective and embodied one. Andrea Bateson, who first entered the HIV/AIDS sector as a community worker on a HIV/AIDS awareness campaign with the National Family Planning Board, narrated her personal experience of this transformation.[52]

> **Andrea Bateson [AB]:** The first time that I actually, physically touched someone who had HIV. Remember you are talking about 1990 and here it is, someone who is sick, the person cannot help themselves. You can't just talk to them and give them education and comfort them. You actually have to touch them.... Someone called and said there was this young man living somewhere in Kencot and his family abandoned him. They moved out and left him in the apartment and he was really ill. And the neighbors were afraid to help him because they heard rumors that he had AIDS. So myself and [Mr. D], one of the contact investigators, we went to see this

young man. And of course, although [Mr. D] was a contact investigator, you couldn't stand up and let him do everything. So he gave me gloves, [I] helped to clean him up, called an ambulance to come and get him and carry him to KPH [Kingston Public Hospital] and that kind of stuff. So you actually had to do that. You had your gloves, you had your disinfectant, and everything. But afterward when you got home and you're thinking..., "What did I just do? I have a child! I have a young baby!" And the fear comes in. I don't know why, but the fear comes in and you started having issues with the fear and so on.

Author: How long did it take you to get over the fear?

AB: I think by [19]94, we not seeing any health care worker dying. We not seeing any health care worker infected. People get needle stick injury.... I actually got a needle stick injury with a known patient [who had HIV] accidentally and eventually you're realizing it's not so easy to get HIV. You're not hearing of any health care worker getting infected. You're not seeing anyone dying who is taking care of someone with HIV. And so more and more, you're being convinced that it's not so easy to get this disease.

Bateson thus realized that even though she was knowledgeable about HIV/AIDS as a community health outreach worker, it was not until confronted with interacting with someone who was HIV-positive that she had to come to terms with HIV/AIDS at an affective and embodied level.

For other health workers, personal change revolved less around their (affective) relationship to the disease itself and more around their relationship to those who were considered to be vulnerable to contracting HIV. Over time, health workers came to know same-gender-desiring Jamaicans and others considered to be at risk of HIV not only as patients but also as fellow professionals. The implementation of HIV interventions utilizing peer-based models meant that CI's like Samuels began working alongside Jamaicans with job titles like commercial sex worker (CSW) or men who have sex with men (MSM) peer educator. And although sex workers and same-gender-desiring Jamaicans were increasingly gaining publicity on the island—especially in the tabloid news media, as will be discussed later in this chapter—for many frontline HIV/AIDS workers who were largely drawn from the island's Black and brown middle classes, their job served as the first occasion in which they had knowingly come in contact with sex workers and same-gender-desiring women and men. Samuels recalls his first experience with a patient that caused him to reconsider his understandings of same-gender eroticism.

I learned something from him because he said, "Mr. Samuels, I am gay. I have sex with men." He wished with all his heart and he tried to have sex with females but he could never get an erection and although he tried, it's not happening. He said "Mr. Samuels, I would love to, but it's just not happening." [I realized] there and then that these men feel they are attracted to men and just attracted to men. You know? Because before I felt sometimes you know, they pushed themselves before that and they could have pushed themselves in the other way.

Samuels's belief that attraction and sexual intimacy was a matter of individual willpower, determined by how one "pushed" oneself, was unsettled by his experience with his self-identified gay patient.

Frontline HIV/AIDS workers in Jamaica who experienced personal transformations as they cultivated relationships with HIV-positive and HIV-vulnerable individuals, and who adapted the latest advances in HIV research and intervention models from around the world to fit Jamaican realities were pivotal in producing knowledge of HIV/AIDS and sexuality on the island. The interactions between these workers and HIV-positive Jamaicans as well as those considered to be at risk for HIV made possible the reports, statistics, and narratives of the epidemic that informed Jamaica's HIV/AIDS programs and policies. It is (directly or indirectly) through the work of frontline HIV/AIDS workers that HIV/AIDS and sexuality were rendered visible not only to Jamaican state institutions but also to nongovernmental organizations and to international funding agencies tasked with combating the epidemic. Whether it was social workers reporting to the Epidemiology Unit of the Ministry of Health, contact investigators providing input to international funding agencies like USAID, or Helpline volunteers conducting HIV/AIDS training for other service organizations such as the Women's Crisis Centre, frontline HIV/AIDS workers played a key role in shaping how HIV/AIDS and sexuality became objects of knowledge in Jamaican public health.[53]

Examining the role of these workers in the politics of knowledge around HIV/AIDS and sexuality in Jamaica involves not only attending to how, what, and with whom they communicated, but also to the strategic decisions they made to avoid communication altogether. Positioned between powerful state, nongovernmental, and international institutions and the HIV-positive and HIV-vulnerable communities they sought to support, Jamaican frontline HIV/AIDS workers not only shared but safeguarded the knowledge created from their interactions with their patients. They struggled to find the balance between what Kara Keeling describes as practices of "looking for" (reproducing technologies of visibility that increase vulnerability to violence) and "looking after" (enacting practices of care).[54] Well aware of the stigma around HIV/AIDS and same-gender eroticism, these workers recognized that the consequences of information sharing cut both ways: knowledge of one's health status and intimate life may be useful in garnering support, but it may also render one vulnerable to violence. The tension between the two is illustrated by the differences in the reports offered by Jamaica's Helpline and CI representatives at the September 19, 1995, meeting of senior staff of the Ministry of Health's Epidemiological Unit. Henry, the Helpline administrator, stated, "The Helpline has been receiving more calls from persons infected with AIDS as well as calls from students regarding assignments. She said that people are more receptive to their relatives who are infected/affected and are seeking information on how to take care of relatives at home."[55] This helpline update was immediately followed by the report offered by Jamaica's head CI, who "informed that when persons from JAS [Jamaica AIDS Support] visit the clinic, they are not willing to divulge [personal] information."[56] In comparison to the kinds of knowledge generated through anonymous Helpline exchanges that may be used in designing HIV/AIDS programming, the in-person, face-to-face setting of the health clinic did not guarantee patients confidentiality in the same way. In these settings, the same-gender-desiring Jamaicans that JAS was known to serve would often refuse health workers' requests for information as a protective strategy against the violence that such disclosure may engender.[57] These workers were thus challenged to support those affected and infected by HIV/AIDS without rendering them visible to those who might cause them harm.

The way that Jamaican frontline HIV/AIDS workers such as CI's navigated the politics of knowledge around HIV/AIDS and sexuality in relationship to dynamics of violence and care has important implications for the well-being of same-gender-desiring Jamaicans and HIV-infected and affected communities as well as for the construction of what comes to be the archives of HIV/AIDS. As the knowledge generated between health care worker and patient moved outside of this relationship, it shaped how HIV/AIDS and same-gender eroticism came to be inscribed in Jamaican history. These workers found themselves navigating dual functions of care (seeing to the needs of individuals and communities infected and affected by HIV/AIDS) and surveillance (producing knowledge from these relationships of care for powerful institutions to combat the epidemic). On the one hand, they were compelled to share what they knew about their patients because they did not and could not operate on their own. To properly care for their patients and combat

HIV/AIDS more broadly, they had to share with other health workers what they learned from their exchanges with patients. For instance, as much as CI's were capable of seeing to the medical needs of HIV-positive patients, they still had to get a physician to cosign prescriptions for patients, which inevitably required some form of communication about the specific case at hand.[58] And the reports from these and other frontline HIV/AIDS workers—who operated as the Ministry of Health's eyes and ears on the ground—formed the basis of Jamaica's HIV/AIDS policies and programs.

The fact that these workers were extremely protective of their patients' information suggests that their role in shaping Jamaica's HIV/AIDS archives involved strategic decisions about both sharing and refraining from sharing patient information. This concern about maintaining confidentiality regarding patients' health status and sexual activity was not confined to just HIV/AIDS and same-gender eroticism. For all sexually transmitted infections and all forms of sex, frontline health workers did not want their patients to come to harm because they disclosed such private information. In the case of CI's, if they were seen to be violating confidentiality, they would ruin the trust and good relationships they had built with their patients and with the communities in which they operated that were necessary for carrying out their work. Yet the severity of HIV/AIDS compared to other sexually transmitted infections, and the intense stigma against same-gender eroticism in relation to other forms of illicit sex, made these forms of intimate knowledge particularly sensitive. For no other kind of sex did Jamaicans take to the streets in protest.[59] For no other kind of sexually transmitted illness were CI's compelled to engage in elaborate social practices to support patients in keeping their HIV-positive status a secret by, for instance, picking up a patient's medication from the pharmacy and strategizing how and where the patient might hide it from family members.[60] Especially at the beginning of the epidemic, CI's were reluctant to talk about their HIV-positive patients even with other health professionals who they feared might mistreat their patients given the lack of knowledge of the new disease and the harsh stigma against it.[61] Thus, while the management of health-related records is always subject to anxieties around privacy, the subsequent destruction of CI and Helpline records to safeguard caller confidentiality takes on added significance in the context of the stigma against HIV/AIDS and same-gender eroticism.

The intense pressure that Jamaican health workers experienced to shield the identities of same-gender-desiring and HIV-positive Jamaicans from public view means there are few sources from which to construct histories of sexuality for Jamaica. Indeed, if frontline HIV/AIDS workers were to leave the sorts of traces that historians often later rely on to create representations of the past, they would run the risk of rendering their patients vulnerable to violence, given the intense stigma against HIV/AIDS and same-gender eroticism of this period. Though writing subaltern subjects into history is often interpreted as a process of liberation, and their deliberate exclusion is taken to be a sign of domination, I suggest that another dynamic might be operating in the archival practices of Jamaican frontline HIV/AIDS workers. Through acts of exclusion and evasion, frontline health care workers sought to protect their patients, hiding HIV-positive and same-gender-desiring Jamaicans from the past to secure their existence in the future.

Archiving Same-Gender Intimacy: Reinscribing Race, Class, and Gender Hierarchies

If the efforts of frontline health workers are central to inscribing same-gender intimacy in the materials of Jamaica's HIV/AIDS epidemic, their archival practices reckon with existing social divisions that shape how and what kinds of same-gender intimacies are documented. Even as the emergence of a new illness expanded public discussions around sexuality, existing race, class, and gender hierarchies foregrounded certain queer subjects while hiding others from view. Poor and working-class Black men emerged as the presumed subject of "homosexuality" while middle and upper-class brown and white men largely escaped public scrutiny. Attending to these patterns of queer inscription is useful in illustrating the contours of archival arrangements that differentially distribute visibility among variously positioned same-gender-desiring subjects. The practice of tracing queerness thus surfaces the persistence of archival effects. Rather than a break with the past, queer history making in this chapter reveals the continuity of archival infrastructures to shape historical narratives.

The same-gender intimacy that is inscribed in the materials from the early years of the epidemic in Jamaica is largely male. This is not because women who have sex with women were unconcerned about HIV/AIDS, or because, unlike male prisons, HIV/AIDS was not present in women's prisons during the condom riots.[62] Instead, it was because male homosexuals were considered to be a high-priority HIV/AIDS risk group while women who shared intimacies with each other were illegible within HIV/AIDS discourse at the time. Although the documentation of a woman with HIV/AIDS in Jamaica did not occur until 1987, four years after the initial outbreak of the HIV/AIDS on the island, the interpretation of women's infection with HIV/AIDS was very different from how men's infection was understood.[63] The first case of HIV/AIDS was accompanied by assurances that the male patient did not contract the infection through sex with another man.[64] In contrast, the first case of a woman with HIV/AIDS was understood to signify the increasingly heterosexual nature of HIV/AIDS transmission.[65] Within the social imagination of this period, the possibility of women contracting HIV/AIDS through sex with other women seemed unthinkable.[66]

Compared to men who have sex with men, who occupy a contested space within Jamaica's public sphere, women's eroticism with other women materialized differently. The tropes of sexual abuse, intimate partner violence, and the desire to find like-minded community and intimate partnership that pervaded characterizations of the lives of men who have sex with men also shaped the lives of same-gender-desiring women. However, women's structural positions in Jamaican society meant that their erotic lives apart from men had little value outside the heteronormative role of anchoring male sexuality, masculinity, and national identity.[67] For instance, tabloid journalists not only uniformly denied requests by women to connect them with other same-gender-desiring women on the grounds of refusing to condone such relationships; they also framed "lesbians" in terms of competition with men for women as opposed to constructing desire among women on its own terms.[68] As Makeda Silvera notes, however, this lack of regard for women's erotic relationships with other women did not prevent such women from experiencing gendered forms of violence that are often not overtly articulated in the public sphere.[69]

In comparison to gay men, whose presence overwhelms the strident public debates over HIV/AIDS, the decriminalization of sodomy, and the politics of dancehall in Jamaica, women who love women are most richly rendered in the imaginative realm of the island's literature. Michelle Cliff's 1987 novel *No Telephone to Heaven* and JAS member Robert Cork's 1998 unpublished play *An Existence Mirrored* serve as exemplary texts in this regard. Though they both adopt the structure of the coming-of-age narrative, their female protagonists are positioned differently in Jamaica's racial and class hierarchies; readers are introduced to Cliff's character Clare Savage as an upper-class, light-skinned young woman, and audience members come to know Cork's character Gloria as a young Black woman who turns to higglering (peddling) after being cast out of her wealthy family's home. In both texts, protagonists come into consciousness as women through their intimate relationships with other women. In *No Telephone to Heaven*, Clare sexually, politically, and spiritually reckons with Black Jamaican womanhood through her exchanges with her friend, comrade, and lover Harry/Harriet. In *An Existence Mirrored*, Gloria understands herself as entering womanhood when she reconciles her desires for other women not only with her friend, lover, and workmate Angie, but also with her estranged daughter Hope. The fact that neither of these texts that foreground intimacies between women addresses HIV/AIDS—the disease that becomes almost conceptually inseparable from men who have sex with men—highlights the difference that gender makes in producing knowledge about same-gender eroticism in Jamaica.

Class relations also mediated the construction of HIV/AIDS archives in foregrounding the lives of working-class citizens. The first HIV/AIDS testing system on the island was established in 1985, not through Jamaica's Ministry of Health but through the Ministry of Labor among outgoing migrant farmworkers in compliance with US labor requirements.[70] This means that the largely working-class men who comprised the majority of the island's migrant agricultural workers were the first to systematically become visible to the Jamaican state as HIV-positive as a consequence of the medicalization of the demands of American capital. The year 1985 was also when Jamaica's chief medical officer made HIV infection and AIDS a notifiable disease, requiring those who tested positive for HIV/AIDS to be identified to the Jamaican state.[71] Yet not all Jamaicans were equally subject to this mandate. A 1993 survey found that 38 percent of private physicians had not reported their HIV-positive patients as opposed to only 4 percent of physicians working in the public sector.[72] And a 1987 report to the USAID office in Jamaica noted that "some Jamaicans who believe they may be HIV+ or have the disease are reportedly travelling to the United States for testing and possibly remaining there for treatment."[73] Thus, Jamaicans who were able to afford to see a private physician or to travel abroad to receive medical treatment were able to bypass the Ministry of Health surveillance protocols. These individuals thus avoided the stigma associated not only with being infected with HIV but also with taking a medical test that would implicate them in engaging in illicit sexual activities. To the extent that same-gender eroticism materializes in the archives of HIV/AIDS in Jamaica, it is likely to involve subjects who cannot otherwise afford to escape state documentation.

This overrepresentation of poor and working-class same-gender-desiring Jamaicans was intimately related to broader classed politics of visibility/publicity around same-gender eroticism in late twentieth-century Jamaica. Working-class Jamaicans did not have the same access to privacy and control over the circulation of information about themselves (and its consequences) that Jamaicans with more resources could afford. Thus, in

An Existence Mirrored, other higglers at the market refer to Gloria's stall as "the sadamite corner," a moniker against which she is quick to retort "me a no saddamite . . . me a happymite." Similarly, the Jamaican tabloid publication *XNews* sought to reproduce the belief that "when you are a low class and common b—y man you mus expect your business to come in the paper."[74] Its reporters frequently investigated the intimate lives of young men from Jamaica's inner-city communities, like Drummie, who had the reputation of being "one big b—y man whey nuh watch nuh face and nuh 'fraid fi tell anybody bout him lifestyle."[75] But even if Drummie "nuh 'fraid" of others knowing about his sexual inclinations, this certainly was a concern for other working-class Jamaicans for whom even the rumor of homosexuality could result in loss of employment as well as ostracism from family and community.[76]

Established in 1993, *XNews* was a weekly Jamaican tabloid publication that branded itself as being even more ribald and outrageous than the island's existing daily tabloid, the *Jamaica Star*, which was founded in 1951. *XNews* became wildly popular, boasting a circulation of some 250,00 for its first issue and claiming title to being the fastest-growing newspaper in Jamaica by the mid-1990s.[77] That this newspaper's debut was marked by the bold front-page headline "Gays Attack Shabba" foreshadowed the way that same-gender eroticism (alongside other forms of illicit sex) would become a major topic of the tabloid in the late twentieth century.[78] *XNews* developed an intense fascination with same-gender eroticism, and its journalists went to great lengths to publicize the intimate lives of the island's same-gender-desiring subjects, disingenuously posing as homosexuals to gain trust and develop relationships with interviewees and explicitly writing about the sexual lives of their interlocutors in almost pornographic detail. Yet, as will be discussed below, *XNews* journalists quickly learned that Jamaicans' willingness to speak about their intimate lives cleaved along the lines of class.

The way that homosexuality became the subject of a national state of emergency through the riots over the distribution of condoms to prevent HIV/AIDS in prisons in 1997 also suggests that class relations played an important role in Jamaican processes of sexual formation. In the 1980s and 1990s, poor and working-class Jamaicans increasingly found themselves in prison as a consequence of their survival efforts within a context of severe economic constraints and growing economic inequality. Since the mid-1970s, Jamaica's protracted economic crisis, which unfolded in relationship to structural adjustment policies imposed by international financial institutions, resulted in high levels of unemployment, inflation, indebtedness, and currency devaluation.[79] The subsequent decline in wages, made worse by inflation, resulted in a shrinkage of participation in the formal labor market as individuals, especially young men, turned to the informal economy and illegal activities to eke out a living.[80] The 1997 prison riots brought together HIV/AIDS and homosexuality in the minds of Jamaicans, and it was largely men of this class strata who were the presumed subjects of same-gender eroticism.[81]

This is to say, not that Jamaicans at the other end of the island's class spectrum were not visible, but that the conditions under which they were perceptible in the public sphere were different. While middle- and upper-class gay activists such as Donna Smith and Brian Williamson intentionally positioned themselves in the Jamaican public, same-gender-desiring Jamaicans of means generally sought to avoid visibility. This is evidenced in Jamaican critics' reception of the play *One of Our Sons Is Missing* by Trinidadian playwright Godfrey Sealy when the piece was first performed on the island in 1993. Set in Trinidad, the play follows the life story of Miguel Alonzo, a twenty-two-year-old young man who finds out that he has contracted HIV, presumably from unsafe sex with other men even as he pursues a relationship with his girlfriend Lesley. Employed as an accounts clerk in an insurance agency, Miguel's character comes from a solidly middle-class background; his father works as an assistant manager at an architecture firm, and his mother is employed as a caterer. Even though content explicitly alluding to same-gender eroticism was toned down in the performance, one reviewer described Miguel's erotic interactions with other men as "indiscreet."[82] What is worth commenting on is not that Miguel is having sex with other men but that he is doing it indiscreetly. On finding out about Miguel's relationships with other men, his father bemoans, "If anybody finds out about this we will be the talk of Diamond Vale," to which his mother replies, "Edrick, calm yourself. Nobody have to know anything."[83] The reassurance that Miguel's mother offers to his father suggests that middle-class men's same-gender erotic activities may be acceptable as long as they are circumspect.

Such expectations are borne out by *XNews* articles featuring middle- and upper-class men that more often than not follow the narrative structure of these men being dramatically caught in the act of sex with other men. Even if the names of these participants were not disclosed, telltale markers of middle- and upper-class status, such as the kind of car driven (Pajero), location (Upper St. Andrew), and type of employment (financial services), were embedded in stories that described men being caught unaware as they engage in illicit sexual encounters.[84] Thus, while it may be no surprise that poor and working-class Jamaican men boldly cruise other men on Kingston's waterfront, men higher up in Jamaica's class hierarchy are expected to be discreet in their same-gender intimacies; if knowledge of their same-gender relationships is circulated, it is often without their consent.[85] This could occur not always in such obvious ways as surprising two men in the act of sex, but also through, for instance, one lover blackmailing another, or one's employees opening a letter (complete with a nude picture) from one's paramour.[86] Thus, if the archives of HIV/AIDS in Jamaica are characterized by an overrepresentation of poor and working-class iterations of same-gender eroticism, this is not necessarily because homosexuality disproportionately takes place within the lower ranks of the island's class hierarchy. Perhaps, instead, it is because protocols of sexual respectability shield the same-gender erotic activities of Jamaica's middle and upper classes from public view.

To the extent that class relations structure the ways same-gender eroticism becomes perceptible in Jamaican society, it is useful to outline relations not only among but between class distinctions. One of the most common iterations of same-gender eroticism among men that materializes in late twentieth-century Jamaica involves intimate relationships that cross the lines of class and often age. These kinds of relationships pervade Powell's *A Small Gathering of Bones*. The intimate relationship between Dale and Nevin begins while Dale is in high school, and he approaches the older man, whom he notices repeatedly watching the cricket games Dale plays with his friends. The two become closer, Dale's mother passes away, and the young man moves in with Nevin, who supports him financially and pays his school fees. When Dale complains of his relationship to Ian, Ian retorts that while he has Bill, an older paramour who buys him gifts, he wishes that Bill showed him the same level of commitment and care that Nevin shows Dale. The differences between Nevin and Dale's relationship and Ian and Bill's illustrate that these cross-class, same-gender intimate relationships take various forms of intensity and emotional investment. Though Jamaica's racial hierarchy does not always neatly map onto class divisions, it is worth noting that Powell describes the wealthy lovers with whom Dale and Ian become involved using terms that index whiteness—Bill's hazel eyes, the blond in Nevin's mustache, the pale-skinned Englishman Dale meets at church.

The social world that Powell evokes in her novel aligns with the first qualitative study on homosexuality conducted in Jamaica in 1993, which was primarily concerned with the implications of men's sexual activity for HIV/STD prevention. In this research, six focus groups were conducted among men mostly twenty to thirty-five years of age from lower-middle-class and lower-socioeconomic backgrounds. One of the major themes of discussion was "older middle-class men who picked up younger, lower-class boys—or even 'kept' them. . . . Younger men may have a high school education, but have a difficult time getting ahead in Jamaica. They are often attracted to the glittery social life of certain circles that admit, or even revolve around successful or entertaining gays."[87]

Jamaica's print news, particularly those outlets that took on tabloid form and content, emphasized three themes in their coverage of erotic interactions among males that cross the lines of class, age, and race. The first focused on the sexual abuse of young boys in vulnerable circumstances by men in power, such as pastors and older family or community members.[88] Though the delicate nature of the issue prevented even *XNews* from discussing such events in any detail, Cliff's articulation of child sexual abuse in the realm of fiction sidesteps the strictures that would otherwise prevent frank discussion of this deviant form of sex. And yet even in *No Telephone to Heaven* when Harry/Harriet graphically recounts to Clare the incident when they were raped as a child by a white army officer, this violation is kept secret. In tending to Harry/Harriet's wounds from the assault, Hyacinth hid the rape from Harry/Harriet's family. Recognizing Harry/Harriet's precarious position as the child of the master and maid, Hyacinth feared that knowledge of this violation would ruin Harry/Harriet, effecting a conversion from "son to servant."[89]

The second theme focused on erotic relationships that occurred in the context of the transfer of resources. These relationships might be a onetime encounter that involved the exchange of cash, or a longer-term situation much like what Powell describes between Dale and Nevin, where the older man provides housing and connections to employment for his lover. The Jamaican news media sought to warn parents to watch out for their sons' falling victim to such older men who would lure their boys into a "homosexual" lifestyle through gifts, travel, and access to fancy cars.[90] While women engaging in sex work had long been a somewhat public secret in Jamaican society, the late twentieth century witnessed a greater prominence of male sex workers engaging men as clients.[91] These men were identified in the island's first medical study examining HIV prevalence rates among homosexual and bisexual men.[92] Yet it took several years for the development of any kind of intervention specifically focused on male sex work and sexual health in the form of JAS's Beach Boy program on Jamaica's north coast (the most tourist-heavy region on the island).[93] The *Jamaica Star* and *XNews* carried salacious front-page headlines such as "Gays Invade Hookers Beat" and "Male Hookers 'Full Up' Park" with accompanying articles filled with lurid details to ensure that readers knew that such sexual encounters were taking place among men.[94] These and other articles highlighted the lives of young men from Kingston's low-income communities, whom they described as having "rude boy face and b—man heart."[95] While these macho-looking men would not necessarily describe themselves as "gay" or "homosexual" nor hesitate in complying with Jamaican DJs' popular exhortation "all who nuh like b—y man put up oonu han," they would nevertheless engage in sexual relationships with other men for economic gain.[96] Often having wives, girlfriends, and/or children, these men considered such encounters to be reflective less of an inner subjectivity and more as an income-generating activity.

The final major theme of sex among men across the lines of class, age, and race addressed in Jamaican print news focused on intimate partner violence. This theme is evident in *A Small Gathering of Bones* when Dale's anger toward Nevin possesses him so fully that he finds himself unconsciously trying to attack Nevin with an icepick. In the *Star* and *XNews*, such instances of violence between male lovers were often framed in terms of jealousy, with physical altercations taking the form of fistfights, knifings, or shootings.[97] When these incidents resulted in death, the police were quick to identify class and age differences between the lovers as an explanatory factor, reproducing tropes about the violent subjectivities of poor Black young men. A 1993 front-page article in the *Star* noted, "In the past twelve years at least 10 prominent gays have been murdered by their ex-lovers . . . it is true that these (usually upper-class) professional men cling to young men from the lower class, and that is why they (professionals) are killed in such a ruthless manner."[98] A senior officer of the St. Andrew Central Division later explained that such murders could be explained by "youth who grew up in communities where the knife and the gun are murder weapons. These are youth who cannot reason. It's just kill, kill, kill."[99]

While these narratives are troubling because they fail to consider how structural forms of inequality shape intimate violence between men, I am less interested in the kinds of representations they engender than in what they reveal about the workings of Jamaican archival practices. Identifying how same-gender desire comes to be inscribed in the past through efforts to repair Jamaica's social body from HIV/AIDS illustrates the persistence of archival arrangements. If fractals occur through repetition with difference, queerness in this analysis functions to illustrate what stays the same. Even as the epidemic foregrounded sexuality—especially same-gender desire—as a site of repair, health care workers, news journalists, and creative writers constructed archives of HIV/AIDS that reinscribed postcolonial hierarchies of color, class, and gender. Identifying how queerness takes shape in these archives illustrates the continuity of archival disparities that differentially shape the legibility of queer historical subjecthood across Jamaican social hierarchies. By materializing poor and working-class Black men as the subjects of same-gender desire, the archives of HIV/AIDS index not only the inequalities that shape health disparities, but also the social forces that shield color- and class-privileged subjects from the same forms of disciplinary surveillance and their subsequent incorporation into historical narratives. Queerness foregrounds these inequalities and social forces as the passive lines of fractal formations that structure the archives of Jamaica's attempts to address the HIV/AIDS epidemic.

Part II

Narrative Ruptures

4

Performance

The National Dance Theatre Company

Three years after England granted Jamaica independence in 1962, Rex Nettleford, cofounder of Jamaica's National Dance Theatre Company (NDTC), wrote, "Jamaicans are a people who are constantly exposed to external influences, whose economic system traditionally depends on the caprice of other people's palates, whose values are largely imported from an alien set of experiences, and whose dreams and hopes have, at one time or another, been rooted [in another country]."[1] This outward orientation could produce incongruous results, leading Jamaicans to "[dance] European quadrilles under the tropical sun, [sing] the European madrigals beneath the mango trees, [and sit] at European afternoon teas belted and brass-buttoned in our woollen suits in the flaring heat."[2] Even in the wake of flag independence, coloniality continued to enchant British Caribbean societies, such that trauma, inauthenticity, and abnormality constituted the reality of its people.[3] This is because colonialism was not only a process of external political and economic domination but also an internal process of diminishing colonized subjectivity.[4] The juridical end of colonization thus did not automatically undo the sense of disorientation that colonized people experienced from being in "an unstable relationship with their own reality."[5] Decolonization required cultural autonomy alongside political and economic liberation.

In this chapter I explore the relationship between queerness and this decolonizing struggle for selfhood by analyzing the early work of the NDTC. Founded in the same year as Jamaica's independence, the company emerged from within a vibrant local dance scene as well as within a broader movement across the anglophone Caribbean toward the development of dance vocabularies rooted within the specificities of West Indian social life. This trend did not preclude the company from integrating dance forms from other parts of the world in the attempt to counter the colonial debasement of local movement patterns, particularly those associated with African heritage. NDTC quickly became a leading force in establishing Jamaican and Caribbean cultural distinctiveness through dance, not only in Jamaica but across the Caribbean, the United States, Canada, and Europe. I turn to the formative years of NDTC not only because of its widespread success and popularity but also because of the utility of performance in addressing the questions of queerness, fractality, and repair through cultural decolonization that I seek to explore in this chapter. I situate performance in terms of forms of movement that can never be perfectly replicated and thus are always subject to revision.[6] Performance thus resonates not only with the concept of fractals as a form of repetition with difference but also with analyses of queerness that foreground how gender and sexual relations take shape through recurrent practices. Thus, in this chapter I investigate how queer fractals figure into the work of performance in repairing the injuries to colonized subjectivity under empire.

I began this investigation by assembling an archive of repair focusing on NDTC's early performances in three ways. First, I undertook archival research. At NDTC's archive in Kingston, Jamaica, I reviewed dance programs, news clippings, photographs, meeting minutes, rehearsal notes, and letters. I also examined video recordings of the company's performances at the National Library of Jamaica and the Public Broadcasting Corporation of Jamaica. I later reviewed articles on NDTC in dance and performance publications at the New York Public Library of the Performing Arts, the Schomburg Center for Research on Black Culture, and the Toronto Reference Library. Second, I conducted oral history interviews with seven (three men and four women) of the early generation of NDTC's company members. Finally, through a gracious invitation from the company's artistic director, Marlon Simms, I participated in NDTC's company classes. These classes were created by Rex Nettleford to impart the company's movement vocabulary to the company's dancers. Simms informed me that every effort was made to maintain the integrity of this training to ensure the continuity of the company's dance tradition. The relationships among these forms of engagement—archival, oral history, performance—proved to be a powerful way of coming to know the NDTC. They operated as a form of relay between what Diana Taylor calls the archive—"documents, maps, literary texts . . . all those items supposedly resistant to change"—and the repertoire: "performance, gestures, orality . . . all those acts usually thought of as ephemeral, non-reproducible knowledge."[7] I thus created an archive that allowed me to develop a cognitive, relational, and embodied sense of the company's performances.

A queer reading of this archive produces fractal effects at the level of narrative. As a kind of repetition with difference, fractals only make sense through the combination of persistence and rupture. Whereas chapters 2 and 3 mobilized queerness to illustrate the *continued* violence of sociohistorical processes that shape contemporary archival infrastructures, in this chapter and in chapter 5 I make use of queerness to *break* with existing accounts of the past to fashion new narratives of repair. Here, queerness surfaces the active lines in fractal formations, that which changes with each iteration. This chapter uses queerness to generate a narrative that departs from the kinds of historical accounts that Jamaica's post-independence period is often made to index. In these accounts the Jamaican state promotes heteropatriarchal kinship structures as a strategy of national development to counter its anxiety over Black men's capacity to lead emerging nations.[8] Turning to the NDTC generates a different narrative from these accounts that foreground the state's concern with high rates of illegitimacy and population growth that supposedly threatened Jamaica's economic and moral well-being. In addition to NDTC's contemporary reputation for countering the colonial degradation of Jamaican and Caribbean cultural practices, I suggest that thinking about NDTC's work through gender and sexual relations materializes a different approach to state-centered preoccupations with Jamaican intimate life.[9] NDTC's early performances and how they were interpreted highlight the covert but pervasive way that queer intimacies were foundational to Jamaican's self-understanding in the wake of empire.

Jamaica's National Dance Theatre Company

In August 1962, Rex Nettleford and Eddy Thomas co-produced the show "Roots and Rhythms" at the Little Theatre in Kingston, Jamaica's capital city, to celebrate the country's independence from England. Though the show had only eleven performances, it nevertheless was a massive undertaking, as it involved the coordination of seven choreographers and over one hundred dancers from six of the island's major dance groups as well as contributions from four visiting artists.[10] NDTC was established as a result of this show, drawing its membership from fifteen of the show's best dancers. The Company articulated four goals: (1) to provide a vehicle for dancers to perform and create works of artistic merit; (2) to experiment with dance forms in order to develop a style that faithfully reflects the movement patterns of Jamaica and the Caribbean area; (3) to conduct research into Indigenous dance forms on the island; and (4) to promote the training of teachers and students in dance and theater.[11]

NDTC came into being through an existing tradition of dance in Jamaica and the Caribbean that was increasingly concerned with developing local movement vocabularies. Formal Jamaican dance education began with the pioneering efforts of Hazel Johnson, who taught in the idiom of classical ballet. And while leading dance figures such as Madame Soohih, Punky & Betty Rowe, Faye Simpson, and Barbara Fonseca continued to teach traditional European dance forms on the island in its immediate pre-independence era, it was Johnson's student Ivy Baxter who began to transform the field of dance theater by incorporating Jamaican folk into her performances.[12] NDTC owes its existence to these earlier figures, as many of them trained the dancers who would become company members, and the company built on and extended Baxter's work in constructing a uniquely Jamaican style of dance. These transformations were part of a wider cultural movement in the Caribbean with, for instance, the establishment of the Little Carib Theatre in Trinidad by Beryl McBurnie in 1948, and the Haitian Institute of Folklore and Classical Dance in Haiti by Lavinia Williams in 1954.[13]

The NDTC also emerged in Jamaica at a time when dance came to occupy a greater space in Jamaican public life. In the realm of popular dance, the early 1960s marked the rise of ska associated with the rude boy culture of lower-class urban youth, and the subsequent proliferation of sound systems in dance halls and social venues across the island. In these settings young people would gather to listen to the slow tempo of ska, a genre of music fusing Jamaican mento with American jazz and rhythm and blues, while moving their bodies to the dance of the same name.[14] The work of institutions such as the Jamaica Social Welfare Commission and the Jamaica Festival also did much to resuscitate the island's folk dances by promoting and organizing dance classes and events across the island in Jamaican forms of movement that were often closely tied to syncretic Afro-religious contexts such as Myal or social functions such as wakes.[15] But it was in the expanding realm of dance as a performing art (in the traditional sense of theater) that NDTC most clearly made its mark. The arrival of motion pictures to the island in the 1920s and 1930s did much to stimulate the formation of local dance troupes; by the 1940s these began to expand beyond the venues of nightclubs and amateur shows in their efforts to take dance seriously as a creative art form in its own right.[16] By the 1950s the Extra Mural Studies Department at the University of the West Indies (UWI) began to host summer dance workshops, attended by students in Jamaica and across the Caribbean, that featured local and visiting instructors such as Neville Black, a Jamaican choreographer living in Chicago.[17] This growth in dance performance extended to Jamaica's much-celebrated annual pantomime, where those who would eventually become NDTC members began to work together in the shows *Jamaica Way*, *Carib Gold*, and *Banana Boy*. These shows began to more fully integrate dance into programming in ways that broke with a long-standing tendency to segregate movement from other performance dimensions.[18]

In its attempt to construct Jamaican and Caribbean movement patterns, NDTC was committed to the kind of reflexive self-exploration that the company understood Jamaica itself to be experiencing. Nettleford stated, "When we travel, people are expecting a Jamaican show but then we ask ourselves— What is Jamaica? We live in a transplanted society with one common link that was the British connexion. The British overlordship welded together people of African origin, people of European origin who came as merchants or property owners, East Indians, Chinese, Syrians, Portuguese, Jews and so on. This is the kind of mosaic that takes on the look of homogeneity because of the strong British connexion. Nevertheless, there are differences in the society that must jell together and find itself."[19] This expansive understanding of the processes of cultural formation was reflected in the offerings of the company's first performance, which was influenced by Afro-Jamaican rural movement patterns and Haitian folk as well as by European ballet and American modern dance traditions. Such a medley of dance forms was facilitated by the experience of several NDTC members who sought dance training in the United States and England. This eclectic mix of dance styles sometimes confused audiences and critics overseas, but Nettleford was adamant that synthesizing different cultural influences required not only experimentation and adventure but also time and patience. Indeed, it was not until the company's eighth season that it began to take on a reasonably uniform look.[20] Eschewing a purely nativist approach to dance, Nettleford insisted that borrowing from foreign dance styles did not necessarily mean internalizing foreign rubrics of value. Thus, while he encouraged NDTC dancers to take classes in different styles of dance to widen their technical range, he also maintained that "standards set in New York and in the British Royal Ballet, while of much value in themselves, may also conceal prejudices and idiosyncrasies born of American and British experiences of little use to us. The NDTC has a responsibility not to be carried away by the stridency of American movement style or the deliberate aesthetic limpness of Anglo-Saxon London. Nor is the tonality of certain types of African dancing the answer. We must find the 'thing' ourselves."[21]

The excitement of participating in the process of finding this "thing" was a major inspiration for the company's cofounders as well as those who would become NDTC members. As early as the 1940s, Nettleford saw merit in putting folk song to movement in producing plays at Cornwall College.[22] Returning to Jamaica after completing his degree at Oxford University as a Rhodes scholar, Nettleford approached Thomas to create the NDTC after having worked together on several theater productions. Though Thomas already owned his own dance studio, his skills as a dancer, choreographer, musician, and costumer made him an invaluable partner in this endeavor. Barry Moncrieffe, the late NDTC former artistic director and dancer, was only twenty-one when the company was formed. He hailed from a Kingston middle-class family and recalls that he and the other members were enthralled at the prospect of taking part in the process of building something new for Jamaica. "Everybody was so keen and we were learning new things, new folk dances of the island."[23]

Alongside the thrill of contributing to the formation of national culture, company members reveled in each other's camaraderie under NDTC's charismatic leadership. Bridget Casserly, who was enrolled as a political science student at UWI when Nettleford asked her to be a part of the company, recalls the early days of NDTC: "We were a family. We enjoyed what we did. We always did things together. We spent so much time together. In those days, rehearsals would go on forever. Sometimes we would get out by 5 in the morning because we were working things out, we were learning."[24] It is crucial to note that NDTC did not pay its members, which meant that only those who were both able and willing to volunteer their labor could take part in the company. But even if NDTC members were not paid, the nature of the company's leadership, particularly that of Nettleford, was a major draw. Marjorie Whylie became a member in NDTC's orchestra as a UWI student in 1963 and then became the company's musical director in 1967. She explained why she joined: "I couldn't not be involved. It was a natural thing. I was there and they just grabbed me. Everywhere I looked in my life there was Rex. He challenged me and cajoled me into arranging songs."[25] This gives some insight into the demanding and caring nature of Nettleford's leadership. The detailed personal letters of thanks that he penned for every company member at the end of each NDTC season are legendary and very much treasured by their addressees to this day.

Very quickly the company came to be a key player in Jamaican cultural life, not only through its performances but also through its efforts in public dance education. Almost all company members were involved in teaching dance as a way of making a living, primarily in school settings to children and youth in Kingston. Yet the company also became involved in advancing dance across Jamaica as a whole through its partnership with the Ministry of Education to train teachers in local dance idioms.[26] This initiative augmented existing attempts by NDTC to extend its work beyond the capital by conducting lecture demonstrations in schools throughout the island.[27] Through a partnership with Jamaica's Ministry of Trade and Industry, the company also trained those who entertained the island's tourists, in order to reduce the reliance on foreign music and dance and to expose Jamaica's visitors to local idioms of performance.[28] Over time, NDTC members became powerful figures in Jamaican dance in their own right. For instance, Joyce Campbell came into the position of dance officer with the Jamaica Festival, and Sheila Barnett ascended to the position of officer in physical education and dance at Jamaica's Ministry of Education.

From the very beginning, NDTC was engaged in exchanges that extended beyond the island's shores in ways that had important implications for both Jamaican international relations and configurations of Jamaican diaspora. The characteristics of the "Sun of the West Indies" tour to Howard University in 1961, before the NDTC was formed, proved to be an important foreshadowing of how the company would become an important player in Jamaica's relationships with other countries. Seeking to rally support for the tour before arrangements had been finalized, Edna Manley, wife of the premier of Jamaica noted, "It is important at this time when the West Indies is on the verge of independence that ties should be firmly established with the United States and no closer and firmer ties could be found than those based on a free and generous cultural interchange."[29]

This framing of dance as a means of facilitating diplomatic relations between countries continued in the early years of NDTC's existence, with the company often taking on the role of cultural ambassador to advance Jamaican foreign policy. For instance, with Jamaica's entry into the Organization of American States, the country felt it necessary to establish diplomatic relations with

Latin America. In preparing for the NDTC's 1969 Mexican tour, the press and cultural affairs officer at the Jamaican Embassy in Mexico wrote to Nettleford:

> I need not tell you how eager we are to get the National Dance Theatre Company to perform in Mexico in order to enhance the image of Jamaica in Latin America. The Mexican public have, so far, demonstrated an enthusiastic receptivity to Jamaica and to the Jamaican culture. If the NDTC do manage to perform here, you can credit yourselves with having achieved something extremely valuable in Jamaica's international relations . . . I need not emphasize how great a contribution you will be making. Please explain the importance of this event to each member of the troupe. Jamaica has reached a certain level in her relations with Latin America at which we must inform and educate the Latin people about Jamaica, stimulate their interest in our people, our culture and our way of life, and make them realise our potential as a young, developing nation.[30]

Yet, far from being a pawn in Jamaican state machinations, the NDTC was extremely deliberate in navigating its overseas engagements. As an amateur company whose members volunteered their labor and had to request leave from their places of work (often communicated through requests made by the Jamaican government), the NDTC was forced to be selective in deciding which international tours it would take. Further, while it depended on financial support from the government to be able to pay for these tours, the economic situation in Jamaica meant that such state subsidies were never very large. For instance, the Jamaican government contributed £2,000 through the Ministry of Finance and Planning in support of NDTC's Mexico tour.[31] While substantial, this figure did not even fully cover airfare costs for company members, much less the expenses associated with accommodations; per diems; in-country travel; or the transportation of scenery, costumes, musical instruments, and so forth.[32] While some of these costs were absorbed by those who hosted the NDTC, the company was nevertheless burdened with the task of fundraising to cover the inevitable shortfall, as well as with the enormous logistical endeavor of coordinating and scheduling a fifty-person tour.

Despite these challenges, the NDTC benefited on several levels from its international engagements. Developing a Jamaican and Caribbean movement pattern was a relational process that involved reckoning not only with the dance traditions and lived realities of people in the region, but also with various others who had their own expectations about who Jamaican and Caribbean people were and what their dances and dancers should look like. Nettleford maintained that people in the Global North labored under gross misapprehensions about Caribbean people and would, for instance, express surprise at the political sophistication of Jamaica and its ability to successfully run institutions of government that once belonged only to advanced industrialized countries. He claimed that these misapprehensions about "sunlit infants from the tropical isles" was intimately related to requests by foreign hosts that NDTC offerings "should have 'more sex,' our girls should be less clothed, things should be more 'primitive.'"[33] Thus, NDTC's investment in showcasing the diversity of Jamaica's cultural influences was to counter the expectations that the company would present displays of Native exoticism when it performed in North American and European venues.

The company's overseas tours also enhanced NDTC's exposure and reputation in other countries. Other Caribbean territories that were seeking to further their local cultural development turned to the NDTC for support. For instance, having heard of the NDTC's successful visit to the Stratford Festival in Canada in 1963, Alek Zybine, the associate director of the Nassau Civic Ballet, wrote to the NDTC in 1964 seeking to make arrangements for the company's tour to the Bahamas. Zybine sought to establish a connection with NDTC by noting that the Jamaican dancer Eryick Darby, who had moved to the Bahamas, had both taught and choreographed for the Nassau Civic Ballet. Zybine explained that he was inviting groups like the NDTC to generate greater interest and commitment to the local Bahamian dance scene.[34] The NDTC received similar requests from cultural organizations in Grand Cayman, Antigua, and Barbados.[35]

NDTC's influence among Caribbean citizens also extended beyond the region to touch Caribbean communities in the diaspora. Through organizations such as the Jamaican Canadian Association, the Jamaican Barbados Society, and the American–West Indian Association, Jamaicans living abroad sought to have the NDTC visit their countries of residence to advance national pride, further community development, maintain their connection to the island, and encourage tourism. While NDTC's appearance at the 1965 Commonwealth Arts Festival in England was praised for its popularity and received rave reviews from cultural critics, the company also made a lasting impact on the country's Caribbean residents.[36] Jamaica's Ministry of Development and Welfare sent Hugh Nash, an officer with the Jamaica Festival, to England to report on the NDTC, and the *Daily Gleaner* published his impressions. "Mr. Nash said Jamaicans in London, Cardiff, Liverpool and Bournmouth expressed pride and delight at the competent and professional manner in which aspects of their country's cultural background was projected. It was evident, he added, that they were proud to be associated with the hospitality afforded the team. A feature of this delight of Jamaicans in England was that previously held impressions of Jamaica as a culturally backward nation, given by some biased presentations in Press and on television were corrected by the fine performances given."[37] The success of NDTC's performances thus in a sense redeemed Jamaican and Caribbean residents in England who had been compelled to endure the racism and xenophobia that surfaced through events like the 1958 Notting Hill race riots and the passing of the 1962 British Commonwealth Immigration Act deterring immigration from the Caribbean.

Even as the NDTC became a significant actor in Jamaican cultural politics both onshore and offshore, critics took aim at what they perceived to be the company's race, class, and national politics in the early years of its existence. They challenged the NDTC's claim to "national" status and questioned the extent to which the company engaged with the country as a whole. When the NDTC went on its first overseas tour to the Stratford Festival in Canada in 1963, Edward Seaga, the minister of development and welfare who was responsible for partially financing the enterprise, took issue with the repertoire the company planned to present. In a letter to Nettleford, marked "urgent," he stated,

> From the items listed for performance it appears that the principal purpose of the visit will be defeated in that most of the items are not of Jamaican origin at all but West Indian . . . there remains only *Pocomania* as a Jamaican item which I was hoping you would never perform until perfected in order that your presentation of this important indigenous material would break out of the mediocrity and unauthenticity of the past. I would be extremely disappointed if this was not so, as you stand to gain nothing by premature performance. It is apparent that an effort to portray the "Jamaican image" is really portraying a West Indian image which is quite unsatisfactory.[38]

Seaga's quarrel with the NDTC lays bare important questions about what constituted the nation and how the form of national performances should be conceived. As a state representative, Seaga was obliged to promote NDTC as Jamaican. And while the company did not oppose this positioning, the *Guardian* also noted, "Rex Nettleford is strongly nationalistic. His nation being the Caribbean in general, rather than Jamaica in particular."[39] Jamaica's relationship to the Caribbean in the early 1960s was a sensitive topic, given the country's central role in the demise of the West Indian Federation. Even though other Caribbean nations sought out the NDTC in support of their own cultural development, and even though company members expressed both joy and relief in performing in other Caribbean countries because their audiences understood the shows more readily than elsewhere, the company felt that it was important to remind its members of this broader regional political context when it performed at the first Caribbean Arts Festival (CARIFESTA). In its communication to company members, the NDTC noted, "It is important that the Company be on their best behavior in treating with our hosts—the Grenadians. The idea of CARIFESTA requires some nursing particularly where Jamaica is concerned."[40]

As an anthropologist who conducted research among the Jamaican revival cults from which the NDTC drew inspiration for its performances, Seaga was also concerned that the company remain as faithful as possible to the island's folk forms.[41] Given the widespread but superficial use of Pukumina in popular Jamaican performances at the time (as indicated in chapter 2), Seaga was understandably concerned about the "authenticity" of NDTC's representation of Jamaican religious practices.[42] Though the NDTC also recognized the importance of developing a rich understanding (cognitive and corporeal) of the movement traditions that informed its work, it refused to be confined to these traditions.[43] The NDTC situated itself as a dance theater company that was committed to artistic excellence through creative works, and it was not interested in simply reproducing Jamaican traditional dance. Nettleford was often fond of saying that the company sought to create dances composed of the essence (or spirit) rather than the letter of Jamaican and Caribbean folk songs and dances.[44]

If Seaga took issue with how the NDTC performed Jamaica, others were more concerned with the company's claim to "national" status, given its alleged limited ability to engage with Jamaicans of all stripes. The *Daily Gleaner* pushed Nettleford on exactly this question, asking, "Having adopted a 'national' designation, how does the company justify this title? Shouldn't more time be spent taking the NDTC to a wider audience?"[45] Nettleford agreed that this was an area in which the NDTC could improve, but he also pointed out the lack of venues across Jamaica in which a dance theater company like the NDTC could perform and conceded that attempts to both draw country audiences to the theater and send its dancers out to conduct lecture demonstrations across the island would have to suffice until the situation changed. At a seminar on "Arts in the Caribbean Today" jointly hosted by the Caribbean Artist Movement and the New World Group, critiques of the NDTC centered less on the company's reach outside of the capital city and more on its supposed class bias; "the critical question posed was whether the NDTC was not guilty of perpetuating a 'middle class monopoly on 'culture.'"[46] Wynter was even more explicit in her critique of the company, which she maintained "reduc[ed] the power of the cult religion to a prettified exoticism, which smack[ed] of instant folk art designed to suit a bland middle class palate."[47] Over time, the company sought to address the elitism associated with a dance theater by subsidizing admission to its performances and providing scholarships to its training programs.

The NDTC also found itself caught up in the ways that race played into competing notions of nationhood immediately following Jamaica's independence. The creation of the island's national motto "Out of Many One People" indexed the ascendancy of a kind of creole multiracial nationalism that Deborah Thomas argues emphasized Jamaicanness in terms of a shared history and culture.[48] In a country where the overwhelming majority of people were dark-complexioned, creole multiracialism allowed white and brown elites to lay claim on the nation and to project representations of Jamaica in terms of multiracial harmony, both externally to other nations (as a distinctively Jamaican characteristic) and internally to its citizens (as a goal to which they should aspire).[49] The way that creole multiracialism operated to sideline attempts at Black self-determination are evident in critiques of NDTC's Afrocentric orientation. Some Jamaicans felt that the company cleaved too closely to the island's African heritage; its "barefoot" dances and bombastic music (particularly the use of the drum) elicited a range of negative reviews from disapproving audiences. In her article for the *Jamaican Enquirer*, Herma Diaz noted that the island "has a tendency to disregard other cultural and artistic courses in concentrating entirely on the African influence. . . . Perhaps in time when the African cult has had its full run, the need for other sources on which to draw will be recognized."[50] Others took issue not with the overrepresentation of the island's African presence in the company's repertoire but with the turn to Africa as a source of national cultural expression at all. For instance, an anonymous "critic" of the NDTC wrote to the *Daily Gleaner* editor to express their indignation with NDTC's performances and refusal to see the company's "bongo dances."[51]

For others however, the problem was not that NDTC was too Afrocentric, but that it was not Afrocentric enough. These critiques rejected narratives of creole multiracialism and instead politically aligned themselves with Black Power movements in Jamaica that were fueled in part by the Coral Gardens "incident" in 1963 and the Walter Rodney Riots in 1968.[52] For these critics, the reality of the devaluation and impoverishment of Black persons in Jamaica not only revealed the illusion of claims to multiracial harmony but also necessitated engaging in processes of cultural production to correct the workings of anti-Blackness specifically. For instance, when Les Ballet Africans de

La Republique de Guinea (African Ballet Company of Guinea) debuted their Caribbean tour at the Carib Theatre in Kingston in 1968, commenters took aim at the NDTC by urging Jamaican audiences to attend the visiting company to see the kind of traditional African dances NDTC ought to be performing.[53] Others, however, were more concerned with the skin color of the performers who were representing the nation onstage. One audience member was heard remarking, "Was NDTC making a new social commentary this [1970] Season—like saying the brown man has emerged? From coffee to cream— especially the ladies: they seemed on stage to be of one shade of tan, pale, honey. Good for the strong mahogany of [Barry] Moncrieffe, [Gertrude] Sherwood, [Audley] Butler, [Tommy] Pinnock (DON'T YOU THINK)."[54]

Even if NDTC was not always successful in communicating its racial politics to audience members, the company sought to foreground Jamaica's African heritage. Nettleford was convinced that "the universe of Jamaica and the Caribbean—has got to be part of the African Diaspora. For we are all caught up in this tremendous, awesome, complex process of finding self—of rejecting/building, of decolonizing/indigenizing. This contradictory process is the dynamic of Plantation American life and it is what engages and challenges the Antillean soul."[55] Nettleford's work with the NDTC resonated with his other roles as political commentator and scholar in actively engaging in discourses around the role of Blackness in Jamaica. Some of this work included speaking on Jamaican radio as early as the 1950s about the need for Black pride; conducting research into Rastafari groups in Kingston to dispel myths about their supposed threat to Jamaica's social order; and publishing *Mirror, Mirror*, in which he insisted on the need to attend to the realities of Jamaica's Black majority.[56]

NDTC Politics of Intimacy

As the NDTC mobilized performance to work through cultural formation in the aftermath of English colonial rule, questions of gender and sexuality operated as subtexts to the more prominent concerns of race, class, and nation. These questions were not only key themes in NDTC dance pieces but also the (often covert) idiom through which to talk about the company among Jamaican and foreign audiences both on and off the island. The NDTC functioned not only as a major site of cultural formation in Jamaica, the Caribbean, and its diasporas but also as a cultural ambassador to Jamaica by using dance to further the island's diplomatic relations with other countries. Gender and sexuality were prime vectors through which the company accomplished this work. I suggest that attending to both NDTC performances and the way they were received by various audiences facilitates a rethinking of hegemonic gender and sexual relations in Jamaica's immediate post-independence period. This approach enacts a break with existing narratives by surfacing the active lines in fractal formations. It prevents the repetition of these narratives by foregrounding a different representation of the past. Existing narratives of this period foreground the promotion of heterosexual marriage to counter the perceived threat that existing rates of population growth posed for Jamaica's social and economic well-being. I unsettle these narratives by suggesting that NDTC's performance of intimacy highlights the significance of queer relations in formulating Jamaican and Caribbean iterations of culture. This alternative historical account illustrates the significance of queerness within Jamaicans' struggle to understand themselves upon attaining independence from England in 1962.

As noted by a *Daily Gleaner* cultural critic, a favorite topic of the company's choreographers in the early days of NDTC's existence was what they referred to as "matters of mating."[57] In dances such as *Legend of Lover's Leap, Dialogue for Three, Two Drums for Babylon, Country Wedding, Night Shelter,* and *Married Story,* just to name a few, the company committed itself to exploring the nuances of Jamaican and Caribbean forms of intimacy. While these dances foregrounded romance between women and men, they did so in a way that failed to valorize these relationships, especially to the exclusion of other kinds of intimate relations. For instance, *Legend of Lover's Leap*—a dance piece set in the nineteenth century in which a lascivious plantation owner and enslaved Jamaicans thwart the romantic relationship between an enslaved man and woman—indexed the futility of romantic love in the context of colonialism and enslavement.[58] *Two Drums for Babylon* similarly underscored the frustrations of romance between men and women but in a way that covertly drew attention to intimacies among men. By highlighting the difficulty of the choice that the young male protagonist must make between his fiancée and the masculinist Rastafari cult to which he is drawn, the piece speaks more broadly to the challenges facing Jamaicans in struggle for self-determination: "How far is it possible for an individual to accept a way of life which seems to threaten his necessary ties and affection?"[59] Finally, *Night Shelter* was structured around the old penny shelters in Jamaica that were established to provide inexpensive accommodation for rural women who traveled to town to sell their produce. The dance piece emphasizes the shelter as a space that institutionalizes close relationships among women by playing up how the residents chastise the tenant who breaks the "no males allowed" rule to sneak her paramour into the all-women space.

4.1. National Dance Theatre Company's *Dialogue for Three* performed by Bridget Casserly as "wife" (*left*), Bert Rose as "husband" (*middle*), and Barbara Requa as "other woman" (*right*). Photograph taken by Maria LaYacona. Date unknown. Source: NDTC Archives, Kingston.

While these pieces reveal important insights about the performance of Jamaican intimacy, *Dialogue for Three* was arguably NDTC's most important work in its early engagement with the "matters of mating" in Jamaican and Caribbean cultural formations simply because of the piece's enormous popularity both in Jamaica and overseas (see figure 4.1). The piece explores the love triangle among a woman and a married couple. It first premiered on June 16, 1963, at the Odeon Theatre in the city of Mandeville, located in Jamaica's western parish of Manchester. The ten-minute modern dance piece is set to the second movement of "Concierto de Aranjuez" by the Spanish composer Joaquín Rodrigo and takes place before a backdrop of guitars expertly painted by Eugene Hyde. *Dialogue for Three* intervenes in Jamaican social life by emphasizing the visceral and libidinous nature of cultural production and the power embedded in nonheteronormative forms of intimacy.

My reading of *Dialogue* is drawn from a 1969 video recording of the piece produced by the Jamaican company Harvey Film Productions, directed by

Easton Lee; and performed by the NDTC dancers Sheila Barnett as the wife, Barbara Requa as the other woman, and Audley Butler as the husband.[60] Before *Dialogue*'s three protagonists even begin to move, the sensuousness of the piece is made apparent by both the dramatic nature of the recorded guitar music and the revealing costumes of the dancers. The women are robed in sleeveless dresses that hug their torsos and hips, giving audience members a full view of their figures. The wife wears a white dress; the other woman wears a bright red dress and a red flower in her hair. The husband is costumed in close-fitting black pants and a long-sleeved cropped red jacket that is left open to reveal his bare chest. While the erotic gaze offered by NDTC dances is certainly not confined to *Dialogue*—other company pieces had dancers dressed in much more revealing costumes—attending to the costuming of the three dancers in this piece highlights the fact that audience members obtain visceral pleasure from the display of the performers' bodies.[61]

This pleasure is both visual and kinesthetic. It comes from witnessing the bodies, costumes, and *movement* of the dancers. Compared to NDTC's other works of the same period, *Dialogue* is a slow-moving performance. The dancers' movements are measured and unhurried. Rarely are all three dancers in motion at the same time. For the duration of the piece, at least one character consistently remains still while another moves, either alone or with the third character. Aside from a handful of climatic moments in which the dancers' bodies enact a passionate urgency, *Dialogue* has an almost sculptural-like quality, as though the characters are taking part in a languorous tableau. The pacing of the performance, in which *Dialogue*'s characters slowly move in and out of static poses enacting various scenes of relations among them, compels audiences to attend to the details of sensuous movement. Such attentiveness was more difficult to elicit in the company's more quick-footed pieces such as *Plantation Revelry* or *Pocomania*.

Nettleford intentionally choreographed *Dialogue* as a cultural intervention into the gendered politics of intimacy that takes place not only in Jamaica but also in various other national contexts. The company's description of the piece reads, "The deeper meaning of the work revealed the total command a woman is capable of in such a situation, despite the usual conventions of the male-dominated society which dictate that the man must be in control. In fact, the women usually understand each other much better than the man understands either one; they are, after all, sisters in emotional knowledge. Thus, the other woman eventually returns the man to his wife."[62] In the performance, it is only when the wife reveals to the other woman that she is pregnant—by mimicking holding a baby—that the other woman leaves the husband. *Dialogue* unsettles the presumption of male dominance in the love triangle by highlighting the affective bonds between women.

Though the piece ultimately illustrates the triumph of "the Western-capitalist family unit—so much Nettleford's ideal," it also reveals the social power of women's close relationships with each other.[63] The ultimate outcome of the triangle is determined through the women's affective exchanges with each other to the exclusion of the man. Because the relationships among all three characters structure the performance, *Dialogue* is marked by moments in which the gendered directionality of the women's gestures is ambiguous (see figure 4.2). In one moment, the characters stand in a line with the husband positioned between the wife and the other woman. The wife reaches out her arms in what appears to be longing. Yet it is not clear to whom this gesture of desire is directed. Is it toward the husband and/or the other woman? In another moment, nearing the end of the performance, after the wife has revealed her pregnancy to the other woman, the husband reaches for the

4.2. National Dance Theatre Company's *Dialogue for Three* performed by Eddie Thomas as "husband" (*front*), Yvonne DaCosta as "other woman" (*middle*), and Noelle Chutkan as "wife" (*back*). Photograph taken by Maria LaYacona. Date unknown. Source: NDTC Archives, Kingston, Jamaica.

other woman's hand. But instead of taking it for herself, the other woman leads his hand toward the wife and releases it as she walks away from the married couple. To what extent is this a movement away from the intimacy of the husband and/or toward affective intimacy with the wife? The most passionate moments in *Dialogue* are the dramatic lifts and turns as the husband dances with either the wife or the other woman. But as the husband stands downstage, the way that the women dance together after the revelation of the pregnancy takes on a greater sense of tenderness than either of their gestures toward the husband or his dancing toward them. In this moment, the affectionate overtures between the other woman and the pregnant wife gesture toward female-oriented forms of kinship that are common across the Caribbean in which the domestic setting of child rearing takes place largely among women who develop close emotional relationships with each other as they go about the work of social reproduction.

As *Dialogue* works through the complexities of the relationships among the characters, it illustrates the power of performance to counter discourses of desire, eroticism, and intimacy embedded in hegemonic articulations of family in anglophone Caribbean family-planning interventions. Though family planning in the region had begun in the early twentieth century as a grassroots response to citizens demands, in the postwar period these efforts increasingly came under state control, supported by the dramatic increase in funding from international bodies concerned about the supposedly excessive rates of population growth in the Global South.[64] In the post-independence era, family planning in the Caribbean came to be articulated through the necessity of regulating population levels thought to be necessary for economic and social development. Though these efforts were primarily concerned with promoting methods of birth control, they also mobilized older concerns about the moral imperative of particular family forms. For instance, when Jamaica's National Family Planning Board (NFPB) was established in 1967, it sought to reduce the island's birth rate of 38.8 per 1,000 individuals in 1966 to 25 per 1,000 by 1977 not only by increasing the accessibility of different birth control methods to the island's population but also by engaging in widespread public education about birth control and what it referred to as "family life."[65] Len Jacobs, the first director of the NFPB; and Beth Jacobs, director of the Jamaica Family Planning Association, maintained that marriage was the foundation of a stable family and that "the welfare of an ideal family depends on both a father and a mother planning and working together for their own and their children's wellbeing. From that we can see that our island must grow from this solid base."[66] *Dialogue* reinforces the moral imperatives accompanying Jamaican family-planning efforts in its valuation of marriage, but it also points to the significance of women's intimate relationships with one another, suggesting not only their erotic potential but also their capacity to serve as productive forms of kinship. The process of decolonization across the anglophone Caribbean was marked by anxieties around the way that Black men's capacity to lead their countries was tied to their ability to lead their families, but *Dialogue* points to another—albeit ephemeral—possibility. The workings of gender and sexuality in this performance thus break with historical narratives that frame intimacy and its significance for national development in different terms. They enact a rupture with hegemonic representations of the past that otherwise recur if left unchallenged. By performing a fleeting queerness, *Dialogue* produces fractal effects by materializing difference within narrative patterns that repeat. Instead of heteropatriarchal forms of marriage, it suggests that the female-dominated erotic triangle may serve as the basis for cultural identity formation in Jamaica's post-independence era.[67]

It is crucial to note that *Dialogue* was not an obscure intervention into Jamaican cultural political life. It was the NDTC's most celebrated performance on the island. With the exception of the 1970 season, it was performed every year since its debut for the first ten years of the company's existence. Though not without its detractors, *Dialogue* found enormous favor in Jamaican audiences.[68] Jamaican doctor Owen Minott noted that when he first saw the NDTC, "I had no idea that in Jamaica, I would have seen anything as beautiful as *Dialogue for Three*. I kept feeling this dance over and over again. I talked and talked about it. It was easy to understand. It was beautiful to watch."[69] Minott's reaction to *Dialogue* was quite common among theatergoers; a similar response inspired the scholar and writer Mervyn Morris to write a poem about the piece.[70] Rodrigo's "Concierto de Aranjuez" became popular as a result of the performance, and Jamaican audience members came to know this piece of music as simply *Dialogue for Three*.[71] Partly in recognition of its enormous popularity, the Jamaican Tourist Board filmed the piece as part of its promotion of Jamaica overseas.[72] If it is through ephemera, or what is left in the wake of a performance, that it becomes possible to identify the imprints of past performances on the present, the sheer depth and scope of affective resonance marks *Dialogue*'s ephemera.[73]

The company's signature piece was similarly well received on NDTC's international tours. In the company's first decade, the piece was performed not only in England, Canada, and the United States, but also across the Caribbean in Mexico, Guyana, Bermuda, Grenada, Puerto Rico, and the Bahamas. Though *Dialogue* was not universally celebrated, Nettleford recognized its popularity among foreign hosts. He highlighted the use of an image from the performance on the cover of the British dance publication *Dance and Dancers* and observed that "when we leave it out [of our repertoire when we perform], we are asked to put it in."[74] An English critic referred to *Dialogue* as "Nettleford's best work"; a reviewer of the NDTC's show in Miami described the piece as the "most esthetically exquisite of the [company's] presentations."[75] A review of the company's tour to Mexico noted that Dialogue's rousing applause was well earned by the "delicada, fina y preciosamente expresiva [delicate, fine and beautifully expressive]" nature of its choreography.[76] Audience reactions in Puerto Rico and Grenada were similarly enthusiastic.[77] In recalling her performance of *Dialogue* in Grenada at CARIFESTA in 1969, the late Barbara Requa noted that audience members became emotionally attached to the characters of the performance, often taking sides and yelling out encouragements to their favored dancers. Indeed, the extent to which audience members made clear their affective investment in the piece by pressing in on the open performance space made it difficult for Requa to stay in character. She worried that she might come to harm as the other woman at the hands of frenzied audience members who were rooting for the wife.[78]

Dialogue's reception in Mexico highlights the importance of attending to the dynamics of race and class in addition to those of gender and sexuality. As reported in the *Jamaica Star*, "'Dialogue for three' was much applauded, but not because of its Eternal Triangle theme of a man's dilemma of deciding between his wife and his mistress. It seemed that because of the variations in complexion of the three Jamaican dancers, 'Dialogue' was interpreted by some audiences as a struggle over colour. When the love struggle was explained, this was shrugged away as not being particularly interesting."[79] The differences in skin tone noted by Mexican audience members highlight the significance of race and class differences in Jamaican intimate relationships. On the one hand, hierarchies of race, class, and gender on the island suggest that not just any and every Jamaican is likely to assume the role of husband, wife, or other woman. In his observations of mid-twentieth-century Jamaican life, Henriques notes that marriage on the island was principally an economic consideration heavily influenced by a man's capacity to pay for an extravagant wedding and financially support his wife.[80] Men of such class standing tended to be (though not always were) lighter in complexion and to seek wives of the same, if not lighter, skin color. Though the situation was different among the island's ethnic minorities, Henriques maintains that mistresses tended to be of darker complexion and lower class standing than their male partners.[81] On the other hand, the diversity in skin tones among the dancers cast in *Dialogue* meant that any of the three characters could range in skin color from dark to light. During NDTC's time in Mexico, the brown-skinned Barbara Requa played the role of the other woman in *Dialogue*, while the light-skinned Bert Rose and the dark-complexioned Audley Butler rotated the role of the husband. The wife was variously performed by dark-skinned Gertrude Sherwood, brown-skinned Noelle Chutkan and Sheila Barnett, and light-skinned Bridget Casserly.[82] By its very definition, performance—like fractals—is characterized by repetition with difference; performances can never be perfectly replicated. In this case, skin color constitutes the most noticeable space of difference. The differences in skin color of the characters from one iteration of *Dialogue* to the next draw attention, not to performance's unreliability as a source of history, but instead to the capacity of performance to disrupt received narratives about the past. The inability to perfectly replicate performances distinguishes this form of knowledge from the unchanging text-based materials that frequently comprise archival collections.

Dialogue offers a way to conceptualize the relationship between race, intimacy, and nation against the competing discourses of creole multiracialism and Black nationalism in post-independence Jamaica. Though emphasizing different racial (and implicitly classed) configurations of the kinds of intimacies that were thought to promote social development in Jamaica, creole multiracialist and Black nationalist visions aligned in their investment in heteropatriarchy. By foregrounding the brown body, creole multiracialism highlighted racial mixing as the consequence of the erotic relationship between Black and white subjects.[83] Though Black nationalists opposed such unions because they rehearsed the workings of imperial power, they nevertheless reproduced the creole multiracialist call for intimate relationships between women and men, with men in a position of leadership.[84] In contrast, *Dialogue* provides the opportunity to think about the nation differently through configurations of intimacy that vary not only by race but also by gender. What might decentering the husband in the analysis of the multiracial husband–wife–other woman triad reveal about Jamaican nationhood? The performance of the relationship between lighter- and darker-skinned women as intimacy contravenes the way that colonial relations of race, gender, class, and sexuality structure the relationship between white women and brown women in terms of antagonism. Upon the emergence of a "mulatto" population in Jamaica, it became customary for white men of means to have both white wives and brown mistresses. This situation positioned these women to compete for the resources of the men they shared.[85] Omise'eke Tinsley's analysis of the relationship between the dark-skinned male woman Harry/Harriet and the light-skinned woman Clare Savage in Michelle Cliff's novel *No Telephone to Heaven* suggests the emancipatory potential in forms of same-gender intimacy that cross raced and class lines. Tinsley contends that while Harry/Harriet ushers Clare into Black womanhood and lesbian eroticism, Clare's mutually loving gaze upon Harriet transforms the "plantation's yield so their formations of racialized gender no longer cut her/him."[86] The intimacy between these characters operates as a "methodology of the oppressed" that transforms the "colonizations of gender, sex, race, class, or any social identities of styles of analysis."[87] Intimate formations do not automatically preclude the workings of exploitation, oppression, and/or violence, but applying Tinsley's analysis to *Dialogue* offers an opportunity to unsettle the presumed relationship between intimacy and cultural identity in Jamaica's immediate post-independence period. In contrast to patriarchal heteronormative forms of inter- or intra-racial kinship that Jamaicans sought to promote for the socioeconomic betterment of the island, *Dialogue* gestures to the possibility that intimacy among women across raced and classed lines may operate as a framework for social reproduction and the basis of nation building.

The sexual politics of NDTC involved not only the enactment of intimacy in its performances but also the ways that sexuality pervaded discussions about the company among Jamaican audiences. These discussions are not perceptible in official accounts of the NDTC. Mervyn Morris discusses the difficulties of discerning such accounts, stating that "given the attitudes of its Artistic Director [Rex Nettleford], writing on the NDTC is a high risk activity unless you come out mostly in praise . . . [w]hich suggests we should all confine ourselves to whatever information reaches us through the NDTC's pervasive, truly excellent PR [public relations]; to seem to know anything else is to be involved in 'theatre politics and kas-kas' or 'hearsay and su-su.' Though Mr. Nettleford surely knows, as the rest of us do, that kas-kas can be of serious significance."[88] The challenges of freely discussing sex, gender, and the NDTC in public suggests the productivity of attending to gossip—what Morris describes as the "hearsay and susu"—about the company.

Gossip functions as a prime site to analyze sex talk about the NDTC because the properties of this form of speech align with how illicit intimacies and performance manifest in everyday conversation. Gossip operates as an evaluative form of talk about subjects in their (presumed) absence. Talk of same-gender intimacy often takes the form of gossip because the taboo nature of this subject tends to foreclose communication through more stable and transparent means. Gossip is also an idiom of intimacy. It presumes and creates bonds of closeness among speakers and listeners and enacts forms of speech that tend to be more personal than the dialogue that occurs in other contexts. As it discloses intimacies that trouble hegemonic systems of sex and gender, gossip thus also *enacts* intimacies that contravene positivistic approaches to historical research. This is because gossip operates as a kind of embodied and affective vocal performance that leaves no permanent trace. And gossip—like performance and like fractals—can never be perfectly replicated. Thus, even as it fails to conform to conventional archival protocols, gossip's formal properties make it an excellent subject to analyze how the relationships between same-gender intimacy and performance are constructed in talk about the NDTC.

The most blatant iteration of talk about same-gender eroticism and the NDTC surfaces in three letters Nettleford wrote in which he insisted that his addressees desist from gossiping about the sexual deviancy of NDTC members. These addressees were the artistic director of another Jamaican dance company, a physician who treated the medical ailments of an NDTC member, and a visual artist with whom the company collaborated. In these letters Nettleford attributed to his addressees the gossip he had heard about the company being nothing but "a bunch of fairies" with "awful sexual morals."[89] Nettleford expressed his disappointment that successful Jamaican individuals would engage in such petty gossip, and he insisted on the need to squelch this kind of talk in the future. For instance, in his letter to the artistic director, Nettleford wrote:

It has been brought to my attention (as indeed to other members in the Company) that certain remarks about the company have been attributed to you. They have to do with ladies coming to train and dance with the NDTC. We are told that you advise them not to because a) our work will spoil their line and b) the NDTC is full of homosexuals.

I am writing this to you in confidence because I feel I ought to. For one thing, I feel that the NDTC is in debt to both yourself and [name withheld] for your kind offer and actual help in training some of our members. I have always assumed sincerity of purpose on your part and have always made Company members appreciate this. Secondly, the work of the NDTC deserves from fellow artists constructive criticism rather than defamation. I do expect to hear of accusations of a deleterious nature from ignorant people and from leisurely verandahs but not from serious artists. I was therefore disappointed to hear your name in connexion with the remarks above....

On the homosexual matter: this kind of image is a cliché with dance companies—particularly ballet companies. In Jamaica, I have even been told that our women are libertarian in sex habits, having illegitimate children and abortions. One ballet teacher here forbade a student from touring with us in 1961 on this account. [Name withheld], we have got to lick this sort of nonsense in the dance-theatre and not make people's sexual credentials take precedence over people's talents.

Let me assure you that one of my hopes is to see a serious classical ballet company emerge with the dedication and sustained application that it means for that dance-form. It means a great deal of sacrifice and willingness of people to work together, for no one person can do something like this. Your difficulties are great I know—men are scarce (largely because of that homosexual image which irresponsible people have projected) and ladies get married and depart. But if ever you were to find the opportunity to hold them, be assured that my support and help (if ever wanted) would be forthcoming. I believe that much in the vital place of the theatre-arts in the lives of individuals (bar none) and the country.

Believe me too when I say that I hold no grudge or malice on the words attribute to you: they may not even be true. But I felt I should in all honesty, let you know how distressed I was to hear that they came from someone like yourself.

Kind regards,

Sincerely
RN[90]

This letter and Nettleford's other two letters are significant in several ways. First, he shifted the register of communication from a chain of individual speech acts whose contents and affective character can never be perfectly replicated (and therefore never fully verified) into text. This process of entextualization more easily facilitated the identification of this talk that associated NDTC with sexual deviance after its enunciation. Second, Nettleford was not concerned about the truth value of these speech acts. He did not attempt to protect the reputation of the NDTC by denying the veracity of the alleged sexual depravity of NDTC members. Third, even though Nettleford was not bothered by the actual sexual preferences of his dancers, he was concerned about the consequences of the talk about such preferences (whether true or not). The issue was not about what gossip is, but what gossip does. Morris was not wrong in his evaluation that "kas-kas can be of serious significance." In this case, Nettleford identified how this gossip made it difficult to attract and maintain dancers. This chapter follows the approach that Nettleford codifies by sidestepping the inevitable questions about company members' erotic/intimate inclinations.[91] It refuses the demand for a kind of visibility that characterizes contemporary North Atlantic contexts where the concept of "outness" structures the workings of gender and sexual minority politics.[92] In so doing, this chapter calls into question the necessity or even the desirability of "outness" for doing the work of historical criticism. Finally, it is because of the potentially damaging nature of this communication that Nettleford sought to establish the rules under which such talk can or should take place. He was not trying to stop this talk from happening altogether. Rather, he was implicitly making a case for when, how, and among whom such talk should occur. As noted in his letter quoted above, it was expected for such gossip to take place among "ignorant people" and even in informal social settings ("leisurely verandahs") among the educated. However, according to Nettleford, such gossip should have no place in the serious business of the art world.

The kinds of communication that Nettleford codified in his letters is "drawn from a store of historical allusions that have been kept alive and given new and renewed meanings by the gossip and arguments of diverse groups."[93] These fugitive forms of speech are related to broader associations of the company with male queerness. When it was first established, the NDTC was unique among dance companies in Jamaica in that it was led two men (Eddie Thomas and Rex Nettleford) when all of the other major dance groups at the time were led by women.[94] Marjorie Whylie, the company's musical director, was also unique in that she was one of the very few women on the island who played the drums, because playing this instrument was predominantly associated with men.[95] The gendered distribution of labor in the company contravened dominant ideologies of the kinds of cultural work expected of women and men. Though it was acceptable for men to participate in both traditional folk and popular dances, Jamaicans looked askance upon men who formally danced onstage. For instance, in contrast to the Jamaican folk dance Jonkunno, which is traditionally performed only by men and young boys, or the ska-influenced "rudie dance" primarily associated with young men from Kingston's low-income neighborhoods, the world of ballet and contemporary dance was understood to be the domain of women.[96] It was therefore not surprising that when Hazel Johnston was the first to feature a local male dancer (Patrick Vermont) in her trio of ballet suites in 1942, Jamaican audiences greeted the performance with laughter.[97] This "queer notion that ballet is sissy for males" made it difficult for NDTC to attract male dancers.[98] Boys with a natural talent for dance or who very much enjoyed it would simply not want to participate because of what would be said about them. The first generation of NDTC male dancers shared that by engaging in what was thought to be women's activities, they were assumed to be gay. Barry Moncrieffe stated, "You always felt that if you went somewhere in pubic everyone is going to talk. From they hear you dance at that time, they think you are gay, which isn't true." Coming from a rural background, with his family involved in agriculture as a way of making a living, he noted, "My father didn't want me to dance because of the stigma, and where he worked was a really macho place."[99] Yet Moncrieffe's passion outweighed his concerns about this stigma, and eventually his father came to see him dance. After that he never missed one of his son's performances and even came to boast about him to his friends. Though the association of this kind of dancing with gender and sexual non-normativity did not stop Moncrieffe from getting involved in NDTC, he was one of the few exceptions.

The ways that gossip functioned to associate NDTC with gender and sexual deviancy compel a serious consideration of this informal means of communication as a form of knowledge and source of history. This is because gossip runs alongside and transforms what persists as NDTC's "official" narrative. The company is now publicly positioned as an important historical actor in its construction of new forms of Jamaican and Caribbean culture in the aftermath of European colonial rule, so it is significant that the bodies engaged in this creative labor were produced as sexual and gender dissidents in the informal realm of gossip. The very birth of the nation was therefore heralded by performances that not only troubled expectations of heteropatriarchal intimacies but also were created by women and men who contravened dominant expectations of gender and sexuality. This queer reading of NDTC's archive produces fractal effects by rupturing existing historical narratives about the gender and sexual politics of nationalism and decolonization in Jamaican's immediate post-independence period. Such a reading pushes against oft-cited historical accounts about the heteronormativity of state-based citizenship models in the aftermath of empire and gestures to queer forms of kinship articulated in the realm of cultural performance.

5

Politics

The Gay Freedom Movement

B eginning in the sixteenth century, Caribbean territories such as Jamaica were transformed into plantation systems as a way to introduce agricultural capitalism into the region and integrate it into an expanding European-dominated transatlantic economy. Yet the plantation was far from just an agricultural and economic arrangement. It became the template for a social and political order characterized by the rule of a free European minority over enslaved African and later indentured Asian populations.[1] The plantation persisted as a remarkably durable set of structuring principles for Caribbean societies such that a class color hierarchy continued to pervade late-colonial Jamaican society even after the abolition of enslavement and the collapse of the sugar industry in the region.[2] And the island's attainment of flag independence in 1962 did not fundamentally alter the way plantation dynamics shaped the country's position within global political economies or its internal racial and economic disparities. The dependent position of new Caribbean nations within a global marketplace prompted them to "deliberately assume the role of house slave to metropolitan businesses" as a development strategy.[3] Though this approach produced some economic gains for Jamaica in the post–World War II period, much of the benefit accrued to foreign entities at the expense of the majority of the island's population, who faced an increasingly unequal distribution of income and massive rates of unemployment.[4]

In this chapter I explore the relationship between queerness and the attempt to redress these local and transnational disparities by assembling and analyzing an archive of the anglophone Caribbean's first self-proclaimed gay activist organization, Jamaica's Gay Freedom Movement (GFM), which operated from 1977 to 1984. GFM was established in a moment when post-independence anglophone Caribbean societies sought to deconstruct colonial modes of being and construct a collective sense of self.[5] It took root in the wake of Michael Manley's election as Jamaica's prime minister in 1972—an event that signaled to Jamaicans, albeit to varying degrees, the possibility of real change.[6] This sense of possibility animated widespread intensive participation in Jamaican public life and the flourishing of feminist, Black Power, and labor movements across the island.[7] During this period, Jamaicans witnessed not only attempts to transform inequitable social relations on the island, but also the state's leadership on the international stage in advocating for the New International Economic Order and Third World solidarity.[8] In this chapter I examine how GFM's politics function as a site through which to reevaluate Jamaica's domestic visions for radical transformation and GFM's leadership in challenging unequal arrangements of power in the global arena.

I constructed an archive of GFM in two ways. First, I conducted archival research across the Atlantic in digital, personal, and "brick and mortar" archives. I reviewed GFM materials in person at the ArQuives in Toronto and the Schomburg Center for Research on Black Culture in New York.[9] I also accessed GFM materials electronically from IHLIA LGBT Heritage in Amsterdam and the Digital Library of the Caribbean (DLOC).[10] And one of the founders of GFM, Laurence (Larry) Chang, graciously allowed me to access his personal archive, which was in the possession of a close friend in Kingston, Jamaica's capital city. Across these various sites, I pieced together all eighty-one issues of GFM's newsletter *Jamaica Gaily News* (*JGN*), as well as letters, flyers, notes, photos, financial documents, and various other materials that GFM and its members generated over the course of its existence.[11] Second, I conducted oral history interviews with seven women and thirteen men who were related to the group in various ways. Some of these individuals were GFM members, others simply attended GFM activities, while others knew of GFM but chose not to be involved with the group at all. In speaking with these twenty interlocutors, I elicited narratives about their personal and social histories, how they understood themselves during GFM's existence, their involvement in GFM (if any), and their impressions of the group's work.

Using this queer archive to revisit existing accounts of the period produces fractal effects at the narrative level. While fractals take shape through both repetition (passive lines) and difference (active lines), in this chapter I mobilize queerness to illustrate sites of rupture with existing representations of the past. Historical accounts of Jamaica in the 1970s highlight the ways that gender and sexuality emerge as sites of contestation for Jamaicans in both global and national contexts. In these accounts, women in Jamaica and other Caribbean countries played a central role in advocating for women's rights at the international level.[12] Narrations of the period also foreground attempts to transform gender and sexual relations on the island by challenging sexual violence, advocating for maternity leave, and ameliorating the legal status of children born out of wedlock. Even though these accounts are significant in highlighting how feminist struggle shifted gender hierarchies in Jamaica and the island's positioning within global politics, same-gender desire marks their limits. Turning to GFM's archive produces a different narrative. The group pushed for same-gender erotic autonomy by creating new forms of sociality and challenging existing expectations of "respectable" sexuality in post-independence Jamaican society.[13] Through its transnational community-building work and its simultaneous adoption and alteration of North American and European ideologies of sexual subjectivity and activism, GFM also articulated a more equitable vision of international gay relations. By using GFM as a point of departure to revisit existing representations of the past, I use queerness as a site of difference to illustrate its capacity for narrative rupture. Identifying how its efforts challenged heteronormativity in Jamaican society and Euro-American dominance of global gay politics unsettles existing accounts of the period that emphasize Jamaica's attempts to redress domestic and international structures of inequality. In this chapter, queerness generates fractality by marking the space of difference in an otherwise familiar story about Jamaican political repair.

The Gay Freedom Movement

GFM emerged in the context of a vibrant, albeit underground, social scene among same-gender-desiring Jamaicans. Dennis, who was born in the rural parish of St. Thomas in 1934 and moved to Kingston in 1952, recalled that prior to Jamaica's independence, the city was home to numerous cruising spots where men would meet each other for casual sex—along South Camp

Road, Marescaux Road, East Queen Street, and so on—as well as other sites of gay male gathering that ranged from small home-based affairs and clandestine bars to nighttime outdoor dances.[14] In the 1960s, as Dennis remembers it, Kingston's gay scene began to really take off, prompting him to start his own gay bar. By the time GFM began publishing JGN in 1977, the newsletter reported on the events of numerous gay bars in Kingston, such as The Closet, Speakeasy, Maddams, Fanny Hill, and the Keyhole, as well as White Lady in Spanish Town. Though these establishments had difficulty remaining open due to the economic hardships of the period, they nevertheless operated as sites of sociality for same-gender-desiring Jamaicans that supported GFM's emergence, despite their ephemeral nature.

Violence was the immediate impetus for GFM's formation. Though Jamaicans often objected to homosexuality by appealing to biblical scripture or the need to maintain something like "the natural order," reporter Jennifer Ffrench theorized violence against same-gender-desiring Jamaicans in terms of "madness."[15] She noted, "The question of morality is one which has always affected our society in peculiar ways. When this morality has to do with sex, the effect oftentimes goes beyond peculiarity and borders more on madness."[16] The pages of JGN are replete with stories of such "madness," including beatings, stonings, and stabbings; discriminatory employment termination; and severe ostracism.[17] These iterations of violence rarely attracted the attention of the island's mainstream media. JGN contributors recognized that these acts of violence were perpetrated, not always by "straight" individuals, but also by other same-gender-desiring Jamaicans who might become involved in "gay bashing" for various reasons, such as to avoid being identified as "gay" themselves.[18] Indeed, it was repeated acts of intracommunity violence at The Closet, a gay club in Kingston, that led freelance designer Larry Chang to organize the meeting in September 1977 that precipitated GFM's formation.[19] During the meeting, a committee of six was formed to investigate the issue and come up with recommendations. The committee was composed of Chang, John Harriet (a white American college student participating in an extended exchange program in Jamaica), and four Black and brown men of middle- and working-class backgrounds.[20]

For Chang and Harriet, their life experiences were a major impetus for their involvement in this initiative. Chang was born into a Chinese Jamaican family in Brownstown, St. Ann, in 1949. Having attend the California College of Arts and Crafts in Berkeley in 1967, he became politicized by the feminist, Black Power, and gay liberation movements sweeping across the United States. In his final year of college, he began answering gay personal ads

5.1. Photograph of Laurence Chang as a stereotypical Chinese shopkeeper taken in 1982 during an advertising campaign for the Jamaican company Grace Kennedy. Photographer unknown. Source: Laurence Chang personal archives.

in underground publications and having his first dating and sexual experiences with men. He returned to Jamaica in 1973 with the goal of contributing to Jamaica's nation building while also finding a way to honor the erotic subjectivity and community building he had begun in the United States (see figure 5.1).[21] Conversely, Harriet began to develop his political personhood in Jamaica. Born in 1948 and raised in a middle-class white family in Boston, Harriet found himself transformed upon signing up for a college exchange program in Jamaica. Laboring alongside agricultural workers in St. Thomas during the week and socializing in Kingston's gay bars on the weekend helped him to recognize both the pernicious workings of racism in the United States as well as the sex negativity that permeated his devout Irish Catholic upbringing. Harriet's involvement in what was to become GFM grew from the development of his critical consciousness of race and sexuality in Jamaica.[22]

In January 1978, the Jamaican newspaper the *Daily Gleaner* published a letter that Chang wrote to the editor highlighting the validity of homosexuality as a form of intimacy. His letter was significant in two respects.[23] First, unlike other Jamaicans who submitted similar letters to the editors of the island's newspapers in support of homosexuality using pseudonyms,

Chang deliberately chose to use his real name. Second, Chang identified himself as "General Secretary, Gay Freedom Movement, P.O. Box 343, Stony Hill," thereby introducing the first self-proclaimed gay activist organization in the anglophone Caribbean to the *Gleaner's* reading public and providing a way to communicate with the organization. Other Jamaicans would come to learn of GFM and reach out to Chang upon reading the letters he wrote not only to the *Daily Gleaner* but also the *Jamaica Daily News* and the *Jamaica Star*.[24] With Chang's name and GFM's address appearing frequently in Jamaica's newspapers, Chang soon found himself communicating by mail with individuals across the island.

In writing to GFM, many Jamaicans expressed both surprise and happiness that a gay activist group existed on the island and requested more information about GFM and how they could get involved and meet others.[25] Those living in rural areas expressed strong sentiments of loneliness and isolation and indicated an especially strong desire to connect with other Jamaicans "like them."[26] In his responses, Chang not only found himself telling interlocutors about GFM and how they could participate, but also providing counseling in letter form and his telephone number should individuals wish to speak with him further.[27] Donna Smith was in sixth form at Immaculate Conception High School and living with her grandmother in the Harborview neighborhood of Kingston when she first learned about GFM (see figure 5.2.).[28] Upon realizing her sexual attraction to other women, she decided to focus one of her research papers on the topics of homosexuality and the gay revolution to develop a better understanding of her desires. Having made her topic known in her class, several of her classmates brought her material that they thought that she could use, including one of Chang's letters in the newspaper. Smith was elated to learn of the existence of a gay organization on the island and immediately wrote to Chang. Chang not only put her in touch with other gay women, whom Smith interviewed for her research paper, but also encouraged her to participate in GFM. She became an active member in the organization and a regular contributor to *JGN*, penning the column "Girl Talk" under the penname "M'Lady."

Yet some of GFM's interlocutors sought much more than a connection to other gay Jamaicans and involvement in the organization's activities, because they experienced the same material hardships as other Jamaicans in the late 1970s. In this period the island experienced an economic recession occasioned by its agreement with the International Monetary Fund that drastically reduced Jamaica's standard of living by a quarter and resulted in a national unemployment rate of almost 30 percent in 1980.[29] GFM fielded letters from gay Jamaicans who, in addition to searching for community, struggled with incarceration, poverty, and hostile family members who threatened to kick them out of their homes. In a handwritten letter dated January 8, 1980, Winston Smalls requested Chang's help because he was soon to be released from prison:[30]

I wish to let you know that I am due to start attending C.A.S.T [College of Arts, Science and Technology] on the 21st of January to pursue a course in social science, which will last for six months and September of the said year I am suppose to report to Churches Teachers College in Mandeville, but I am worried. Larry, what really cause me to be worried is that when I

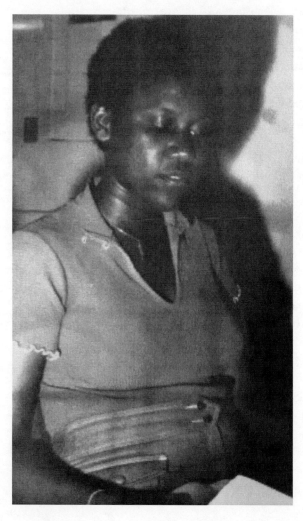

5.2. Photograph of Donna Smith taken in early 1980s at a Gay Freedom Movement art exhibit and poetry reading held in Beverly Hills, Kingston. Photographer unknown. Source: Laurence Chang, personal archives.

leave here I don't know where I am going [to live] neighter [neither] where or how I am going to gain meaningful employment so I am asking you very kindly to see what you can work out between you and ... [Name of GFM Prison Program Coordinator]. I want you to know that if I can't find honest employment within reasonable time then I decide to end everything in my own way because I don't decide to be involved with the police again because of any criminal offence so if I can't make it then death is the only answer.[31]

While Winston may have overemphasized his sentiments of need and despair because he was seeking Chang's support, it is also important not to dismiss his letter. In 1987 the US State Department noted that the situation of police station jails in Jamaica was "substandard" as "overcrowding, unsanitary conditions, inadequate food, and limited medical care for inmates are the norm for these detention facilities. According to the Ombudsman, conditions in the two maximum security prisons are marginally better than in the police station jails, but similar problems plague the prisons."[32] If this representation resonated with the lived experience of incarcerated Jamaicans, it is no surprise that Winston expressed an urgent desire to find "honest employment" and a place to live so that he did not have to resort to activities that would land him in prison again.

It was partly by responding to letters like those from Smith and Smalls that GFM fully took shape. When Chang first called the meeting to address violence at The Closet, the goal was not to establish an activist organization but to resolve a community problem. Similarly, the *Jamaica Gaily News* arose less out of a plan to create a regular publication and more out of a pragmatic need to galvanize support to resolve The Closet's challenges. Indeed, it was only after hearing from readers that they wanted the newsletter to continue that Chang took the newsletter more seriously and changed the name from *Toilet Paper*—something to be used once and then discarded—to *Jamaica Gaily News*. The initial meeting to address the problems at The Closet morphed into a more sustained initiative, and Chang developed a logo for the emergent organization that combined the lambda and triangle symbols typically associated with gay liberation (see figure 5.3). GFM came to understand itself as a group that sought to provide structures of support and community building for gay men and women on the island while also tackling the homophobic conditions of Jamaican society. GFM's formation elicited considerable ideological diversity among its members because of the emergent nature of its attempts to institutionalize "gay" as a kind of personhood and relationality.

5.3. Gay Freedom Movement logo. Source: GFM brochure, accessed March 6, 2023, https://dloc.com/AA00002992/00001/images.

How should GFM function? What should be its goals? How should they be achieved? Who should GFM try to engage? The ideological differences of those involved in GFM led to conflicts in the group; combined with a lack of resources, this led to breaks in the organization's activities. In the short history of its existence, GFM undertook an ambitious array of activities, such as a sexual health clinic, a speaker's bureau, a youth program, and a prisoner-support program, just to name a few. Yet this "organization" was essentially a do-it-yourself, grassroots initiative composed of a floating network of a dozen or so committed individuals and resourced through donations and volunteer labor. Though GFM was never very large—reporting a membership of eighty-one individuals during its most active period—it made significant inroads in advocating for erotic autonomy as a positive dimension of community and national formation.[33]

From the beginning, GFM battled with the overrepresentation of men in its membership and the presumption of its male character. In *JGN*'s second issue, columnist Andromeda pleaded, "With the present situation in Jamaica today, both economically and on the gay scene, it would do us gay women well to come out as a team and give the much needed support."[34] In September 1979, GFM received a letter from Bernice Bell of Kingston who queried "if you admit women to your organization."[35] A few months later in March 1980, it received a letter from Mrs. Paulette Baker of Mandeville, who wondered "whether or not there should be some form of movement also, for the interested ladies."[36] In responding to Baker, Chang wrote:

> Dear [Paulette]
>
> Thank you very much for writing. It is good to get your letters since we know how much courage it often takes to make contact.
>
> We would like to inform you that gay women are very much a part of our movement. In fact, one of our directors is female. I have referred your letter to her also, so you may be hearing from her soon. We feel that no one can relate to a woman more than another woman, especially if they are gay.
>
> We admit that there are not as many women as we would like to see in the movement . . . those few that are involved, however, are very active and contribute a great deal. Whether there should be a separate movement for gay women is entirely up to them to decide, although we would regret a split. What we would like very much to see is a strong women's liberation movement both gay and straight.[37]

It is true that there were women who actively participated in GFM, such as Donna Smith and Frances Camden, GFM's treasurer, but men were overrepresented in GFM in spite of ongoing efforts to solicit greater women's involvement.[38] This was largely due to the gendered nature of Jamaican society's relationship to homosexuality, as same-gender-desiring men and women had different experiences on the island, particularly with respect to violence. Women's disruptions of patriarchy, whether engaging in activism to end domestic violence or turning down a stranger's sexual advances, were met with the derogatory epithet "sodomite" (in Jamaica, a term for a woman who has sex with other women).[39] Indeed, another Jamaican creole term used to refer to same-gender-desiring women was "manroyal," which pejoratively indexed women who acted like men in behavior and/or dress. Makeda Silvera notes that even though these women did not occupy as large a space in Jamaica's public imaginaries as men did, they were nonetheless subject to violations, such as gang rape by men who perceived these women as committing gender transgressions or suspected that they might share sexual intimacies with other women.[40] The pages of JGN reveal that gay men also experienced various forms of physical violence, such as beatings, stabbings, and stonings.[41] The fact that in the most spectacular forms of this violence, women were assaulted sexually but men generally were not, suggests that gender made a difference in the kinds of violent responses to actual or perceived gender and/

or sexual difference. Extreme forms of this violence functioned to maintain a particular iteration of manhood that had different gendered consequences. Directed toward men, it worked to eradicate effeminacy and the desire for other men. Conversely, violence against women operated as a form of power oriented less toward extermination and more toward bringing women into a "proper" relationship with men. In this context, rape functioned as a way of controlling all women who were considered to be "out of line," which made it difficult to differentiate violence motivated by the suspicion of a woman's same-gender sexual inclinations from violence against women in general. As I discuss below, the different ways that women and men were positioned in relationship to homophobic violence may help to explain the differences in the kinds of activisms they undertook.

GFM emerged in the context of the island's post-independence social movements. Women's liberation, labor organizing, and Black Power and Rastafari movements were all active in this period, partly because of the economic and social welfare policies of the ruling political party—the People's National Party (PNP)—that had the effect of strengthening civil society and popular organizations. GFM was established in the same year that Sistren, a grassroots working-class women's theater collective, was formed. This collective was created to "perform drama about how women suffer and how men treat them bad," and as a means of consciousness-raising and entertainment.[42] Drawing on the momentum of women's empowerment that achieved results such as the formation of the Women's Bureau based in the prime minister's office in 1973, this group was one of the many initiatives that Rhoda Reddock identifies as part of a new era of women's struggle not only in Jamaica but across the Caribbean region.[43] The 1970s also witnessed the establishment of sugar cooperatives, in which sugar workers across the island took advantage of the state's attempts to improve their often abysmal living and working conditions.[44] These and other like-minded initiatives drew from the island's history of worker resistance in the 1930s, in which labor organizations such as the Bustamante Industrial Trade Union arose in response to the economic hardships occasioned by the Great Depression.[45] The post-independence period also witnessed riots initiated by students at the University of the West Indies (UWI), when the Jamaican state refused to grant entry to Walter Rodney, Afro-Guyanese historian, activist, and UWI lecturer. Returning from a Black Power conference in Montreal, Rodney was barred from the island in 1968 for fear that he would promote racial unrest. These riots tapped into Jamaica's long-standing concerns over Black pride and self-determination, as articulated earlier through Marcus Garvey's Black nationalism and later through the increasing popularization of Rastafari ideologies.[46] GFM's struggle for sexual agency took place within broader impulses of decolonization and creolization then sweeping across the island and with unprecedented levels of popular participation in determining the nature of Jamaican life.

GFM in Jamaica

GFM's intervention into the relationship between sexuality and nationalism was one of its most significant contributions to Jamaican politics. As general secretary of GFM in 1978, Chang penned a *JGN* editorial in which he wrote, "While our nation celebrates sixteen years of political independence, it would do us well to pause and think of our own struggle for sexual freedom and independence. While we are not clamouring for secession or autonomy we are demanding our basic human right to choose our partners, associates, and lifestyles, while remaining within the system to contribute to nation-building as patriotic Jamaicans. We have much to offer, and being free, equal citizens of this country, [it] is only just that we be afforded the rest and position in society that we truly merit."[47] This editorial is significant because it indexes the way that GFM ties the struggle for sexual freedom to the project of nation building. GFM's work facilitates a rethinking of existing accounts of sexual politics in 1970s Jamaica. Focusing on this organization's efforts enacts a break with existing narratives by surfacing the active lines in fractal formations. This approach forestalls the repetition of these narratives by foregrounding a different representation of the past.

GFM was not the only organization in Jamaica that took sexuality as the focus of its change work, but it differed from other initiatives in important ways. For instance, the advocacy efforts of the People's National Party Women's Movement were key to the passage of Jamaica's Status of Children's Act in 1976 and later the Maternity Leave Act in 1979.[48] And Sistren's theater-based work played an important role in exploring women's experiences of sexual violence in the realm of popular culture.[49] While GFM aligned with these efforts by insisting that intimate matters were not just private affairs but also public and political ones, it diverged from these women's organizations in three respects. First, GFM explicitly articulated its work in terms of sexuality, whereas women's organizations addressed issues of sexuality to the extent to which they coincided with their primary aim of redressing gendered imbalances in power. For instance, sexuality became the focus of Jamaican women in pushing for the Maternity Leave Act because the lack of accounting for reproductive labor hindered women's participation in other domains of the island's workforce.[50] Second, unlike GFM, whose work focused specifically on same-gender intimacies, Jamaican women's organizations largely addressed sexual relations only between women and men. For example, Sistren's powerful critiques of sexual violence against women were confined to heterosexual relations, even though some of its members shared intimacies with other women and even though they were labeled "sodomites" for challenging unequal gender dynamics.[51] Finally, GFM could not rely on existing forms of political power or on a network of local organizations as could many Jamaican women's groups. In speaking of her time as the head of Jamaica's Women's Bureau, Peggy Antrobus noted, "My most strategic support came from the women in the People's National Party (PNP), who put aside their disappointment at getting a non-Jamaican, non-Party woman in the post they had struggled for and they worked closely with me in devising a strategy of three interlocking components: the bureaucracy [Women's Bureau], women within the ruling political party, and autonomous women's organizations (A most effective combination for generating action!)."[52] In contrast, aside from the Revolutionary Marxist League, GFM had no other local organizations it could turn to for support in its struggle for sexual freedom.[53]

GFM sought to connect the struggle for erotic autonomy to nation building in two ways: through community building and through efforts to transform Jamaican society. GFM built on and created new forms of gay sociality. The group expanded on Kingston's existing underground gay nightlife by holding events at the city's clandestine bars and clubs, venues it depended on, given the difficulty of procuring spaces elsewhere. For instance, on off-hours at the bar Maddams, GFM hosted community meetings and a low-cost community sexual health clinic.[54] Maddams was so important to GFM's efforts that when the bar threatened to close because of financial difficulties, GFM sought (unsuccessfully) to enter into a joint ownership arrangement with Maddams to keep the business going.[55] As a grassroots initiative, GFM's work was rooted not only in the institutional life of Kingston's gay bars and clubs, but also in the informal life of home-based socializing. Chang's residence at 27 Gallery Way near Emancipation Park in Kingston housed GFM's library and served as an informal community center where gay women and men would drop by to chat, drink, play cards, and hopefully meet new people for friendship and/or sex. Lena Knight, the daughter of a mechanic and milliner who jokingly described herself as "red ibo" because of her lighter skin color, was in her early twenties when GFM started.[56] Knight, who had begun experiencing desires for women, recalls, "I was always at his [Larry's] house because I lived around the corner from him. I would be there reading because he had a lot of books on the subject matter. It was the first time I had ever seen a book or any literature having to do with gay life or gay emotions."[57] Through her interest in reading GFM's library materials, Knight came to enjoy the company and friendship of same-gender-desiring Jamaicans who frequented Chang's house.

GFM not only built on existing forms of gay community but created new ones. For the first time, it brought together same-gender-desiring Jamaicans who may not have previously known each other into the same space to both support one another and address the conditions of oppression, violence, and discrimination that marked their lives. This initially took place through events like a workshop to identify community problems and later in the form of action meetings where GFM members sorted themselves into committees to accomplish the various dimensions of the group's social change work.[58] GFM also established initiatives to build relationships across generations and between incarcerated and nonincarcerated same-gender-desiring Jamaicans. GFM's Gay Youth Movement (GYM) was formed to address the unique challenges the island's gay youth faced, such as the risk of family ostracism and being thrown out of their homes. They also experienced difficulties in finding support because existing avenues of gay social life (bars and clubs) were not always available to them and because their older counterparts (and potential mentors) were not above taking advantage of their inexperience (sexually or otherwise).[59] Though short-lived, GYM built structures of support among gay youth, provided mentorship, and established avenues of socializing beyond bar life, such as beach trips, picnics, and movie outings. GFM's prison program took shape because of the unsolicited letters the organization received from prisoners like Smalls, discussed earlier. In this fellowship- and charity-based initiative, GFM members visited incarcerated Jamaicans in the men's facilities of Kingston's General Penitentiary and the St. Catherine District Prison as well as in the women's facilities of Fort Augusta Prison in Portmore to provide much-needed company, reading material, and toiletries.[60] As much as possible, GFM tried to ensure that incarcerated Jamaicans were part of the community it tried to build, reminding *JGN* readers to donate funds to incarcerated GFM members, involving these members in its pen-pal program, and publishing their writing in *JGN*.[61] The initiative petered out because its leader passed away, but at the height of the program, prison visits took place every week.

The *Jamaica Gaily News* also fostered new forms of gay sociality. Over the course of its existence, GFM produced eighty-one issues, and it put out 250 copies of each issue every two weeks in its heyday. Members of *JGN*'s production team would type up the eight- to twelve-page issue on a typewriter and painstakingly copy it using a mimeograph machine. Initially it was only distributed in Kingston's gay clubs and by individual GFM members. However, GFM soon began to mail its newsletter (in discreet, confidential packaging) to those who could afford the subscription costs. It was not cheap to keep *JGN* in production; and GFM continually had to rely on donations of money, paper, ink, and equipment to ensure *JGN*'s continued circulation.

Through its pen-pal program "Gay Friends," *JGN* connected same-gender-desiring Jamaicans to those who wished to correspond with them. Starting in 1978, *JGN* readers were invited to "Write to Gay Friends, PO Box 343, Kingston 9, giving us your full name, pen-name if you like, age, address, description, preference and interests. Your name and address will NOT be published, so prospective pen pals will send their letters to us to be forwarded to you."[62] One of the responses to this program was from John Trenton from the Jamaican parish of Manchester, who, in a letter to *JGN* dated October 18, 1978, wrote:

Hi friends,

I wish to extend happy returns to all members of "the Jamaica Gaily News."

It was a relief to me to hear that we are having a bit of exposure as I am tired of being pushed aside by a group of people "rough necks" who felt as if a gay person isn't as normal and worthwhile in a society as anyone else. Keep the torch burning my friends.

Well, I must tell a bit about myself.

I am 27 years of age—Libran—185 lbs.

Good educational background—handsome, very tall 6ft 2 inches tall.

I have been involved from age 21 but unable to find my type of man. I therefore wish you to publish my request in the next series of Gaily News.

I am looking for a responsible man, age between 30 and 60. Should be understanding, very loving, respectful, dark complexion and of a fair educational standard. I do not want a person who wish to run competition as I always live a quiet life. Right now, I am lonely, without a lover and because of this I am very frustrated {no young guys need apply}.

I am asking you to send full details of everything as I wish to get involve in this movement.

Is there any charges? If so, how much?

God bless your wonderful effort and help you to expand this movement throughout Jamaica.

Is there any other way that you assist your members to find mates without publishing? If so assist me. I am badly in need of someone to settle with permanently.

Reply quickly please.

All the best to "Gaily News." Remember, the word is love. I remain one of you.

John Trenton[63]

Although it is unclear how the *JGN* editorial team responded to Trenton's letter, his pen-pal entry appeared in the next issue of the newsletter as "27 YEAR OLD LIBRAN, 185 lbs. 6'- 2", handsome, with good education seeks mature man 30–60, dark, loving with good education, to write soon as he is lonely and frustrated (30–3)."[64] The "(30–3)" in the entry indexed the coding system that *JGN* established to ensure public anonymity while also internally keeping track of the identities of those requesting pen pals. In his letter to Chang two months later, Trenton wrote:

Dear Larry

How is everything? I guess fine. Well I am not fine at all. Your missive has come to hand safely and I have seen where you have published my request in our magazine. I have gone through both letters enclosed and I am sorry to say that both of these men who wrote to me are well in friendship with people in Mandeville. I know of their ways that what they are interested in is one-night intercourse. That's not my motive Larry. What I need is a friend who I can share my joys and sorrows with. Right at this instant, writing this letter, I am maybe the saddest gay person in Jamaica. I am badly in need of a friend.[65]

While there are numerous points to be made about this exchange, I highlight three. First, even though GFM sought to provide support to those struggling with their desires, individuals like Trenton had come to an understanding of their desires without such coordinated intervention. The fact that Trenton was familiar with the two men who wrote to him also suggests that forms of same-gender-desiring sociality—or at least a knowledge of other same-gender-desiring men—preceded GFM's establishment in the parish of Manchester. Second, Trenton had so strongly come to terms with his sexual subjectivity that he cheered *JGN* efforts to normalize "gay" people and asked to be involved in the movement. Finally, Trenton's letters highlight the senti-

ments of loneliness and the urgent desire for intimacy that often characterized the lives of same-gender-desiring Jamaicans at this time. Although, it
is not clear what additional correspondence Trenton may have received—if
any—from his entry in *JGN*, it is worth noting that, unlike other requests for
pen pals that were repeatedly printed issue after issue, Trenton's was not. I
would like to imagine that he was able to find the kind of relationship he so
desired.

JGN connected individuals not only through lettered communication
but also through the act of reading the newsletter itself. In this case, *JGN* is
characteristic of what Michael Warner refers to as the kind of public that
comes into being in relation to texts and their circulation.[66] As *JGN* editor,
Chang mobilized the newsletter to represent and recruit across different
positions within Jamaica's racialized hierarchy to build as broad a gay movement as possible. As I have written elsewhere, Chang's contributed to *JGN* not
only as editor but also as the fictional characters Tony Long and Mamapala
Morgan.[67] Writing in "standard" English, Long was figured as a normatively
masculine, middle-class gay man who was intended to engage international
interlocutors and Jamaica's white and brown middle and upper classes. In
contrast, Mampala Morgan wrote exclusively in Jamaican patois and was
constructed to be a gender-ambiguous, lower-class Black subject intended
to encourage the participation of the island's Black masses. As a Chinese
subject, Chang thus engaged in a form of race, class, and gender crossing as an activist strategy. The fact that his efforts took on literary form is
significant not only because the taboo nature of homosexuality at the time
made it difficult to undertake more embodied forms of social and political
engagement, but also because the written word allowed for transgressions of
race, class, and gender in ways that would be considerably more difficult to
enact in person.

Though intended primarily for same-gender-desiring Jamaicans, Jamaicans of all stripes read the newsletter. Thus, even though not all its readers
were gay, these readers were nevertheless brought into a kind of gay publicity as *JGN* audience members. *JGN*'s writers actively sought to cultivate this
kind of wide-ranging readership. For instance, *JGN* contributor Aquarius
advocated using *JGN* as a public education tool, asking their readers, "Why
not 'accidentally' drop a *JGN* in the school library, the doctor's office, in a
place where a relative or young lonely gay can see it?"[68] While *JGN*'s editorial
team intended the newsletter to challenge the negative attitudes of "straight"
Jamaicans toward same-gender-desiring Jamaicans, Lamar Brown's letter to
JGN illustrated the harm that may result from such widespread circulation,

There is one thing I would like to advice your movement that you are to be more careful as to the manner in which you outlet information. . . . A young lady employee at the Bata Shoe Company on Spanish Town Road had the privilege of obtaining a copy of the Gaily News and after reading this paper she pose as a male and write seeking information on receiving reply and pamphlets she took the letter to her workplace and there it becomes a number one topic it was her desire to send it to the Gleaner Company for it to be publish but she was force not to do so by a friend of mine who is not gay but moves with the gay people. . . . [T]his kind of a thing cannot be allow to continue.[69]

Brown's letter highlights the challenges *JGN* faced in balancing the desire to publicly share information about Jamaica's gay community while also safeguarding against injurious use of this information. In an attempt to protect against the widespread problem of blackmail, faced especially by same-gender-desiring men, *JGN* implemented an editorial policy in which real names were not to be used in the newsletter unless *JGN* was granted permission. Each issue came to be accompanied by the tagline "Names appearing in the Jamaica Gaily News do not indicate sexual preference."[70]

Alongside its community-building efforts, the second way GFM sought to connect the struggle for sexual freedom to nation building was through its attempts at transforming Jamaican society through public education and media intervention. GFM member Garret Elliot Murray played a pivotal role in the formation of the group's speaker's bureau, which operated as an important component of GFM's public education program.[71] Born in 1952 in the Jamaican parish of St. Elizabeth, Murray at the time was a light-skinned man who had completed a laboratory sciences degree in the United States and returned to Jamaica to take up a job as a health instructor at the University of the West Indies. He described how GFM's speaker's bureau started:

As part of my class, we had a health seminar and students would talk about their role in medicine, their role in society etc. So, I asked Larry and Frances [Camden] to come to my class and speak to them. That went great. I think we had them for two hours and that was extremely popular. Larry said, "What happen if we had a speaker's bureau?" And we would respond to requests for talks or we would even reach out and say we were available. And so that's how we started. . . . We started getting requests from people in academia and friends of friends. Someone who knew someone who was a teacher, and they would ask permission for us to speak to an upper level class or something like that. Sometimes it would be just social gatherings. People would have a group of people at their house, 90% of them were straight but they just had this question: "I just want to hear about this thing." "How did this happen?" "Did something happen to you early in life?" "Did you get raped?" Just some ignorant questions. But at least it was someone who was open enough to ask questions.[72]

Murray's description of how the speaker's bureau began further illustrates the ad hoc and improvisational nature of GFM's programing. It also suggests that while same-gender-desiring subjects experienced various levels of violence on the island, Jamaicans also actively sought to learn more about "homosexuality." That Murray's health seminar went over the allotted time was characteristic of many of the bureau's engagements. These sessions were often the first time that many Jamaicans were openly having substantive conversations about homosexuality and also meeting individuals who publicly identified themselves as "gay" or "homosexual" or "lesbian," so it is no surprise that many of these meetings exceeded their allotted time. GFM was adamant that there should be a variety of people leading seminars for the speaker's bureau, so that attendees would encounter a variety of same-gender-desiring persons. This mobilization of difference in and of itself was to serve as a pedagogical function: to illustrate to audience members that Jamaicans of all different stripes could be "gay."

One of the bureau's first major engagements was with the Jamaica Psychological Association (JPA), which on November 27, 1979, hosted GFM at the Priory School in Kingston for a discussion on homosexuality, as its members had been wanting to learn more about the topic. JGN's report of the discussion noted:

> Using the popular workshop style of conducting the meeting, small groups were given hypothetical gay situations to discuss. The opinions of the members were shared with the large total group. Discussion was spirited and revealing. Many of the 50 persons present were pro-gay and open minded, making the task of the 20 GFM members present an easy one. The meeting was recorded on tape for our library and lasted about four hours. It ended on a very positive note with many of those attending eagerly requesting extra copies of the literature hand out. The GFM Public Education Group had prepared a Fact Sheet on homosexuality in time for the occasion. Copies of this were available on request. The most significant achievement, however, was that almost all of the gays present came out to their small groups.[73]

This description of the event indicates that GFM members used popular education techniques and narratives of their own experiences to guide the discussion with the JPA. Reports not only from JGN but also from the *Jamaica Star* and the *Jamaica Daily News* suggest that GFM was successful in creating a dialogue with Jamaican psychologists who sought information about homosexuality as part of their professional development.[74] The following year, GFM returned to the JPA to discuss homophobia as it related to women and youth.[75] In addition to psychologists, GFM also offered training to Jamaican guidance counselors and nurses to better support their same-gender-desiring patients.[76]

While some of GFM's public education engagements were successful, others proved to be more challenging. Murray recalls:

> [In 1982] Frances, Keisha, and I went to speak to a sixth form class at Excelsior College on Mountainview Avenue.[77] That was one of the things that was scheduled for an hour, and it went for about an hour and a half. They asked questions about the mechanics of sex, like "What do you guys do together?" They also asked like, "Are you Jamaican?" "Is it [homosexuality] something that foreigners were bringing to Jamaica?" [Sigh] By the time we were finished talking, word had gotten around campus that there was this lesbian and this gay person speaking to the sixth form class. It was on one of the upper floors and we basically had to fight our way down to the car. They were hostile, these students, shouting "Oh my god! Battyman!" whatever. Nobody punched or shoved us, but we had to jostle. By the time we got down to the first floor, we had to fight our way to the car. Students were surrounding the car. We had to fight to get into the car, close the door, and then they sat on top of the car and then they started pushing the car, so the car was physically rocking back and forth.

The subsequent backlash was sufficiently intense for Mrs. Dorothy Austin to write a letter to the editor of the *Daily Gleaner* protesting, "I think the whole venture is disgusting, we do not send our children to college to be taught the pros and cons of homosexuals or lesbians' life. This is outrageous. The teacher involved and the homosexuals and lesbians should be stoned. They ought to be ashamed of themselves." The editor took a personal interest in Austin's correspondence and included his response immediately below her letter in the printing of the newspaper that day. "Excelsior Community College tells us the subject was one in its series of discussions on controversial matters where speakers for and against are invited. Miss Ffrench was invited to speak on 'homosexuality' in view of her Gleaner articles. As she could not attend, she suggested to the agent for the College that a member of the Gay Freedom Movement be invited. Three members turned up without the teacher responsible knowing of the new turn of events. The three 'gays' were given a stormy reception and were stoned by students."[78] The GFM Speaker's Bureau visit to Excelsior College highlights the importance of attending to the various contexts of GFM's change efforts. In narrating his recollection of the event, Murray was adamant that unlike other sessions in which attendees expressed overt hostility to GFM members, the problem at Excelsior lay not with the sixth-form student participants. Instead, the violence that they experienced came from other Excelsior students who did not meet and interact with GFM members. In the aftermath of this event, what emerges as significant is not the dialogue that occurred in the sixth-form classroom but what transpired in the spaces and times *around* that dialogue. Indeed, the sixth-form students' reactions to Francine, Garret, and Keisha had little bearing on how the other Excelsior students later violently mobbed them or how Mrs. Austin denounced homosexuality as a "disgusting" subject for education.

For this reason, GFM knew that its public education work with small groups of Jamaican psychologists, guidance counselors, nurses, and high school students had to take place alongside efforts to transform the broader contexts in which these groups operated. They had to change existing discourses circulating in Jamaican society that condemned homosexuality as immoral and unnatural. GFM sought to do this by intervening in Jamaican television, radio, and print media, insisting on the normalcy of homosexuality and the need to stop violence and discrimination against same-gender-desiring subjects. For instance, the group publicized the letter it wrote to Jamaica's major political parties calling for an end to the use of anti-homosexuality rhetoric in contests over control of state power.[79] While GFM's public emergence netted positive coverage among some of the island's journalists who advocated understanding and acceptance, Jamaica's newspapers also published articles and letters to the editor that railed against the existence of homosexuality.[80] In response to negative media coverage and current events, GFM members submitted letters to the island's newspapers in an attempt to counter anti-homosexuality discourse. For instance, in response to the *Jamaica Star* reporter who characterized gays as "aggressive" and insisted that Jamaica's economic problems were the result of what she saw as the increasing permissiveness toward homosexuality, which contravened biblical teachings, GFM's Eve Fuller wrote:

> I am not saying that one woman has the right to force herself on another woman (if indeed that was the case) . . . [but] I don't see the point in using this to the point branding gays as aggressive. There is good and bad in every human being whether gay or otherwise. My dear Ms. Thomas, you

spoke of Jamaica being a little Sodom and that it is for this reason that we are suffering. I think you are being naïve if you really believe such a thing. One does not need a microscope to see the reasons for the country's deplorable economic condition. I'm sure that it is not us gays that have caused it, so don't fool yourself. We are all here to enjoy the gifts of the earth and to endure the adversities. The greatest gift is LOVE.[81]

Partly as a result of GFM's efforts in writing to Jamaican newspapers and calling into the island's talk-show radio programs, homosexuality became a prominent topic of public discourse. JGN itself pointed to the storm of publicity accompanying the announcement of GFM's formation.[82] Of particular note is reporter Jennifer Ffrench's five-part series on homosexuality published in the *Daily Gleaner* that drew from research with GFM in its evenhanded discussion of gay women, gay youth, and bisexual men, among other topics.[83] The rise in dialogue around homosexuality transformed language practices such that Jamaicans increasingly became aware that "gay" indexed not just an affective state of happiness but also same-gender desire.[84] Reporter DeB noted, "It has recently become impossible to describe our cheerful and lively friends as GAY without the risk of misunderstanding. For some time longer, it has been impossible to describe our eccentric and funny friends as queer without running the same risk. GAY is a kinder, less hostile epithet for our homosexual friends than queer and it has established itself."[85]

Contrary to GFM's intention, the increase in public discourse elicited intense backlash against homosexuality in the media, churches, and local government. Some Christian leaders, such as Rev. Ernle Gordon, were adamant that "homosexuals are made in the image and likeness of God and they too must be provided with a caring environment by the Christian Church," but many largely agreed with Rev. Dunn of St. Ann, who insisted that "the Church ... [needs] to speak out against this dreaded EVIL that is feeding at the roots of Society. This EVIL has been festering for years and ought not to be taken lightly as it is now seeking prominence in our society."[86] Indeed, it was this perception of the increasing prominence of homosexuality in Jamaica that led the Kingston and St. Andrew Corporation (KSAC)—the municipal department of housing and urban development for Jamaica's capital city—to pass a resolution to "stamp out homosexuality activities in the society."[87] The resolution called for an investigation into the city's gay clubs and for the Jamaican Council of Churches to condemn homosexuality. Though the KSAC resolution was "more noise than anything else," the fact that this municipal body perceived homosexuality as being significant enough to warrant condemnation highlights the extent to which homosexuality had become part of mainstream Jamaican discourse.[88] Many Jamaicans writing to the island's newspapers vociferously criticized editors for giving so much space to the deviant topic of homosexuality. In his letter to the editor of the *Jamaica Daily News*, Glendon Cooper wrote, "An atmosphere of excessive liberalism is beginning to take root in Jamaica. The issue of homosexuality is having so wide a publicity that one is left to ask why is it so. The impact this can have on the society is significant if commentators do not just define, compare and give examples but also impart the evils of homosexuality."[89]

Although some Jamaicans criticized the island's media outlets for giving space to GFM, the fledgling organization fought against the way it was both censored and misrepresented by these outlets. Jamaican media houses ignored the news releases that GFM submitted regarding their events. And even when they reported on these events, they downplayed or avoided the topic of sexuality altogether. When Chang hosted his first solo art exhibition at the Bolivar Gallery in 1980, entitled "Homoerotica: The Art That Dare Speak Its Name," the media releases that he wrote described the body of work as "Jamaica's first public show of homosexual art" comprising "male homoerotic fantasy in which nude male figures and phallic images predominate."[90] Yet news coverage of the show declined to mention homosexuality, and the *Daily Gleaner* even avoided imparting the exhibit's name, which unavoidably indexed its homoerotic subject matter.[91] In 1981 the *Daily Gleaner* and the *Jamaica Daily News* also declined to publish advertisements that GFM purchased for the Pride celebrations it had planned, because doing so "would encourage homosexuality."[92] And after GFM participated in a panel discussion on homosexuality hosted by the Jamaica Broadcast Company (JBC) television program "Say It Loud," JBC officials declined to air the recording, noting that it was not fit for public viewing.[93] Jamaican journalists proved to be correct in their initial assessment that even though they admired the gumption and daring of Jamaica's gay activists for pushing public dialogue on homosexuality, these change makers would be met with stiff resistance.[94]

GFM in the World

GFM marks the space of difference in existing narratives not only about sexual activism in 1970s Jamaica but also about Jamaica's role in international politics during the same period. During Prime Minister Manley's reign, Jamaican emerged as a leader in advocating for the New International Economic Order and for political and economic cooperation among countries of the Global South as the Jamaican state took an active role in the Non-Aligned Movement.[95] In this era, Jamaican feminists also gained international notoriety. The island became one of the first countries in the world to establish a Women's Bureau. And Lucille Mathurin Mair, who became general secretary of the World Conference for the United Nations Decade for Women, was only one of the many Jamaican women who took on important global leadership positions during this period. These accounts of Jamaica's leadership in fostering political solidarity, especially among women of the Global South, typically do not intersect with the narratives of global gay activism of the same period. Instead, Jamaica goes missing from histories of the 1970s and 1980s that emphasize the vibrancy of same-gender-desiring activist organizations in different parts of the world and the formation of relationships between them.[96] Mobilizing GFM to highlight Jamaica's role in these exchanges not only transforms existing narratives of Jamaica's international leadership but also challenges the North Atlantic–centric nature of historical studies of global gay social movements.[97] Attending to the changes that GFM enacted beyond the island illustrates how countries of the Global South like Jamaica are not just the sites of local histories but operate as key vantage points from which to analyze the workings of sexual politics across national borders.

Despite its limitations as a small, cash-strapped, grassroots organization, GFM sought to make change both within and beyond Jamaica. In 1981, GFM's general secretary penned a *JGN* editorial in which he noted, "At the international level, we have certain rights along with certain responsibilities to our gay sisters and brothers in our common fight against oppression."[98] GFM's commitment to transforming Jamaican society thus did not preclude it from extending its struggle for sexual freedom to those beyond the island's shores. In the fight for erotic autonomy, GFM intervened not only in the politics of Jamaican nationalism but also in the politics of international gay activism. In its fight for sexual freedom, GFM's international efforts are most evident in its transnational community-building work and its simultaneous adoption and transformation of North Atlantic discourses of sexuality and social change. GFM's newsletter was key to the way that it established relationships among individuals and organizations outside of Jamaica. *JGN* circulated not only within but beyond the island, as suggested by the inclusion of subscription information and rates for the United States, Canada, and the UK, in addition to Jamaica.[99] GFM's pen-pal program thus established relationships between same-gender-desiring subjects in Jamaica as well as between these subjects and their international counterparts. The first round of pen-pal requests was published in *JGN*'s fifteenth issue and were written by young men in the Jamaican parishes of St. Thomas, St. James, and Kingston. This first set of personal ads indicated not only that *JGN*'s readership extended across Jamaica but also that its readers were well aware of *JGN*'s international audience. For instance, one ad read, "KINGSTON POSTAL WORKER, 35, 5'9, dark complexion would like pen pal between 20–30 also dark and who is quiet. Would also like to hear from foreigners. (#15–5)."[100] Within five months of the launch of *JGN*'s "Gay Friends" feature, the first pen-pal request from outside of Jamaica was published: "BRITISHER, 40, 5'–7", 160 lbs. enjoys reading, writing, foreign travel and meeting people from other countries. Would like tall active Jamaican male friend over 25. Hopes to visit Jamaica soon. (20–2) Note: Please enclose 50-cents in stamps if replying to this Gayfriend."[101] Within three years, those placing pen-pal requests in *JGN* were primarily from outside the country. *JGN*'s seventy-fifth issue published pen-pal requests from England, Guyana, Denmark, Montserrat, and Ireland.

Many of the letters that GFM received from abroad suggested a desire to know Jamaica and Jamaicans on a level playing field. These letters included, for instance, twenty-four-year-old Remy from Zurich, Switzerland, who had written to GFM in 1980, hoping to connect with young Jamaicans over his love of reggae music in advance of his trip to the island; and seventeen-year-old Yuda from Jakarta, Indonesia, who in his 1979 letter to GFM sought a Jamaican pen pal with whom he could discuss his hobbies of souvenir collecting, playing guitar, and reading.[102] Other letters that GFM received indexed the way that foreigners constructed the island and its inhabitants through racialized fantasies of sexual availability. In 1978, Chang received the following letter—typed in all caps—from Daniel Jones of Johannesburg, South Africa:

DEAR LAURENCE,

MANY THANKS FOR THE LETTER THAT I RECEIVED A FEW DAYS AGO AND ALSO FOR THE BROCHURE YOU SENT.

LAURENCE, AS I HAVE NEVER BEEN TO THE FAR EAST AS YET, BUT WOULD LIKE TO ASK YOU A FEW QUESTIONS ABOUT THE GAY LIFE OVER IN YOUR COUNTRY. HOW MANY GAYS ARE THERE, BY THAT I MEAN QUITE A LOT, OR ARE THERE NOT SO MANY. ARE THERE ANY CLUBS THAT THE GAYS CAN GO TO. ANY SAUNA BATHS, GAY CINEMAS, ARE LIVE STAGE SHOWS PERMITTED, IS THE GAY SCENE JUST FOR EN-JOYMENT, ARE THERE RENT AS WELL. I MEAN BOYS THAT YOU HAVE TO PAY. LIKE IN MOST PLACES IN THE WORLD, INCLUDING MY COUNTRY.

WHAT SORT OF PEOPLE DO YOU [HAVE] MOSTLY IN YOUR COUNTRY, I MEAN THE COLOUR OF THE DIFFERENT SKINS. LIKE IN OUR COUNTRY THEY ARE MOSTLY BLACK AND WHITE, BUT I HAVE AN IDEA THAT IN YOUR COUNTRY YOU HAVE LIGHT BROWN AND DARK BROWN PEOPLE, I'M VERY CURIOUS TO KNOW LAURENCE.

THEN BESIDES JAMAICA, CAN YOU TELL ME OF ANY OTHER PLACE IN YOUR PART OF THE WORLD THAT YOU CAN RECOMMEND, WHERE THE GAY LIFE IS PLENTIFUL AND OPEN, I MEAN LEGAL. AS I WOULD LIKE TO GO THERE AS WELL. I HAVE ALREADY BEEN TO AMSTERDAM, PARIS, COPENHAGEN, LONDON, LISBON, RIO, NEW YORK AND GERMANY. SO I DO NOT WISH TO GO THERE AGAIN, BUT IF YOU HAVE ANY PERSONAL EXPERIENCE OR SUGGESTIONS. THEY WILL BE VERY WELCOME INDEED.

WHAT LANGUAGES ARE SPOKEN IN JAMAICA, AND WHAT WOULD A REASONABLY CLEAN AND COMFORTABLY HOTEL COST PER DAY, IN U.S. DOLLARS. SO THAT I CAN HAVE SOME IDEA OF HOW MUCH POCKET MONEY I'LL NEED WHEN I COME OVER, AND PLEASE TELL ME WHAT WHISKY COSTS, AS WE GET IT VERY CHEAP HERE, AND I WOULD BE DELIGHTED TO BRING SOME OVER FOR YOU.

LASTLY LAURENCE PLEASE TELL ME WHERE I CAN GET SOME NICE PHOTOS OF LOVELY BIG COCKS IRRESPECTIVE OF WHAT COLOR THEY ARE. AS I GET AN ENORMOUS THRILL AND LOTS OF EXCITEMENT OUT OF LOOKING AT THEM. PLEASE BE SO KIND AS TO SEND ME TWO OR THREE, IF YOU POSSIBLY CAN AS THEY ARE EXTREMELY HARD TO GET OVER HERE.

SHOULD YOU BE ABLE TO SEND ME ANY PLEASE SEND THEM IN A SEALED ENVELOPE. I SHALL MAKE IT UP TO YOU IN MORE WAYS THAN ONE. HOPING THAT YOU ARE REALLY KEEPING WELL AND LOOK FOR-WARD TO HEARING FROM YOU SOON. SHOULD YOU NOT HAVE ANY PHOTOS PERSONALLY, COULD YOU PLACE AN ADVERT IN YOUR MAGA-ZINE NEXT ISSUE, SEND ME THE PHOTOS AND ACCOUNT TOGETHER AND I WILL SEND YOU A BANK DRAFT FOR THE COST PLUS 12 DOLLARS MEMBERSHIP

FOR 1 YEAR. YOUR FRIEND, DANIEL JONES[103]

Unlike Remy or Yuda's letters, which suggest an interest in cultivating Jamaican friends, Jones's correspondence with Chang reflected a desire to construct himself through a sexual relationship to a racialized foreign other. His questions about Jamaica revolved around the availability of gays presumably for sexual relations and the variation in their skin color. Given that he mistakenly situated Jamaica as part of the "Far East," it is unclear how he differentiated the island from the other countries that he visited in the search for places "where the gay life is plentiful." His extensive listing of cities that are quite far from his address in South Africa suggests that Jones had access to significant resources to be able to afford this travel.[104] Finally, his request that Chang mail him photos of "lovely big cocks" indexed Jones's sense of entitlement not only to the erotic visual consumption of others' bodies but also the labor required to produce and procure these images. It also presumed that Chang was able and willing to incur the costs of obtaining such photographs and that he was open to accepting the sexual overture implied in Jones's statement, "I shall make it up to you in more ways than one." Jones's letter enacted a foreign expectation of local service.

GFM established relationships between same-gender-desiring subjects in Jamaica and "foreign" individuals and collectives as well as other Jamaicans living in the diaspora. By the time GFM came into existence, long-standing patterns of Jamaican immigration had resulted in the formation of sizable populations of Jamaicans living in countries across the Caribbean region, the Global South, and the North Atlantic (especially England, the United States, and Canada).[105] Jamaican migration during this period involved not so much a severing of homeland ties as a reworking of existing relationships across nation-state borders. Whether through the reconfiguration of family practices, the formation of remittance economies, or the eventual return of migrants, the movement of Jamaicans to other countries created a variegated transnational network of exchanges that worked to transform the nature of life "back home."[106] In addition to brokering exchanges around concerns such as family, employment, and education, Jamaicans on the island and those living overseas also trafficked in sex, desire, and intimacy.

As GFM's default "community center," Chang's house served as a meeting place where Jamaicans living abroad who returned home over the holidays would meet up with local Jamaicans for friendship, socializing, and opportunities for sex. These kinds of informal exchanges gave rise to more sustained political connections. Yet it was difficult for those who were not "in the know" to find out about these social venues. In her letter to Chang, Patricia Campbell, a Jamaican young woman attending college in New York, wrote:

> I am dropping you a few lines in response to some information given to me by [Name] concerning the GFM. When I was in Ja[maica] last summer, I sought high and low for someone to contact but everyone was so

secretive and their information so sketchy, that I left with the same feeling that I did at the age of sixteen: 'Hopeless! absolutely hopeless! There are no gay people in Jamaica!' Of course that could not be true. Intellectually I knew that but where were they? Anyway, I'm quite relieved to learn that we actually exist and are acknowledged (if even only by a few people) and I look forward to some kind of communication soon.[107]

Yet Campbell's engagement with GFM indicated the potential differences and dynamics of power that emerged among Jamaicans on the island and in the diaspora. Upon her return to Jamaica in the summer of 1980, Campbell penned an article in JGN aptly titled "Looking In" in which she wrote:

Well, for someone who has been unmercifully "checked" and finally abandoned by disillusioned straight men on each vacation, I was extremely happy to learn of GFM. I proudly announced the news to SALSA and they too were happy as there are a number of Jamaicans there who had been yearning for a gay community at home. They made donations of literature and have promised their continued support.

My dear reader, you must imagine my distress when I learned on my arrival of the closing of the club and the discontinuation of the meetings. That was bad enough but learning that the failure of the gay community was accelerated by the apathetic attitudes of the members is real grief. Grief! . . .

We need to emerge from the cloak of hypocrisy and fear that surrounds us. It is irrelevant whether people know our names or not. What we want them to know is our strength and power, our love of life, and the way we choose to live it. The majority of people in this world are in one type of closet or another. We just happen to be closeted (predominantly) in our sexuality. But do we have to be closeted in every aspect of our lives? I say no. The gay (international) community too, is largely underground but within that, there are communication networks that would boggle the straight mind. The work is getting done but we need to generate more activity in this part of the world. I do hope my frustration has been understood and I will continue in the struggle because I am tired of wishing that Maddams was still open and now I think we should move forward and find another meeting place for discussions etc.

To all those who are still in the closet: Almost everybody knows that you are gay. Weh yu still a hide fah!

Please let us unite to a more positive state of existence.[108]

The SALSA that Campbell mentioned in her article refers to the Salsa Soul Sisters, a New York–based Third World lesbian community organization to which she belonged. After contacting GFM, SALSA donated gay literature to the group and solicited material from Jamaican lesbians in the hopes of producing a Third World gay publication.[109] Partly through relationships with groups like SALSA, Jamaicans in the 1970s and 1980s became well versed in North American gay liberation literature such as Laud Humphrey's *Sociology of Homosexual Liberation* and Karla Jay's *Voices of Gay Liberation*.

But even as Jamaicans like Campbell and groups with Jamaican membership like SALSA contributed to GFM's efforts, Campbell's *JGN* article highlights the differences among Jamaicans living on and off the island. Campbell problematized what she interpreted as apathy among GFM members, the lack of action toward social change among gays "in this part of the world," and Jamaicans who were "in the closet." Yet Campbell was unfamiliar with the social organization of sexuality in Jamaica. Though she grew up on the island, it was only in the very summer that she wrote "Looking In" that she began to interact with other gays in Jamaica for the first time. Rather than trying to understand the Jamaica's same-gender-desiring communities on their own terms or interrogating her own assumptions about these communities' supposed deficits, Campbell issued critiques based on her experiences of gay life in the United States. These critiques lay bare the difference that place makes in debates about sexuality among same-gender-desiring Jamaicans.

In addition to forging new relations across Jamaica's borders, the second way that GFM enacted change at the international level was through its adoption and transformation of North Atlantic discourses of sexuality and activism.[110] North Atlantic ideologies played an important role in how same-gender-desiring subjects in Jamaica understood their erotic subjectivities and conceived of political action. In 1978 Larry Chang, under his pseudonym "Tony Long," published a set of articles in *JGN* collectively titled "On Being Gay," written in a series of installments outlining an idealized set of stages through which those with same-gender attractions progress, from "realization" to "trauma" to "self-acceptance" and "reinforcement" to "coming out" to "activism." An excerpt from the self-acceptance article reads:

> After we have been through the trauma of realizing we are gay and all that being "sexually deviant" means to society, we must at some point arrive at some degree of self-acceptance. From the status of being labelled perverts, inverts, sick and diseased, non-persons and even demons, our egos must rebel and reassert themselves. We alone know our true selves, our intrinsic

nature, our innermost thoughts. Knowing this, we know that we cannot be as bad, worthless, evil and degenerate as we are made out to be. How could being gay ever be wrong when it is such an integral part of our spirit, personality and disposition, as natural and easy for us as breathing?[111]

In this article, same-gender desire indexed an interior subjectivity that constituted an individual as a particular kind of person. Within this configuration of sexuality-as-personhood, GFM identified the acceptance of one's desires and "coming out" or "being prepared at any time to freely admit to being gay" as a prerequisite to effective political action.[112] The series concluded with the sentiment that "having come out and removed the fear of exposure, we must get together with other free spirits to carry out certain necessary actions. These have to do with legal reform, community development and defence, and public education."[113]

Chang's articulation of subjectivity and political action around same-gender desire aligns with the views of GFM's counterparts in North America and Europe. Eve Kosofsky Sedgwick maintains that the construction of homosexuality as a defining feature of personhood is intimately related to the mappings of secrecy and disclosure and of the private and the public in twentieth-century Western culture. Within this context, the salience of the distinction between heterosexuality and homosexuality highlights the extent to which knowledge and sex become conceptually inseparable. "The closet," with its ramifications of homosexual secrecy, emerges as "the defining structure for gay oppression," such that "coming out of the closet becomes "a salvational epistemology."[114] These logics shaped the work of two of GFM's interlocutors, the British lesbian magazine *Sappho* and the Canadian gay publication *The Body Politic*. Animated by the imperatives of gay liberation, the activist bent of these publications focused on building solidarity and collectivity in terms of sexuality. They marshaled sexuality as a point of differentiation from "straight" people, as a call for a particular kind of visibility ("coming out"), and as a site of politicization.[115]

The resonance in discourses of sexuality and social change between GFM and its North Atlantic counterparts is not altogether surprising given the high levels of exchange between them. SALSA was just one of many social justice organizations outside of Jamaica with which GFM interacted. In addition to exchanging publications with initiatives like the Revolutionary Socialist League in New York (*Torch*) and the Body Politic in Toronto (*The Body Politic*), GFM also corresponded with a slew of other organizations, such as the Society for the Protection of Personal Rights in Israel, the newsletter *El Otro* from Colombia, and the publication *Lambda* in Italy.[116] Yet GFM was far from being just a node in an international network of activist organizations. It was also a leader in its own right. In 1978 the group was invited to participate in the annual conference of the British organization Campaign for Homosexual Equality.[117] The following year the Costa Rican organization Movimiento de Liberación Homosexual contacted GFM requesting support for their fledgling initiative.[118] In 1980 the German branch of Amnesty International wrote to GFM requesting their help to inform their deliberations as to whether discrimination on the basis of sexual orientation should be considered a human rights violation.[119] A few months later the Scottish Homosexual Rights Group reached out to GFM to form a "pairing relationship," and the group partially sponsored GFM to participate in the third International Gay Association (IGA) conference held in Italy.[120] At this event, GFM became the liaison to the English-speaking Caribbean for IGA's newly formed Latin American and Caribbean Secretariat.[121]

GFM also played an important role in the production of knowledge about sexuality in Jamaica for international audiences. IGA's Canadian delegation sought GFM's expertise in preparing a report on the exploitation of Third World gays by white male gay tourists, and GFM contributed to the human rights report of the US-based American Friends Service Committee on the status of gay rights on the island.[122] Taken aback by the misinformation about Jamaica in the international gay travel guide *Spartacus*, Chang wrote a new entry for the island and soon became Jamaica's author for the publication in the 1980s.[123] In addition to their active participation in the political realm of rights and organizing, Jamaican gay women and men were also encouraged to contribute to literary and artistic publications by American groups, such as *Blackheart*, a gay Black men's publication in New York; *Ache*, a journal for Black lesbians located in Oakland, California; and Malis Alliance, a bisexual organizational based in Philadelphia.[124]

GFM both adopted and transformed the discourses of sexuality and social change of its international interlocutors. This approach was connected to the emergent nature of GFM itself, such that even though Chang initially identified coming out as key to the group's political work, the participation of new members brought different perspectives and a gradual change in GFM's outlook. In her regular column "Girl Talk," Donna Smith, the young Jamaican woman introduced earlier in the chapter, called for an approach to activism that did not require "coming out." She stated, "It is neither fair nor practical to demand of every Jamaican homosexual that he/she come out indiscriminately and participate in such activities as gay demonstrations and marches."[125] In emphasizing the importance of "those behind the scenes acts of solidarity which are such an essential element of group militancy," Smith argues that "adopting an open position" should not be a prerequisite for participation in GFM. The group began to acknowledge the importance of making space for those for whom coming out was neither possible nor necessarily desirable. Tackling issues such as employment discrimination, the threat of blackmail, and the desire to have one's "own" children, later issues of JGN recognized the difficulty of "outness," particularly for lower-class and poor individuals, as well as how some subjects of same-gender desire chose to live their lives in ways that did not conform to a logic of "coming out."[126] Thus, while GFM members initially criticized manifestations of same-gender desire that failed to adhere to North Atlantic models of subjectivity, they soon came to recognize not only the validity of these various sexual forms but also the capacity of a wider range of individuals to contribute to the group's movement work.

Through the course of its existence, GFM adopted an equivocal position in evaluating itself in relation to North Atlantic counterparts. On the one hand, GFM used the language of progress when comparing its achievements to those of gay movements in countries like the United States. Whether insisting that Jamaica's "narrowness and insularity will only relegate us forever to the Third World backwater," identifying Jamaican gays as "still so far behind North American gays in terms of consciousness," or expressing joy that "Jamaicans joined the rest of the civilized world in the celebration of International Gay Pride Week," GFM members echoed Campbell's sentiments that Jamaica was somehow "behind" the political advances made by gays in the Global North.[127] On the other hand, in keeping with the zeitgeist of this period of high nationalism in Jamaica, GFM was convinced of the importance of the island's cultural and historical specificity. Thus, the editorial of JGN's special heritage issue notes, "Until gay Jamaican history books are written, we have to draw on the history of the world's gay peoples as our single source of pride and inspiration. This is as it should be since our heritage transcends all national boundaries. But we should still like to have a piece of gay heritage that is uniquely our own."[128] In rejecting the tendency "to depend and rely on someone 'from abroad' to come and tell us what to do and how to do it," GFM maintained that it had something significant to offer on the world stage.[129] For instance, while the group was deeply appreciative that the Scottish Homosexual Rights Group had sponsored GFM's participation at the 1981 International Gay Association meeting in Italy, Chang also found the gathering to be deeply problematic. In his report of the conference, he wrote,

"In real terms our participation at this conference amounts to little more than tokenism. The benefits to us from my experience and from the contacts I have made will be immeasurable and far reaching indeed. But until more women and non-white people are included, IGA and by extension, the international gay liberation movement will continue to be dominated by the concerns of gay white males."[130] Even though Chang was willing to engage with offshore interlocutors and accept their support, this did not stop him from critiquing the structure of international organizations and how GFM was incorporated into their work. He thus considered GFM's work, and the (Jamaican) perspective that it brought, to be sufficiently significant to warrant genuine participation on the international stage and to condemn tokenistic overtures.

Ultimately, GFM came to an end in the throes of the island's HIV/AIDS epidemic. As its leaders, members, and communities began to succumb to the disease, GFM's scant institutional form gave way to informal work of HIV/AIDS care. In the short seven years of its existence, this small voluntary organization made important contributions to Jamaican national formation by creating new forms of community and challenging regimes of sexual respectability. It also played an important role in transforming the nature of international relations by building gay forms of sociality across nation-state borders and reshaping hegemonic North Atlantic discourses of sexuality, subjectivity, and activism. GFM's work thus sutured the struggle for same-gender erotic agency to the project of Jamaican nation building while also insisting on Jamaica's significance to the efforts of international gay social movements. This account of GFM differs from existing representations of the period, which highlight the island's efforts to repair local and global structures of inequality by drawing attention to Jamaica's Black Power, feminist, and labor movements and its efforts to redress the colonial architecture of the existing global economic order. Turning to GFM enables the construction of a different historical narrative that foregrounds the contested space of same-gender desire in Jamaica's struggle for domestic and international change. GFM's work illustrates the productivity of queerness as a generative site through which to surface the active lines of fractal formations and circumvent the repetition of existing representations of the past.

Epilogue

Fractal Futures

Fractal Repair explores how the practice of history making can respond to the discursive and material intimacy between queer violence and Jamaica in the present. In so doing, it forwards queer fractals as a theory and method of constructing histories of repair. Fractals are patterns that repeat but never in the same way; queerness marks the space of difference that forecloses exact replication. The physical and psychic harms that queers on the island experience, and the positioning of Jamaica in terms of queerphobic exceptionalism, almost demands a liberatory orientation toward historical inquiry. Yet this romantic visioning of progress fails to align with the recursive nature of Caribbean and queer temporalities, where time seems to proceed in a looping, not linear, fashion. Abolition, revolution, independence, and development in the Caribbean have yet to yield the forms of freedom that their architects imagined, and LGBTQ activist victories have not protected the most vulnerable gender and sexual minorities. Queer fractals suggests that repair takes shape not through an emancipatory break with the past, but through the practice of living with the past that repeats into the present while holding fast to the queer sites of rupture that prevent absolute reiteration.

Queer fractals is not a practice of liberation. As much as it operates on a different register from arithmetic calculations that enable the incorporation of subaltern subjects into the racialized workings of empire, these calculations form the basis on which fractal formations take shape. Queer fractals is discursively inseparable from the biopolitical violence that arithmetic practices facilitate. Fractals materialize through active lines (what changes with each iteration) and passive lines (what stays the same with each iteration), and it is the passive lines that make evident this inseparability. By making queerness visible in key moments of Jamaica's late twentieth-century cultural political formation, this book surfaces both lines. Materializing same-gender intimacy in the making of a local social science tradition and then again in the island's response to HIV/AIDS almost half a century later foregrounds the continuity of archival arrangements that inscribe queerness through hierarchies of race, class, gender, and nation. Making same-gender intimacy perceptible in these moments where Jamaicans attempt to localize knowledge production and combat a deadly epidemic does less to suture queerness to narratives of change than to illustrate the persistence of archival disparities. In contrast, eliciting queerness from within the formative years of Jamaica's National Dance Theatre Company and the heady political period of 1970s Jamaica shows how queerness carries the potential to renarrate existing accounts of the past. Queerness disrupts existing representations of these moments that emphasize how Jamaicans worked toward cultural and political decolonization by showing the heretofore unacknowledged significance of gender and sexual peculiarity to these efforts. This approach to history making uses queerness to reveal the complexity of reparative effects that perform both historical continuity and change. Even as it opens space for imagining the past otherwise, queer fractals cannot fully escape the violence of its recursive effects.

If queer fractals refuses the conceit of total liberation from the past, what are its implications for conceptualizing futurity? Responding to this question requires a broader consideration of how the practice of mathematics structures futural thought. This structuring is perhaps most evident in the "futures" in finance capitalism. Here, the term "futures" refers to an agreement to buy or sell a commodity at a set date in the future for a set price based on derivative calculations. Futures condense logics of time and value in the service of financial speculation. These logics were elaborated during the transatlantic slave trade and later animated the practices that became foundational to the workings of contemporary global capitalism. The lengthy time required to complete the triangular circuit of the trade—from Europe, to Africa, to the Americas—meant that merchants had to conduct their business through a system of credit. This system constructed value not through an actual exchange of goods but instead through an agreement that such goods would be exchanged in the future at a set price. The logics of this agreement sought to identify, quantify, and minimize risk as much as possible in the service of predicting the future with maximum certitude. The 1781 massacre on the slave ship *Zong* spectacularly illustrates the horrific consequences of this economic practice. The ship's slavers threw enslaved Africans overboard to their death, confident that they could collect insurance on them as "lost" property. Their capacity to financially benefit from this mass murder was premised on the certainty that the future would confirm the market value of the enslaved.[1] Contemporary reparations discourses rehearse this consolidation of value and temporality through efforts to secure financial restitution for historical injury. Monetary practices of reparations and the futures of finance capitalism rooted in the transatlantic slave trade engage in the same mathematical grammar of futurity. Though the calculations are now oriented toward economically compensating the survivors (not the perpetrators) of violence, they nevertheless run the risk of reinscribing the logics of racial capitalism that produce value from the disposability of black bodies.

Queer fractals approaches futurity through a different orientation to mathematics. It unsettles the futural grammars of financial capitalism that work to eradicate indeterminacy in the service of progressive profit accumulation. Rather than working to secure the future as a progressive achievement through the certainty of flawless calculations, it engages the problem of futurity through an "investment in the errant, the irrational, the unpredictable."[2] This is a more measured approach than that proposed by José Muñoz's critical utopian methodology of hope that foregrounds queerness "as the warm illumination of a horizon imbued with potentiality."[3] Queer fractals suggest that the future comes into being not as an assured liberation from the past but as a process of living with a past that persists in the present and embracing the moments of indeterminacy where the past fails to repeat exactly.

Conut, the character in Erna Brodber's novel *Nothing's Mat*, gestures to this futural approach in her assertion, "Your end is your beginning."[4] What would it mean to think Jamaican and Caribbean futurity by revisiting the start of the region's fundamental modernity? There are doubtless many entry points to narrate this origin story, but I focus on the letter that Dr. Diego Álvarez Chanca wrote to the Municipal Council of Seville as a physician to Christopher Columbus on his second voyage to the New World. This text is significant because it is considered to be the first written account on the natural history and ethnography of the Americas. Unlike Columbus's first exploratory trip, this higher-status venture carried a significantly larger contingent with the explicit goal of conquest. Aristocrats and clergy from different religious orders peopled the second voyage, which also transported livestock and plants for the purpose of building new lives across the Atlantic. Though Chanca wrote this letter in January 1494 when he had been in the New World for less than three months, it nevertheless offers a sprawling account of the multiple islands the conquistadors visited. The letter provided detailed descriptions of the region's natural landscape and plant and animal life. It also narrated the material culture, architecture, settlement patterns, diet, dress, physical descriptions, and social customs of the various Indigenous people the Spanish contingent encountered.

A queer reading of Chanca's letter gestures toward the fractality of futural thought. This move is not intended to legitimize the content of the account as "true." Chanca's interactions with Caribbean peoples were mediated by a translator, and his portrayal of the region is inseparable from his interest in fostering support for future efforts to extract wealth from the New World. The significance of the letter lies in its capacity to illustrate, not some truth about the Caribbean, but instead the durability of representational forms and their effects. For Chanca, "La costumbre desta gente de Caribes es bestial [The habits of these people of the Caribbean are beastly]."[5] Sylvia Wynter notes that whether these New World peoples were "beastly" was a question about their capacity to be converted to Christianity, and ultimately their status as humans.[6] Within a sixteenth-century moral political order, Spanish practices of dispossession, violence, enslavement, and murder in the Americas were permissible only if enacted upon nonhuman, inhuman, or subhuman populations.

Conquistador assessments of Indigenous gender and sexual practices were foundational to calculations of beastliness and, by extension, humanness. Chanca supports his description of "beastliness" by narrating how the Carib people of Guadeloupe treated other Indigenous groups. He notes, "Esta gente saltea en las otras islas, que traen las mugeres que puedan haber, en especial mozas y hermosas, las cuales tienen para su servicio, é para tener por mancebas . . . Los mochachos que cativan córtanlos el miembro, é sírvense de ellos fasta que son hombres, y despues cuando quieren facer fiesta mátanlos é cómenselos, porque dicen que la carne de los mochachos é de las mogeres no es buena para comer." [When these people attack other islands, they capture as many women as they can, especially those who are young and beautiful and keep them as servants and concubines . . . They cut of the members of the boys they capture and use them until they become men, and after, when they want to make a feast, they kill them and eat them, because they say that the flesh of boys and women is not good to eat."][7] While the trope of cannibalism pervades European colonial discourses about Indigenous people in the Americas, Chanca's account illustrates that gender and sexual violence against women and boys as well as anthropophagy marked Spanish assessments of inhumanity.[8] Chanca's gendered, raced, and sexual inscription of the New World instantiated a new global order of knowledge around human difference and set in motion processes of transatlantic capitalist modernity.

Rendering fractal futurity through queerness entails identifying sites of rupture in the forces of history that repetitively conscript this region and its people into the global workings of racial capitalism. Chanca's letter illustrates that the description of "beastly" discursively initiates these processes of conscription; fractal futurity entails attending to the different ways that this ascription of queerness is mobilized with each conscriptive iteration.[9] This approach counters linear progressive orientations to the future invested in the certainty of calculations that seek to sever violent ties to capitalist modernity. Instead, queer fractals suggests that there is no ultimate liberation from our present that is also our past. The modernity of racial capitalism has simultaneously violated and shaped Caribbean people. We cannot escape how its forces have woven themselves into our very beings even as they subject us to material, cultural, and psychic injury. And yet the recursive nature of this conscription means that it is never complete; each iteration is never exactly the same as the ones that came before. Though beastliness will always stand in for the inferior difference that prompts violent incorporation into the global modernity of racial capitalism, it is impossible to know in advance exactly how coloniality will mark the Caribbean and its people with each iteration. The future lies in this queer site of indeterminacy, the ruptural space that prevents exact repetition. Our queer end is indeed our queer beginning.

Notes

Introduction

1. My experience is similar to the diversion-reversion dynamic that Édouard Glissant (*Caribbean Discourse*) maintains is vital for the construction of
Caribbean subjectivity. Even as he advocates for the relational construction of
Caribbean self-formation outside of the region, he notes, "We must return to the
point from which we started . . . not a return to the longing for origins, to some
immutable state of Being, but a return to the point of entanglement" (26).

2. Padgett, "Most Homophobic Place on Earth."

3. Whether or not Jamaica occupies the top spot, the notion that it is both possible and desirable to rank countries around the world in terms of homophobia
continues unabated. For instance, a *Newsweek* magazine article in 2014 by Max
Strasser listed the "twelve most homophobic nations," pegging Nigeria as "the
most homophobic country in the world." A similar list appeared in 2023 in *World
Population Review*, "Most Homophobic Countries 2023."

4. Discourses about queerness and Jamaica on the island and beyond its
shores are so overdetermined by the framework of homophobia that it is difficult
to even think about the topic in other terms. Responses to the initial ascription
"most homophobic place on earth" tend not to question whether homophobia is
even an appropriate starting point for conversations about Jamaica and queerness. An article in *Time* magazine in 2015 asked whether Jamaica was becoming
less homophobic (A. Jackson, "Is 'the Most Homophobic Place on Earth' Turning
Around?"). Three years later the *Guardian* declared the island to be "no longer
the most homophobic place on earth" (Faber, "Welcome to Jamaica"). In 2020
the University of the West Indies (UWI) published the proceedings of a sympo-
sium (Anderson and MacLeod, *Beyond Homophobia*), held on the island at UWI's
Mona campus, addressing LGBTQ experiences and research in Jamaica. The title
of the edited volume is telling.

5. Sedgwick, "Paranoid Reading and Reparative Reading," 149; D. A. Thomas,
Exceptional Violence, 6.

6. My work is indebted to earlier interventions in Caribbean queer history, including Agard-Jones, "What the Sands Remember"; King, "New Citizens, New Sexualities"; Isenia, "Looking for Kambrada"; Cummings, "Jamaican Female Masculinities"; La Fountain-Stokes, "1898."

7. S. Hall, "Cultural Identity and Diaspora," 225.

8. Theodore Porter (*Trust in Numbers*) discusses the ways that numbers are currently considered to be objective forms of knowledge. Mary Poovey (*History of the Modern Fact*) illustrates how numerical calculations were disparaged in England before the practice of double-entry bookkeeping, which positioned mathematics as yielding universal, modern facts.

9. Rotman, "Semiotics of Mathematics," 13.

10. Historians, anthropologists, and literary scholars have long insisted on the significance of representational form. Hayden White (*Metahistory*) maintains that different components of a historical account carry their own explanatory effects. The convincingness of a historical narrative may derive just as much from the nature of its emplotment as from the nature of its argument. In tracing the delegitimization of literature in the seventeenth century, Terry Eagleton (*Literary Theory*) suggests that this concern about "convincingness" is tied to the hierarchization of modes of expression in which fiction and subjectivity are disparaged in favor of fact and objectivity, respectively. And Johannes Fabian (*Time and the Other*) argues that the textual strategies that anthropologists use in constructing their ethnographic accounts authorize them as experts while relegating their interlocutors to the position of spatial and temporal other. George Lakoff and Mark Johnson, *Metaphors We Live By*—on metaphor, language, knowledge production, and social life—is also useful for thinking about the relationship between mathematics-as-metaphor and practices of history making.

11. On the erasure of Indigenous women under settler colonialism, see A. Simpson, *Mohawk Interruptus*. For additional work on mathematical narratives and Native gender and sexual relations, see, for instance, Kauanui, *Hawaiian Blood*; L. Smith et al., "Fractional Identities." On the commodification of enslaved Black women, see J. L. Morgan, *Reckoning with Slavery*. For further discussion on the relationship between mathematics and Black genders and sexualities, see, for instance, C. A. Smith, "Counting Frequency"; Carby, *Imperial Intimacies*. It is also worth noting that US Black feminist literature on intersectionality offers an implicit critique of additive notions of difference. Kimberle Crenshaw ("Demarginalizing the Intersection") thus argues that the interlocking nature of race and gender-based discrimination in the United States cannot be understood through their addition. On the colonial construction of Indian woman as prostitute, see Mitra, *Indian Sex Life*. For additional work on the enumeration of Indian sexuality under British colonialism, see Levine, "Orientalist Sociology"; Tambe, *Codes of Misconduct*.

12. Saidiya Hartman (*Lose Your Mother*) thus notes that "black lives are still imperiled and devalued by a racial calculus and political arithmetic that were entrenched centuries ago" (6).

13. J. M. Johnson, "Markup Bodies"; Gebru, "Race and Gender"; Stevens, Hoffmann, and Florini, "The Unremarked Optimum"; McPherson, "Why Are the Digital Humanities So White?"

14. McKittrick, "Mathematics Black Life," 23. Mayra Santos-Febres ("The Fractal Caribbean") advocates a similar strategy in seeking to "make the algorithms work in our favor (48:34)."

15. Hammonds, "Black (W)holes," 139.

16. Ron Eglash (*African Fractals*) illustrates how fractal forms characterize the settlement patterns, architectural designs, material culture, and even hairstyles of societies across the African continent such as Cameroon, Burkina Faso, Egypt, and Senegal.

17. For Mandelbrot, part of the process of accounting for supposedly non-uniform natural processes also involved considering fractional dimensions. Mandelbrot (*Fractal Geometry of Nature*) noted that such processes occurred not just in whole-number dimensions such as 2 or 3 but also in dimensions of, for instance, 2.14.

18. Anjali Arondekar ("The Sex of History") asks, "How then can the vernaculars, temporalities and spatialities that make 'sex' intelligible as object and archive summon itinerant geopolitical forms that are often left behind?" (4). I suggest that the vernacular of fractal geometry materializes queer history in ways that summon the Caribbean. In his work on Caribbean queer returns, Rinaldo Walcott makes a similar argument. He forwards a homopoetics of relation to consider the political implications of queer diasporic subjects returning and "speaking back" to the Caribbean in the language of queer rights ("Queer Returns," 10). While Walcott's essay raises many important questions for this study, I am especially interested in pushing his theorization of return through diaspora in a different direction, albeit similarly aiming to "hover in the gaps, spaces, and crevices of the Caribbean's multiple and contradictory inheritances of its queer formations" (10). Where Walcott leans on the spatial aspects of queer return, in this book I consider how an emphasis on temporality offers another angle through which to engage the problem space of queerness in the contemporary Caribbean.

19. In alignment with Mandelbrot's contention that regularity characterizes what appears to be natural disorder, Antonio Benítez-Rojo (*The Repeating Island*) understands the Caribbean as a repeating island, a chaos that endlessly returns. This echoing temporality that marks the region permeates the level of subjectivity such that "every Caribbean person's present is pendular. . . . In the Caribbean one either oscillates toward a utopia or toward a lost paradise" (251). Drawing on J. L. Austin's speech act theory, Judith Butler (*Bodies That Matter*) argues that far from being natural or stable "essences," gender and sexuality take shape through practices in relationship to forms of regulation. Repetition is key to how these practices materialize gender and sexuality. Butler thus notes that "performativity cannot be understood outside of a process of iterability, a regularized and constrained *repetition* of norms" (95, emphasis added).

20. Édouard Glissant (*Poetics of Relation*) forwards a poetics of relation that functions as a language through which to understand Caribbean consciousness and realities. For Glissant, this poetics works against any form of closure, assimilation, or certitude, and "inscribes itself in a circularity . . . a line of energy curved back onto itself" (32). Gilles Deleuze (*Difference and Repetition*) argues that history writing is an erotic practice because it necessarily entails engaging with repetition. He maintains that representing the past requires taking hold of the virtual object that constantly circulates (repeats) between two nodes: the existing present (the time of writing) and the present that was past (the time to be written about). For Deleuze it is the force of desire that reifies this virtual object, tearing it from circulation for the purpose of representation.

21. Brodber, *Nothing's Mat*, 36.

22. Brodber, *Nothings Mat*, 95.

23. Brodber, *Nothings Mat*, 97 (emphasis added).

24. Benítez-Rojo (*The Repeating Island*) notes that "repetition is a practice that *necessarily* entails a difference" (3, emphasis added).

25. Brodber's conception of family resonates with the critique in Macharia, *Frottage*, of the genealogical imperatives of Black diasporic thought that privilege heteronormative forms of kinship.

26. Somerville, "Queer." See also Sayers, "The Etymology of Queer."

27. William Leap (*Word's Out*) states, "'Queer' is one of a handful of terms in English that establish references by opposition and exclusion, not just by simple description. That is, instead of identifying properties that the object under discussion contains, calling something 'queer' suggests that it is out of place in some sense, that it is excessive and overextended, that it disrupts and subverts" (101).

28. J. J. Thomas, *Froudacity*, 117.

29. It is critical to note that Thomas's antiracist critique is not an anti-imperial one, as suggested by his continued faith in colonial institutions of law. For more on Thomas, see F. Smith, *Creole Recitations*; Lewis, "J. J. Thomas"; De Barros, "'Race' and Culture."

30. Sedgwick, *Tendencies*, 7. See also Warner, "Introduction"; Lauretis, "Queer Theory."

31. For Eglash, African approaches to fractals place a greater emphasis on recursion and the social organization of gender and sexuality than do their European counterparts. Eglash thus notes, "While recursion is prominent in African fractals, it has been less so in European fractal geometry." He suggests that "one contributing factor to the African mathematical emphasis on recursion could be this African construction of sexuality through positive public domain expressions." Eglash also points out that European critiques of fractal geometry are closely tied to gender and sexual regulation, as many of the European mathematicians working in this field—such as Ada Lovelace, Rozsa Peter, and Alan Turing—bristled at the gender and sexual limitations of their societies (Eglash, *African Fractals*, 214, 210).

32. Gallagher and Greenblatt, "Counterhistory," 52. My use of fractals in the service of history making differs from that of Ghassan Moussawi (*Disruptive Situations*), who mobilizes fractals to attend to the workings of Orientalism in different contexts. Moussawi's turn to fractal geometry in terms of nested dichotomies facilitates an analysis of the multiple scales and layers in (and through) which Orientalism functions. His fractal Orientalism is concerned less with mathematics and history than with binaries and space.

33. Though reparations initially referred to a relationship between states in the aftermath of war, the rise of a human rights paradigm after World War II has meant that individuals and subnational groups emerge as legitimate actors in reparation debates. It has also meant that the terms of reparations are no longer limited to victorious states' claims over the spoils of war, but are extended to include broader notions of morality, justice, and truth in the aftermath of unjustified (and unjustifiable) violence. See Torpey, *Making Whole*.

34. This approach is evidenced in Eric Williams's famous economic history *Capitalism and Slavery*, in which he argues that the transatlantic slave trade financed the industrial revolution in England and gave rise to the development of industrial capitalism that ultimately precipitated the end of slavery. Williams's study has been foundational to the development of Black Marxism and Caribbean Historiography and has inspired contemporary scholarship on reparations. See, for instance, Beckles, *Britain's Black Debt*. Yet Gordon Rohlehr ("History as Absurdity") takes issue with what he sees as Williams's overwhelming focus on anticolonial revenge and contends that Caribbean history making cannot only constitute "a stockpile of facts to be hurled like bricks against dead and living imperialists" (75).

35. One such example is the "Ten Point Action Plan for Reparatory Justice" that Caribbean Community (CARICOM) nations adopted in an attempt to obtain a formal apology from European nations that accepts responsibility and pledges a commitment to redressing the ongoing legacies of slavery, colonialism, and imperialism. See Shepherd, "Past Imperfect, Future Perfect?"

36. Ferreira da Silva, "Fractal Thinking."

37. For a similar argument about the politics of time for queer subjects of the Global South more broadly, see Rao, *Out of Time*.

38. Édouard Glissant ("Creolization") maintains that history in the Caribbean does not unfold according to the "imperial linear conception of time that Columbus brought with him" (88). David Scott ("The Tragic Vision") thus questions romantic "narratives of longing and vindication that link past, present, and future in a steady rhythm of progressive (sometimes righteously exultant) redemption" (799) and instead proposes a postcolonial tragic sensibility that counters "the drives embodied in progressivist accounts of the past in the present . . . [and offers] a strong doubt about teleologies of history in which heroic subjects of rational self-determination and committed resolve realize their moral and political destinies" (800).

39. Freeman, *Time Binds*; Love, *Feeling Backward*. These and other studies of queer temporality look askance at historical narratives that conceptualize the past in terms of difference. See also Goldberg and Menon, "Queering History"; Freccero, "Queer Times"; Traub, "The New Unhistoricism in Queer Studies."

40. Eglash (*African Fractals*) notes, "Neither fractal nor Euclidean geometries have any inherent ethical content; such meanings arise from the people who use them" (195). Indeed, he argues, "Fractals and chaos theory have increasingly been mentioned in the humanities as either a tool or an object of cultural analysis, but too often the approach of these studies has left the impression of mathematical ink blots allowing writers to see whatever they please" (199).

41. The reparative potential of queer fractals is similar to the way Denise Ferreira da Silva ("Fractal Thinking") conceives "poethical" thinking. Ferreira da Silva notes, "Images of poethical thought are not linear (transparent, abstract, glassy, and determinate) but fractal (immanent, scalar, plenteous, and undetermined), like what exists in the world. When poethical thinking contemplates the present [refugee] situation in Europe, it does not image 'unprecedented crisis' but rather business as usual for global capital. . . . Poethical thinking, deployed as a creative (fractal) imaging to address colonial and racial subjugation, aims to interrupt the repetition characteristic of fractal patterns."

42. Keeling, *Queer Times, Black Futures*, 19.

43. Brian Rotman ("Semiotics of Mathematics") contends that contemporary mathematical practice figures the mathematician as an abstracted subject without temporal of geographical coordinates.

44. Mair, *A Historical Study*, 20. Abigail Swingen (*Competing Visions of Empire*) notes, "Plantation and migration, forced or otherwise, characterized Cromwellian imperialism, and plans to populate Jamaica with hardy laborers and godly servants coincided with similar efforts in Ireland. Often these endeavors involved the same people and families" (50). On the place of Ireland in the Atlantic World, see Richards, "Scotland"; Nicholas, *Kingdom and Colony*.

45. Petty was neither the first nor the only person to bring mathematics to the arts of government, but his work is now recognized as foundational to both classical economics and statistical demography as well as to the history of racial thought. I focus on Petty as an exemplary, not as an exceptional, historical figure. His contemporaries John Graunt, Charles Davenant, and Gregory King also made key contributions to the codification of political arithmetic in England and its empire (Hoppit, "Political Arithmetic"). And English formulations of political arithmetic were not the first to apply quantitative techniques to the arts of government. For instance, Arjun Appadurai ("Number in the Colonial Imagination") notes that prior to British rule, Mughal leaders in India engaged in practices of enumeration and mapmaking to facilitate revenue generation through taxation.

46. Petty, *Political Anatomy of Ireland*.

47. Marquis of Landsdowne, *The Petty Papers*, 119.

48. Petty, *Political Arithmetick*.

49. Yet Jennifer Morgan notes that even if Petty's political arithmetic functioned as a kind of racial alchemy that positioned Irish and Native women as carrying the potential for reproducing an English populace in support of colonial conquest, this potential was denied to African women with the solidification of hereditary slavery. The conversion of Africans into commodities prevented the kind of assimilation into whiteness afforded to Native and Irish people (J. L. Morgan, *Reckoning with Slavery*, 103).

50. Foucault, *The History of Sexuality*, vol. 1.

51. Black, *War against the Weak*.

52. Young, *Colonial Desire*.

53. Stocking, *Race, Culture and Evolution*.

54. It is therefore not surprising that Petty (*Political Anatomy of Ireland*) draws people of Irish and African descent into a commensurate relationship. In attempting to calculate the losses of Ireland's late rebellion, he estimates that "if you value the people who have been destroyed in Ireland, as Slaves and Negroes are usually rated, viz., at about £15 one with another; Men being sold for £25 and children £5 each; the value of the people lost will be about £10,355,00" (21).

55. Davenport, "Race Crossing in Jamaica," 227.

56. Bashford and Levine, *Oxford Handbook*; Dikötter, "Race Culture."

57. Davenport and Steggerda, *Race Crossing in Jamaica*. Punch cards produced "a two-dimensional portrait of people, people abstracted into numbers that machines could use," and the Jamaica study became the occasion for the racialization of this technology to quantify the worrying consequences of interracial sex (Lubar, "'Do Not Fold,'" 44).

58. Black, *IBM and the Holocaust*.

59. Deborah Thomas (*Exceptional Violence*) notes, "Within the Caribbean, if one wants to study violence, one goes to Jamaica" (1). I suggest that this geopolitical discursive process is also at work in the construction of queer violence.

60. T. Chin, "'Bullers' and 'Battymen'"; Cliff, *No Telephone to Heaven*; Powell, *Small Gathering of Bones*; Silvera, "Man Royals and Sodomites."

61. Human Rights Watch, "Hated to Death."

62. Padgett, "Most Homophobic Place."

63. Reports on the violence that gender and sexual minorities on the island experience include Human Rights Watch, *Not Safe at Home*; J-FLAG, *Annual Country Status Update*; Women's Empowerment for Change, *Health Seeking Behavior*; Inter-American Commission on Human Rights, "Discrimination"; J-FLAG, *Human Rights Violations*.

64. In his memoir, *The Fractalist*, Mandelbrot notes how the use of punch cards was part of the process of conducting computerized mathematical research at the company. The use of punch cards continued until the late 1960s, when punch cards were replaced by disk storage technology (Pugh, *Building IBM*).

65. Franklin E. Frazier is most associated with the argument about the destructive consequences of plantation society on Black forms of kinship in the New World. See Frazier, *The Negro Family*. The notion of repair that cannot fully escape conditions of violence is evident in J. S. Lewis, *Scammer's Yard*.

66. For more on this point, see Noxolo, "Caribbean In/Securities."

67. Higman, *Writing West Indian Histories*.

68. Sheller, *Citizenship from Below*, 3.

69. Queer scholars' engagements with the Global South often unfold in such a way that these sites "provide the exemplars, but rarely the epistemologies" (Arondekar and Patel, "Area Impossible," 152). On the contrary, like Arondekar, I see "an understanding of area studies as vitally constitutive of the histories of sexuality and vice versa" (Arondekar, *For the Record*, 5).

70. Eng and Puar, "Introduction: Left of Queer," 2; Amin, "Genealogies of Queer Theory," 17.

71. Higman, "Development of Historical Disciplines," 17–18.

72. Gupta and Ferguson, "Beyond 'Culture.'" Ghisyawan (*Erotic Cartographies*) takes on the question of space in a different way and considers the contemporary subjective space making practices of same gender desiring Trinidadian women as a site of decolonization.

73. Mitchell, "The Stage of Modernity." Trouillot ("North Atlantic Universals") makes a similar claim in describing the material and organizational features of world capitalism as a condition for the possibility of modernity.

74. Foucault, *The History of Sexuality*, 1:141, 143. John D'Emilio's discussion of capitalism and sexual subjectivity in the United States similarly envisions a geographically bounded modernity (D'Emilio, "Capitalism and Gay Identity"). D'Emilio maintains that it was only in the nineteenth century with the development of a system of wage labor, which allowed individuals to make a living independent of existing family structures, that it became possible for same-gender eroticism to coalesce into personal identity. US imperialism does not figure into his analysis of the sexual politics of capitalist transformation in the United States. His characterization of capitalism as enabling greater individual autonomy also does not necessarily apply in settings like the Caribbean, where capitalist incorporation produced not liberated workers but various forms of unfree labor.

75. Spivak, "Can the Subaltern Speak?," 290. Ann Stoler (*Race*) tackles Foucault's Eurocentrism from another angle, pursuing a chronological proposition that "colonial regimes anticipated the policing of sexuality in modern Europe" (42).

76. Trouillot, "North Atlantic Universals." David Scott (*Conscripts of Modernity*) refers to this process as being "conscripted into modernity."

77. Mintz, "Enduring Substances, Trying Theories," 298.

78. Higman, *Writing West Indian Histories*; Bolland, "Creolisation and Creole Societies."

79. Palmié, "Creolization and Its Discontents."

80. E. K. Brathwaite, *Contradictory Omens*.

81. Caribbean scholars have illustrated the ways that creolization discourses reproduce existing hierarchies of power to the exclusion of Black and Indigenous as well as poor and working-class subjects. See D. A. Thomas, *Modern Blackness*; S. Jackson, *Creole Indigeneity*; Kamugisha, *Beyond Coloniality*. While recognizing the material violences enacted in the name of creolization, I remain invested in what Kamau Brathwaite describes as the fluidity and open-endedness of this concept. Brathwaite's thinking about creolization in *The Development of Creole Society in Jamaica* (1971) takes on new forms in his *Contradictory Omens* (1974) and then again in "Caliban, Ariel, and Unprospero in the Conflict of Creoliza-tion" (1977). In this 1977 discussion of creolization, he notes, "My model of cre-olization has therefore in many senses been considerably extended; it has become, for one thing, less linear and 'progressive,' more prismatic, and includes more comprehensively than formerly a sense of cultural interaction not only among all elements of the 'tropical plantation' but also between these elements at certain metropolitan aspects (look at popular music for instance) of the continent" (41).

82. Khan, "Journey to the Center." It is worth noting that this association was at work in Charles Davenport's interest in Jamaica for his 1926 eugenics study, given the way that it invoked the danger of interracial intimacies.

83. For Sidney Mintz ("Enduring Substances, Trying Theories"), this modernity necessarily entailed being open to forms of difference and "ways of socializing without recourse to previously learned forms" (296).

84. Brathwaite, *Contradictory Omens*, 19. Sidney Mintz (*Caribbean Trans-formations*) notes, "Masters might acquire temporary sexual partners of slave status and different culture, while aspiring eventually to return to Europe and marry legitimately there; or they might maintain mistresses though married to European wives who accompanied them in their Caribbean exile; or, finally, they might marry wives who were originally of slave status and different culture and legitimize their children (if legally permitted) as part of their settling down in the Caribbean colony. All three patterns occurred in the Caribbean area; each suggests a somewhat different answer to the problems of creolization, and the emergence of national cultures in the area" (308).

85. For this reason, Faith Smith ("Sexing the Citizen") contends that "by virtue of being indigenous, African or Asian, and even by residing in the tropics, one is probably already marked as deviant, queer, or perverse" (8).

86. This position differs from that of DeCaires Narain and Ilmonen, who distinguish between queer and creole as analytical practices. DeCaires Narain, "Naming Same-Sex Desire"; Ilmonen, "Creolizing the Queer."

87. Foucault, *The Archaeology of Knowledge*, 145.

88. E. K. Brathwaite, "Caribbean Man," 9. Halberstam (*Female Masculinity*) notes that scavenger methodology "uses different methods to collect and produce information on subjects who have been deliberately or accidentally excluded from traditional studies of human behavior" (13).

Chapter One. Queer Jamaica, 1494–1998

1. To take a fractal approach to Jamaican queerness is to adopt Mayra Santos-Febres's insistence that fractals illustrate the multiplicity of what appears to be one (Santos-Febres, "The Fractal Caribbean").

2. Indeed, Charles Davenport's 1926 survey on race crossing, which I discussed in the introduction, included data collection in Grand Cayman because it was considered to be part of Jamaica at the time. Davenport and Steggerda, *Race Crossing in Jamaica*.

3. C. J. Robinson, *Black Marxism*; Kempadoo, *Sexing the Caribbean*; Hong, *Ruptures of American Capital*; Speed, *Incarcerated Stories*; Ferguson, *Aberrations in Black*.

4. For narratives of Jamaica and its Indigenous people prior to European arrival, see Atkinson, *The Earliest Inhabitants*.

5. Hulme, *Colonial Encounters*.

6. Trexler, *Sex and Conquest*; Goldberg, "Sodomy in the New World"; Morgensen, "Settler Homonationalism."

7. Burg, *Sodomy*.

8. E. K. Brathwaite, *Development of Creole Society*.

9. Mair, *Historical Study*.

10. Walker, *Jamaica Ladies*.

11. Tinsley, "Black Atlantic, Queer Atlantic."

12. Hortense Spillers has referred to this process as ungendering. Spillers, "Mama's Baby, Papa's Maybe."

13. Bush, *Slave Women*.

14. Higman, *Slave Population*.

15. S. Turner, *Contested Bodies*; Morgan, "Slave Women."

16. Richard Price ("Introduction") maintains that this gender "imbalance" was generally characteristic of maroon communities across the Americas.

17. Kopytoff, "Early Political Development"; Thompson, "Gender and Marronage."

18. F. Smith, "Sexing the Citizen," 2.

19. Nugent, *Lady Nugent's Journal*.

20. Spillers, "Mama's Baby, Papa's Maybe."

21. D. Hall, *In Miserable Slavery*. While colonial authorities constructed enslaved men's sexuality as a threat, particularly to European women, few studies have examined sexual relations between enslaved men and free (or freed) people in the Caribbean. Exceptions include Bost, "Traumatizing Black Masculinities"; A. Thomas, "'Outcasts from the World.'"

22. Jordan, "American Chiaroscuro."

23. Hurwitz and Hurwitz, "A Token of Freedom."

24. Mair, *Historical Study*.

25. Holt, "Essence of the Contract."

26. C. Hall, "Gender Politics."

27. Brereton, "Family Strategies."

28. Deborah Thomas (*Modern Blackness*) describes respectability as "a value complex emphasizing the cultivation of education, thrift, industry, self-sufficiency via landownership, moderate Christian living, community uplift, the constitution of family through legal marriage and related gendered expectations, and leadership by the educated middle classes" (5–6). See also Wilson, "Reputation and Respectability"; Besson, "Reputation and Respectability Reconsidered."

29. Though sexual offenses amounted to only 1 percent of total prosecutions (30 cases) between 1750 and 1834, in the two decades after emancipation they constituted 14 percent of total prosecutions (371 cases). Dalby, "'Such a Mass,'" 136–37.

30. Sheller, "Quasheba, Mother, Queen."

31. Sheller, "Acting as Free Men."

32. A. Thomas, "'Outcasts from the World.'"

33. Colonial authorities experimented with European indentureship as a means of fostering white settlement. Brathwaite refers to these workers as "secondary whites." E. K. Brathwaite, *Development of Creole Society*.

34. Look Lai, *Indentured Labor, Caribbean Sugar*.

35. Verene Shepherd (*Transients to Settlers*) notes that Jamaican planters "saw [Indian] women as desirable immigrants only in light of their ability to satisfy the domestic and sexual needs of male workers and would support single women only if they formed permanent attachments to male laborers on arrival. The feeling was that 'a woman who is not occupied other than in cooking her husband's food is more likely to get into mischief.' This was a euphemism for 'sexual mischief,' the planters being of the view that single women were generally prostitutes and 'women of doubtful character'" (50).

36. Lokaisingh-Meighoo, "Jahaji Bhai"; Khan, "Voyages across Indenture."

37. Shepherd, *Transients to Settlers*.

38. Moore and Johnson, "'We Are Heathen.'"

39. Look Lai, *Indentured Labor, Caribbean Sugar*.

40. Walton Look Lai (*Indentured Labor, Caribbean Sugar*) refers to an instance of an Indian indentured worker in British Guiana who fled the plantation to live in an Amerindian community. While it is unclear whether Indian workers either during or after their indentureship developed relationships with Jamaican Maroon communities, perhaps the practice of Islam among some Maroon communities may have been a draw to some Indian Muslims. See Afroz, "The Manifestation of Tawhid."

41. Look Lai, *Indentured Labor, Caribbean Sugar*.

42. Lowe, *Intimacy of Four Continents*; Lee-Loy, *Searching for Mr. Chin*. Jamaican planters spatially separated indentured and formerly enslaved workers not only via housing but also through gendered distribution of work. They assigned Africans to work gangs for rigorous labor on the basis of their supposed physical

superiority to Indians. In contrast, Indian women and men were grouped together to perform "women's work" (Shepherd, *Transients to Settlers*).

43. Look Lai, *Indentured Labor, Caribbean Sugar.*

44. Bryan, "Creolisation."

45. Both elite and ex-slave classes in the British West Indies engaged in practices of migration in the post-emancipation period. Thomas-Hope ("Establishment of a Migration Tradition") states, "The preoccupation of the post-emancipation upper class with maintaining its wealth was matched by lower-class dedication to consolidating its freedom. It should not be surprising, therefore, that when their economic base was threatened by economic depression, upper class families left the islands, taking their money with them" (66).

46. Though travel was less available to Indian indentured workers, who were required to stay in Jamaica for the duration of their contracts and remain on the island for at least five years afterward, several hundred Indians did migrate from Jamaica to Panama, Cuba, and other Latin American countries in the late nineteenth century. Look Lai, *Indentured Labor, Caribbean Sugar*, 117; Shepherd, *Transients to Settlers*, 112, 137.

47. Roberts, *The Population of Jamaica.*

48. Senior, "The Colon People, Part 2."

49. Putnam, *The Company They Kept.*

50. Though Jamaican migrant women may have had more economic flexibility than men, their economic existence was more precarious, and they often resorted to taking on a mix of jobs—domestic labor, laundry service, huckstering—to make ends meet (Flores-Villalobos, "'Freak Letters'").

51. J. Parker, "Empire's Angst." These and other forms of discipline predominantly impacted Jamaica's poor and Black migrants and had less effect on the much smaller segment of the island's mobile white and brown professional and merchant classes who were able to find commonalities with elites in their host countries. Olive Senior ("The Colon People") thus notes, "While the white and near white Jamaican merchant, professional or 'white collar' classes could identify with and share in the life of an Isthmus 'elite' of other nationalities, the labouring class frequently met with antagonism and hostility" (62). She goes on to highlight the vulnerabilities that women across Jamaica's class strata faced, given the heightened economic precarity of the period: "Opportunities in Jamaica were scarce for everyone. For the young women who had been thrown out of work as seamstresses with the introduction of the sewing machine, prostitution seemingly offered the only alternative means of livelihood" (64).

52. Reena Goldthree ("'Vive La France!'") notes that although the British War Office eventually permitted Indian subjects from the West Indies to enlist, it initially restricted these recruits on the basis that Indians were already considered to be well represented among the fighting forces of the empire. World War I prevented indentured workers from returning to India at the end of their contracts—no repatriations took place between 1916 and 1923—but it is not clear

to what extent this may have affected their decisions about whether to become involved in the war (Shepherd, *Transients to Settlers*, 99).

53. R. Smith, *Jamaican Volunteers*.

54. Bean, *Jamaican Women*.

55. Vassell, "Movement for the Vote."

56. Bean, *Jamaican Women*. Patrick Bryan also notes that Chinese Jamaican women obtained employment in the American Naval Department ("Creolisation," 199).

57. Goldthree, "Writing New Histories."

58. Bean, "'Dangerous Class of Woman.'"

59. Bolland, "Labor Protests."

60. H. Johnson, "The Anti-Chinese Riots." Tensions of interracial sex also precipitated the anti-Chinese riots of 1965, which were a response to the perceived injustice of a Chinese man setting aside his Black mistress to marry a Chinese wife (Lee, "The Chinese in Jamaica").

61. If they were forced to return to Jamaica owing to changing circumstances in their host societies, migrant laborers questioned why Indian and Chinese subjects were not similarly required to leave Jamaica. See Shepherd, *Transients to Settlers*; Bryan, "Creolisation."

62. Lind, "Adjustment Patterns"; J. Levy, "Economic Role."

63. Bryan, "Creolisation."

64. Bandopadhyay, "Romancing Jamaica."

65. Bair, "True Women, Real Men."

66. French and Ford-Smith, *Women and Organization*.

67. Ford-Smith, "Unruly Virtues."

68. French, "Colonial Policy towards Women." It is also noteworthy that the commission commented on Indian intimacies and recommended that the marriages conducted by Indian religious officials be considered valid and legitimate. Shepherd, *Transients to Settlers*.

69. De Barros, *Reproducing the British Caribbean*.

70. T. Robinson, "Mass Weddings in Jamaica."

71. Edmondson, *Making Men*.

72. T. Robinson, "The Properties of Citizens"; French, "Colonial Policy towards Women."

73. French, "Colonial Policy towards Women."

74. Cook, *Queer Domesticities*. Here it is worth noting that Thomas Foster (*Rethinking Rufus*) found enslaved valets to be particularly vulnerable to sexual violence from white men in the United States.

75. Romain, *Race, Sexuality and Identity*. Cobham's analysis of the intimate relationship between Jamaican writer Claude McKay and his English patron, Walter Jekyll, shares structural similarities with the relationship between Nelson and Stanley (Cobham, "Jekyll and Claude").

76. De Barros, *Reproducing the British Caribbean*.

77. Bourbonnais, *Birth Control*.

78. Roberts, *The Population of Jamaica*.

79. Bourbonnais, "'Dangerously Large.'"

80. While early birth control efforts did not conceive of men as their primary target audience, the unexpected interest of men prompted these interventions to consider men in future iterations of their programming. But it was not until the late 1970s that Jamaican academics and social welfare workers began to see men as legitimate subjects of family-planning initiatives. See, for instance, Whitehead, "Men, Family and Family Planning."

81. Bourbonnais, "Class, Colour and Contraception."

82. By the time Jamaica gained independence in 1962, birth control—reframed as an issue of family planning—had become accepted as a matter of national concern and would be further enforced with the establishment of the Family Planning Unit in the island's Ministry of Health in 1966 and the foundation of Jamaica's National Family Planning Board in 1967.

83. Rex Nettleford ("Introduction: The Fledgling Years") recalls that Jamaica's independence "brought no sense of fundamental change. Things certainly did not fall apart. In fact, a great many things, like the class structure, underlined in color, continued to appear immutable. The social order did not collapse. The political order merely moved from one phase to the next" (3). In contrast, Faith Smith ("Soundings with My Sisters") recounts her parents' joyous celebration upon learning of Jamaica's new government elected in 1972, noting, "In this view, Jamaica's 1960s were not yet distinguishable from colonial time, and genuine independence, falsely promised since August 1962, could not properly begin until 1972" (124). Straddling the middle ground of these assessments, Deborah Thomas (*Political Life*) notes that the immediate post-independence period was marked by an affective register of expectancy that produced technologies of prophetic waiting.

84. Antrobus, *The Rise and Fall*; Reddock, "Women's Organizations"; Rosenberg, "The New Woman."

85. DeVeer, "Sex Roles."

86. Ford-Smith, *Lionheart Gal*.

87. Henry-Wilson, "Status of the Jamaican Woman."

88. LaFont and Pruitt, "The Colonial Legacy."

89. Lewis, "Walter Rodney"; Nettleford, Smith, and Augier, *Report on the Rastafari Movement*.

90. Stuart Hall ("Minimal Selves") notes, "Black is an identity which had to be learned and could only be learned in a certain moment. In Jamaica that moment is the 1970s" (45).

91. Chevannes, "Healing the Nation."

92. The replacement of "concubinage" with "common-law marriage" in the 1943 and 1946 West Indian censuses made it difficult to trace the way these race and gender asymmetries continued to pervade interclass nonmarital intimacies. Tracy Robinson ("The Properties of Citizens") notes that this transformation

marked a reorientation in the accounting practices of the colonial state, "from the hybrid, interracial, and hierarchical intimacies associated with concubinage, to the intra-racial, intra-class, and less fluid Black unions associated with common-law marriage" (426).

93. Because their standing as men is tied to their sexual exploits and their ability to provide for their families, elite men's "outside relations" do not harm—and in fact may enhance—their masculinity. On the other hand, the fact that elite women's status as "ladies" is tied to their positions as mothers, wives, and family members, means that they are encouraged to accept (or at least tolerate) their husbands' philandering while also refraining from affairs of their own that may jeopardize their marriage and therefore class standing. See Douglas, *The Power of Sentiment*.

94. Lisa Douglas (*The Power of Sentiment*) maintains that elite women (whether single or married) face greater condemnation for inappropriate intimate relationships than do elite men and often participate in them only when they leave the island.

95. Douglas, *The Power of Sentiment*, 159.

96. Jamaica's experience was not unique but instead was part of the foreclosure of the global conditions of possibility for postcolonial socialism and the kind of nonaligned sovereignty envisioned by Bandung with the collapse of the Grenada Revolution in 1983 (Scott, *Omens of Adversity*, 4).

97. These policies included the privatization of public sectors, cutting back social services, devaluing the Jamaican dollar, imposing restraints on wages, liberalizing imports, and removing subsidies on consumer goods, including food. These policies stimulated export production, but they also produced greater unemployment, a dramatic rise in the cost of living, a decrease in wages, the deterioration of public health, and an increase in violence (including domestic violence). See McAfee, *Storm Signals*; LeFranc, *Consequences of Structural Adjustment*.

98. Antrobus, "Crisis, Challenge"; Harrison, "Gendered Politics and Violence"; Bolles, "Kitchens Hit by Priorities"; Antrobus, *The Rise and Fall*; Castello, "Where Have All the Feminists Gone."

99. Mullings, "Globalization, Tourism." Scholars such as Angelique Nixon (*Resisting Paradise*) investigate how Caribbean people unsettle the ways that neocolonial forms of power position them as objects of desire for Global North tourists, but in this chapter I attend more closely to the processes of positioning itself.

100. Pruitt and LaFont, "For Love and Money."

101. Although less scholarship of this period discusses male sex workers with male clients, Royes (*Jamaican Men*) makes note of "bisexual hustlers or prostitutes, who work primarily in Kingston or tourist areas; for them, sexual activities are simply a way of earning a living" (9). The fact that men were turning to sex with men as a means of survival prompted greater acceptance of homosexuality among some Jamaicans. One of Chevannes's informants stated, "'Wi no support batty-ism but me kinda get a understandin.' For if is a uman pussy cause her fi be

so lucky, then some man, realizing se [that] price de 'pon dem batty, wi' sell it! Das why mi woulda never beat a battyman again!'" (Chevannes, *Learning to Be a Man*, 203).

102. S. Campbell, Perkins, and Mohammed, "'Come to Jamaica.'"

103. In one of the earliest studies of sex work, Ross-Frankson (*The Economic Crisis*) notes five types of sex workers, including "hospitality prostitutes," who are "usually from middle class backgrounds and may have regular office or bank jobs," as well as "kept prostitutes," whose "economic mainstay is entirely dependent on a wealthy man. They live well and don't intend to drop below a certain level" (12).

104. Stolzoff, *Wake the Town*.

105. Ulysse, "Uptown Ladies."

106. D. A. Thomas, *Modern Blackness*.

107. C. Cooper, "Slackness Hiding from Culture."

108. C. Cooper, *Sound Clash*.

109. Harrison, "International Drug Economy."

110. T. Chin, "'Bullers' and 'Battymen'"; Gutzmore, "Casting the First Stone!"

111. Barry Chevannes ("Sexual Practices") thus notes that "attitudes toward homosexuality are changing, at least among the middle classes, at which level male homosexuals can function openly" (24–25). This might be because middle-class men do not have the same kind of homosocial networks as lower-class men and their sense of masculinity is not as tied to their sense of their peer group. See De Veer, "Sex Roles." Yet even in working-class communities, Chevannes concedes, known homosexuals "are tolerated in the community. Because they were born and grew up there, people have learned to accept them and do them no harm provided 'dem never iina fuss wid anybody'" (*Learning to Be a Man*, 203). Sobo's observations in *One Blood* suggest that this insight may be true of lesbians in rural communities. "The village woman most infamous for lesbianism, Sarah, was well liked by many young men and by some young women. Other people scorned her, but Sarah was never beaten or strongly accosted. Occasionally (and rarely in public), people might 'pass remarks' about her masculine and jealous personality (while she kept many intimate 'friends' she allowed her 'inside' lover no one else), but Sarah made it a point to 'live good' with others so no one had cause to 'trace' her experiences" (217).

112. Though Ellis ("Out and Bad") notes that a later period of dancehall makes space for queerness even amid its supposed articulations of homophobia.

113. Skelton, "Boom, Bye, Bye"; Saunders, "Is Not Everything Good to Eat."

114. L. Williams, "Homophobia."

Chapter Two. Knowledge

1. Bush, "Colonial Research"; French, "Colonial Policy."

2. *Daily Gleaner*, "Lady Foot Hits at Illegitimacy," January 11, 1952, 1.

3. Kempadoo, *Sexing the Caribbean*; Barrow, *Family in the Caribbean*.

4. T. Robinson, "The Properties of Citizens," 435.

5. Yet the work of these early social scientists did not constitute a complete break with coloniality. The emergence of kinship as an object of inquiry, the methods developed to study it, and the institutional infrastructure that supported this research were intimately connected to colonial knowledge formations. For instance, Jamaica's first generation of anthropologists were trained in British social anthropology dominated by structural functionalist paradigms. M. G. Smith, Edith Clarke, and Fernando Henriques studied with Daryll Forde, Bronislaw Malinowski, and Meyer Fortes, respectively. Charles Carnegie ("The Fate of Ethnography") maintains that UCWI was "formed and nurtured in a colonial matrix" in which the "official sponsorship of social scientific research . . . owes in part to changing views about the methods of colonial rule being formulated in other parts of the Empire" (6).

6. T. Robinson, "The Properties of Citizens."

7. Una Marson, "That 'Smelly Alley' Is the Fruit of Slavery," *Daily Gleaner*, January 20, 1952, 6.

8. Wills Isaacs, "'Smelly Alley,'" *Daily Gleaner*, January 22, 1952, 6.

9. Erman Brumwall, "Labour Gave Unanimous Backing to Isaac's Call for Inquiry," *Jamaica Times*, March 3, 1951, 3.

10. Munroe, *The Politics*.

11. Government of Jamaica, "Report of the Commission of Enquiry into the Police Force," 10.

12. *Jamaica Daily Express*, "Enquiry Hears Hint at Immoral Practice: Promotion Grouse Is Heavy," April 12, 1951, 3; *Jamaica Daily Express*, "Many Denials Are Heard as Inquiry Nears Close," May 12, 1951, 2; *Jamaica Daily Express*. "Force Gone Is Gone in Reverse under Its Present Rule," May 11, 1951, 4.

13. M. Chin, "Antihomosexuality."

14. D. K. Johnson, *The Lavender Scare*.

15. D. K. Johnson, "America's Cold War Empire."

16. *Daily Gleaner*, "KSAC Motion Asks for Anti-Communist Organization," June 14, 1948, 13.

17. Suffee, "Homosexuality and the Law"; Ellis, "Black Migrants, White Queers."

18. Interview with Sir John Wolfenden during his visit to the University College of the West Indies on January 17, 1960, University of the West Indies Archives.

19. Though focused on an earlier period, Rhonda Cobham's "Jekyll and Claude" explores the relationship between foreign men and same-gender eroticism in her analysis of the relationship between Englishman Walter Jekyll and Jamaican writer Claude McKay.

20. Wynter, *The Hills of Hebron*, 81–82.

21. Though focused on the United States, Woodward and Foster identify the complex relationships between slave masters and their valets, which often involved intimate violations. Woodard, *The Delectable Negro*; Foster, *Rethinking Rufus*.

22. Wynter, "Novel and History."

23. Morris Gilbert, "The Rise and Fall of Prophet Moses," *New York Times*, July, 15, 1962, 24; George Patton, "Bedward—in New Guise," *Daily Gleaner*, July 22, 1962, 14.

24. In his 1955 surveys of Kingston and eight rural communities, M. G. Smith (*West Indian Family Structure*) described the difficulty of obtaining information from research participants about their "mating" experience, noting that women were considerably more forthcoming with information about children and intimate relationships than men were. Such challenges were also noted in Blake, *Family Structure in Jamaica*, 34; Clarke, *My Mother Who Fathered Me*, 90–92.

25. M. G. Smith, *Kinship and Community*; Apter, "M. G. Smith"; Barrow, "Mating and Sexuality."

26. Henriques, *Jamaica*, 168–69.

27. F. F. Taylor, *To Hell with Paradise*, 160.

28. F. F. Taylor, *To Hell with Paradise*, 159.

29. Austin-Broos, "Gay Nights."

30. F. F. Taylor, *To Hell with Paradise*, 171.

31. Sheller, *Consuming the Caribbean*.

32. *Daily Gleaner*, "Wills O. Isaacs—Man of the Year," December, 25, 1960, 6.

33. Vendryes, *Barthé*.

34. M. Parker, *Goldeneye*, 86. The associations among whiteness, homosexuality, and foreignness also occluded the intimate lives of white Jamaicans Trevor Owens, a pioneer in Jamaica's fashion industry; and Archie Lindo, a leader in Jamaica's cultural nationalist movement. See Gregory, "The Fading History"; Lawrence, "Through Archie Lindo's Lens."

35. *Daily Gleaner*, "Archbishop Condemns Mobay Morals," February 16, 1954, 13.

36. *Daily Gleaner*, "6 Months for Indecent Assault," June 10, 1955, 22.

37. Henriques, *Family and Colour*, 86.

38. The religious practice is various spelled "Pocomania," "Pukkumania," and "Pukumania." Wedenoja ("Quest for Justice") notes that the term "Pocomania" has often been used derisively. Following Besson and Chevannes ("The Continuity-Creativity Debate"), I adopt the terminological convention "Pukumina."

39. Wynter, *The Hills of Hebron*, 61.

40. Curtin, *Two Jamaicas*.

41. G. E. Simpson, "Jamaican Revivalist Cults."

42. Henriques, *Family and Colour*.

43. G. E. Simpson, "Jamaican Revivalist Cults."

44. *Daily Gleaner*, "Ex-Councillor's Wife Gets Decree Nisi," July 2, 1954, 5.

45. G. E. Simpson, "Jamaican Revivalist Cults."

46. Kerr, *Personality and Conflict*, 89–90.

47. G. E. Simpson, "Jamaican Revivalist Cults," 404, 402.

48. G. E. Simpson, "Jamaican Revivalist Cults."

49. Kerr, *Personality and Conflict*, 90.

50. M. G. Smith, *A Framework for Caribbean Studies*, 5.

51. A recent *Gleaner* article on Revivalism in Jamaica gestured to this association. It noted, "There are two branches, the 60 Order or Revival Zion, and the 61 Order or Pocomania . . . for whatever reasons, Pocomania is much berated, even by some Zion Revivalists themselves. This negative attitude was vocalized recently in an interview with a pilgrim at the Zion Headquarters at Watt Town in St. Ann. 'In everything, there is good and bad. We have 60 and 61, 60 is clean, let me not say a thing more,' Linda Edwards, a long-time Zion Revival said" (P. Williams, "In the Spirit of Revival," *Daily Gleaner*, June 10, 2015).

52. Wekker, *The Politics of Passion*; Conner and Sparks, *Queering Creole Spiritual Traditions*; Tinsley, *Ezili's Mirrors*; Brown, "Mermaids and Journeymen" (229). On contemporary queer spiritual practices in the context of Hinduism in Trinidad, see Ghisyawan, *Erotic Cartographies*.

53. Alexander, *Pedagogies of Crossing*. See also Decena, *Circuits of the Sacred*; Lara, *Queer Freedom*.

54. John Forkman, "On the Level," *Daily Gleaner*, March 10, 1962, 9; Susan Lewis, "Jamaica: 'Most Beautiful Island,'" *Daily Gleaner*, April 16, 1957, 12; Susan Lewis, "First Guests at Arawak," *Daily Gleaner*, February 26, 1957, 16; *Daily Gleaner*, "Pocomania Cult Act for Visitors," January 30, 1957, 15.

55. Calvin Bowen, "Reception for Queen at King's House: It Was a Glittering Welcome," *Daily Gleaner*, November 27, 1953, 6.

56. *Daily Gleaner*, "Della: An Unfaithful Picture of a Shepard's Life," June 29, 1954, 8.

57. G. E. Simpson, "Jamaican Revivalist Cults," 342.

58. Henriques, *Jamaica*, 128.

59. Ranny Williams, "Nearly but Never," *Daily Gleaner*, June 14, 1954, 11; Adolphe Roberts, "Bedward the Revivalist," *Daily Gleaner*, January 31, 1960, 14; *Daily Gleaner*, "Bogus Bishops in Island-Wide Religious Racket," October 13, 1949, 1.

60. *Daily Gleaner*, "Man Shot in Riot at 'Poco' Orgy," July 2, 1952, 1; Curtin, *Two Jamaicas*, 171.

61. Seaga, "Cults in Jamaica."

62. Thames, "Two Happy People," 28–29.

63. Silvera, "Man Royals and Sodomites," 524–25.

64. Central Bureau of Statistics, *Population Census of Jamaica 1960*.

65. Henriques, *Family and Colour*.

66. Edmondson, *Caribbean Middlebrow*, 7.

67. Gray, *Radicalism and Social Change*.

68. Curtin, *Two Jamaicas*; Heuman, *Between Black and White*; M. C. Campbell, *The Dynamics of Change*.

69. D. A. Thomas, *Modern Blackness*, 30.

70. T. Robinson, "The Properties of Citizens."

71. Henriques, *Family and Colour*, 98.

72. Ellis, "Between Windrush and Wolfden"; Romain, *Race, Sexuality and Identity*.

73. He initially volunteered as a special constable in 1938 to quell the labor riots in Kingston, which were part of a broader pattern of social unrest across the island and the Caribbean region during the Great Depression. However, witnessing the plight of the masses prompted a social and political conversion that led him to join the insurgency.

74. Before his passing in 1955, he wrote more than two hundred short stories and poems and more than sixty stage and radio plays (E. K. Brathwaite, "The Unborn Body").

75. Hawthorne, *The Writer in Transition*, 7–8.

76. Hawthorne, *The Writer in Transition*, 41. Jean D'Costa has also taken note of Mais's preoccupation with sexuality (Jean D'Costa, "The Treatment of Sexuality in the Novels of Roger Mais" [1974], Special Library, University Pamphlet PR9349. M15.z6, University of the West Indies Special Collections, Mona, Jamaica).

77. Carr, "Roger Mais."

78. Mais, *Black Lightning*, 68–69.

79. Mais, *Black Lightning*, 33.

80. In the novel, Amos plays the accordion.

81. Mais, *Black Lightning*, 92–93. It is worth noting that Jake and Amos's discussion about whether the unnamed thing that draws them together is a result of "being born that way" or "we did it to ourselves" mirrors Henriques discussion of "natural" and "induced" homosexuality. Henriques, *Jamaica*.

82. Mais, *Black Lightning*, 163.

83. Mais, *Black Lightning*, 171–72.

84. E. K. Brathwaite, "The Unborn Body," 18. The Akan are a West African people with a cosmological spiritual tradition.

85. Carr, "Roger Mais," 4.

86. Edmondson, *Caribbean Middlebrow*, 11–12.

87. Wilson, "Reputation and Respectability." For a feminist critique of Wilson's thesis, see Besson, "Reputation and Respectability Reconsidered."

88. Rose Van Cuylenburg, "Smelly Alley," *Daily Gleaner*, January 26, 1952, 6.

Chapter Three. The Body

1. *Daily Gleaner*, "AIDS Is Here," September 22, 1983, 1.

2. *Daily Gleaner*, "AIDS Kills Twenty in Canada," August 15, 1983, 11; *Daily Gleaner*, "Diseases That Plague Homosexuals," January 17, 1982, 25.

3. Jamaica Ministry of Health, *National Plan for AIDS*.

4. Figueroa et al., "HIV/AIDS Epidemic in Jamaica."

5. On syphilis and gonorrhea, see A. Brathwaite, *Some Facts about V.D.*; Jamaica Medical Department, *Report of the Medical Services*. On family planning and population control, see J. Briggs, "'As Fool-Proof as Possible'"; Bourbonnais, "Class, Colour and Contraception."

6. Author interview with Ian McKnight, July 10, 2018.

7. Kempadoo, *Sexing the Caribbean*, 170.

8. I chose HIV/AIDS as the entry point from which to construct representations of same-gender eroticism in Jamaica's past, but it is unclear how, or the extent to which, this illness played a role in the ways that same-gender-desiring Jamaicans from across the island's interlocking hierarchies of race, class, and gender understood themselves in the period under study. (For an exception, see Brotherton, "Contagious Bodies.") The overt hostility toward homosexuality articulated in Jamaica's public sphere discouraged same-gender-desiring Jamaicans in this era from crafting first-person narratives that might otherwise serve as a counterhistory to the account offered here. It would not be until J-FLAG was established in 1998 that (some) same-gender-desiring subjects would have an institutionalized base from which to articulate their understandings of themselves and their concerns—separate and apart from HIV/AIDS—in the Jamaican public sphere.

9. Briggs, *Reproducing Empire*; Levine, *Prostitution, Race and Politics*.

10. Although the novel is set in 1978, when AIDS had not yet been officially diagnosed in Jamaica, Powell describes this work as reckoning with the politics of HIV (K. Campbell, "Patricia Powell").

11. In the context of addressing sexually transmitted infections (STI's) more broadly, history making played an important role in the work of CI's, because the type and stage of STI determined how much of the infected person's sexual history the CI's had to construct. For instance, in the case of primary syphilis, CI's had to obtain the sexual contacts of the patient within the past three to four weeks. Epidemiological Research and Training Unit, *Role of the Contact Investigator*, 2.

12. Reddock and Roberts, "Introduction."

13. Jamaican media (newspaper, television, radio, film) occasionally carried "homosexual" content from or about other countries—particularly North American and Western European countries—but overt discussions of Jamaican same-gender intimacies were limited before the 1980s. When they were discussed at all, they largely included news coverage of crimes under the Offences Against the Persons Act involving sexual relations between two men. The work of the Jamaican activist organizations, The Gay Freedom Movement (1977–84), and later Jamaica AIDS Support were important exceptions to this trend; members of these groups called in to Jamaican radio stations, wrote letters to the editors of Jamaican newspapers, and attempted to get on Jamaican television to normalize and combat violence directed toward same-gender intimacies and gender nonconformity.

14. *Daily Gleaner*, "3219 AIDS Virus Cases Here," November 3, 1987, 1.

15. S. J. Smith and Stover, *Impact*.

16. Figueroa et al., "HIV/AIDS Epidemic in Jamaica."

17. Figueroa et al., "HIV/STD Control." In his important work on HIV/AIDS in Trinidad and Tobago, Lyndon Gill (*Erotic Islands*) critically analyzes and contests the claim that men who have sex with men (MSM) have disproportionately high rates of HIV/AIDS. My aim here is less about deconstructing the facticity of such claims and more about what such claims do.

18. Jamaican medical authorities certainly held that the risk of contracting HIV/AIDS also applied to other groups, such as sex workers, intravenous drug users, and those whose work involved travel, including migrant farmworkers and informal commercial importers (ICI's). These groups differed from men who have sex with men in that they were already identified by Jamaican state, medical, and/or academic institutions as worthy of documentation, study, and/or intervention.

19. In 1988, in the first nationwide survey conducted by the Ministry of Health to determine Jamaicans' knowledge of AIDS, virtually all respondents maintained that HIV could be spread through sex, blood, and mother-to-child transmission (Smith and Stover, *AIDS and Sexually Transmitted Diseases*). Yet many respondents also believed that the virus could be contracted through mosquitoes, touching someone who had AIDS, or coming into contact with something that someone with AIDS had touched (such as a toilet seat). Similarly, when the term "homosexuality" was used in the Jamaican news media, it was often accompanied by a definition, such as "homosexuality is sexual relations between people of the same sex," as though readers would be unaware of the term. Yet actual usage of the word often extended beyond erotic activity to include descriptions of non-normative gender expression/presentation. And even when "homosexuality" was used to describe sex between men, it was not always clear that both parties necessarily understood themselves as "men." Accounts of the period reveal that it was not uncommon for one of the participants in such "homosexual" encounters to use a name or wear clothing conventionally associated with women, which suggests that the gender attribution of "men" may be misplaced. As the topic came into widespread public conversation, Jamaicans raised several questions about homosexuality. Was homosexuality to be understood as a kind of person-hood, such that homosexuals should be granted certain human/civil rights? Or was homosexuality simply a behavior to be evaluated in terms of morality and Christian principles? And to what extent might the social and medical sciences, with their investigations into family relations and biological patterning, be constructive in interpreting homosexuality?

20. Hope Enterprises, *Report on Pretest*, 3. Rosie Stone, in *No Stone Unturned*, noted that she was compelled to dispel rumors about her husband's sexual orientation when it became known that he was HIV-positive. In contrast, although one of Sobo's rural Jamaican informants maintained that AIDS was primarily a disease associated with men who have sex with men, Sobo suggests that most of her interlocutors did not share the belief that only male homosexuals contract AIDS.

21. Jamaica Ministry of Health, *National Plan for AIDS*.

22. Figueroa et al., "HIV/STD Control."

23. One television public service announcement (PSA) produced by the Ministry of Health involved three men drinking in a bar, discussing AIDS. One of the PSA's main messages, which was well understood by test audiences, was the notion that "anybody can have AIDS . . . not just homosexuals" (Hope Enterprises, *Evaluation of AIDS Messages*, 43). Despite the success of this messaging, Jamaicans

continued to conflate employment in the sexual health sector with sexual orientation. (Author interview with Peter Figueroa, June 27, 2018.)

24. In a focus group created to determine the effectiveness of existing public health messaging about HIV and STI's, one middle-class Jamaican man stated, "If yuh nuh get one or two episodes [of an STI] yuh nuh hard, when you get them you have yuh stripe" (Hope Enterprises, *Report on Pretest*, 15).

25. Author interview with Dr. Tina Hilton Kong, July 4, 2018.

26. Hope Enterprises, *Evaluation of AIDS Messages*.

27. On Buju Banton and homophobia in this period, see V. E. Turner, "Gay Communities Attack Buju Banton Lyrics," *Daily Gleaner*, October 24, 1992, 1. It is critical to note that Buju Banton has recently removed "Boom Bye Bye" from his discography. Yet even within this period, as lesbian and gay groups opposed the content of his lyrics, they also praised the Jamaican artist for his anti-AIDS initiatives. *XNews*, "'Gay' Groups Praise Buju Banton," June 28, 1994, 3. On the 1993 anti-gay rally in Kingston, see *Daily Gleaner*, "Civilians Turn Out for Gay Bashing," June 10, 1993, 3; *Jamaica Star*, "Gays Not Marching Today," June 16, 1993, 1; Norman Cuff, "Gays in for Attack If They March in Kingston," *Jamaica Herald*, June 6, 1993, 3A.

28. *Jamaica Observer*, "Prisoners Killed as Warders Strike," August 21, 1997, 1.

29. *Daily Gleaner*, "Army, Police Quell Riots," August 25, 1997, 1.

30. "Devon" is a pseudonym.

31. Heart-wrenching personal accounts of being mistreated by family members and others began appearing in the Jamaican news media in the early 1990s. See *Jamaica Herald*, "Driving AIDS Victims to Suicide," June 21, 1993, 1.

32. *Daily Gleaner*, "Terri-Ann Speaks about AIDS," October 4, 1994, 6.

33. Jafari Allen ("Friendship as a Mode") and Lyndon Gill ("Chatting Back an Epidemic") also illustrate how HIV/AIDS operates as a site through which to organize forms of sociality around same-gender eroticism in Cuba and Trinidad and Tobago, respectively.

34. JAS reported that during the years 1992–94, more than four hundred men had attended its weekly support groups (Jamaica Ministry of Health, *AIDS Control and Prevention Project*, 1994, 17). Gender became a critical issue in the sexual politics of JAS, and women within GLABCOM soon established the group Women for Women to address the specific experiences and needs of same-gender-loving women (author interview with Lena [pseudonym], July 6, 2018).

35. Hopwood, "Study of Gender Relationships."

36. *Daily Gleaner*, "Worried about AIDS? Call the Helpline," October 16, 1994, 12.

37. *Daily Gleaner*, "Worried about AIDS?," 12.

38. *Daily Gleaner*, "Worried about AIDS?," 12.

39. "Patricia Henry" is a pseudonym. The following quotations from Henry are from the author's interview with her on June 18, 2019.

40. A. Brathwaite, *Contact Investigation*.

41. Freidlob and Emerson, *Evaluation*.

42. Epidemiological Research and Training Unit, *Role of the Contact Investigator*.

43. "Tony Samuels" is a pseudonym. The following quotations from Samuels are from the author's interview with him on July 24, 2018.

44. Epidemiological Research and Training Unit, *Role of the Contact Investigator*, 9.

45. Although it is outside the scope of this chapter, the ways CI's came to know the economies of sex work in Jamaica is a topic that deserves future study. For instance, the rise of go-go clubs in Jamaica in the 1990s and the movement of women through these clubs across the island—so as to avoid recognition in their hometowns—meant that CI's were compelled to develop techniques of tracking hypermobile forms of eroticism.

46. This initial strategy involved two enzyme-linked immunosorbent assay (ELISA) tests followed by one rapid HIV test (author interview with Dr. Evadne Williams, July 2, 2019).

47. A. Brathwaite, *Contact Investigation*.

48. A. Brathwaite, *Contact Investigation*.

49. A. Brathwaite, *Contact Investigation*.

50. Author interview with Patricia Henry, June 18, 2019.

51. *Jamaica Herald*, "HIV/AIDS Prejudice," May 19, 1994, 6.

52. "Andrea Bateson" is a pseudonym. The following quotations from Bateson are from the author's interview with her on July 19, 2019.

53. Ministry of Health Epidemiological Unit, "Minutes and Report of Senior Staff Meeting," Kingston, April 12, 1995; Jillson-Boostrom, *AIDS in Jamaica*; author interview with Patricia Henry, June 18, 2019.

54. Keeling, "Looking for M."

55. Ministry of Health Epidemiological Unit, "Minutes and Report," 4.

56. Ministry of Health Epidemiological Unit, "Minutes and Report," 4.

57. Powell's novel *A Small Gathering of Bones* imaginatively maps how same-gender-desiring Jamaicans refuse health workers' requests for information as a protective strategy against the violence that such disclosures may produce. When Dale goes to visit Ian, who has been brought to the hospital to be treated for the symptoms of what are presumably AIDS-related conditions, the receptionist greets Dale with hostility and scorn when he requests Ian's room number. She discloses that Ian was found in Nanny Sharpe Park—a cruising spot where men were known to share erotic encounters. Dale later finds Ian's physician, who begins grilling him for information on his patient. "'They find him in the park, you know. Him go there often? Him one of them funny types? Where you know him from?' . . . Him didn't see what it matter; a sick man is a sick man. Why it should matter who him sleep with, where they find him? Dale clear his throat, voice cold, dull 'We attend the same church.'" In response to the demand for knowledge about Ian's sexuality that is both irrelevant to his health and serves as the basis on which to malign him further, Dale refuses the doctor's terms of engagement and instead shifts the register of the interaction from one space (Nanny Sharpe Park) to another (Ebenezer Open Bible Church) (Powell, *A Small Gathering of Bones*, 82).

58. A. Brathwaite, *Contact Investigation.*

59. *Daily Gleaner*, "Civilians Turn Out"; Norman Cuff, "Gays in for Attack."

60. Trevor Dennis (pseudonym), the first CI assigned to Jamaica's parish of Portland, recalled the lengths he went to, to maintain the secret of his patient's HIV status. "The first time, she asked me to collect her medication for her because she couldn't be seen going there [health center]. And when I collect the medication and went to her, she tear [up] the package. She tear [up] the package and throw it in the garbage bin. So nobody can tie her to that. She couldn't take the medication home. She had to hide it. She never come here, she used to go to University [of the West Indies in Kingston] for consultation. Up to now, I don't think anybody in the parish aside from me know about her" (author interview with Trevor Dennis, June 26, 2019). Rosie Stone's autobiographical text *No Stone Unturned*, in which she details her life and the life of her family after she has found out that her husband, Carl Stone, has given her HIV/AIDS, similarly illustrates how she solicited the support of health professionals to keep Carl's HIV status a secret.

61. Dr. Tina Hilton Kong recalls needing to educate CI's who were too tight-lipped about their patients. "In the early days we kind of had to 'deprogram' contact investigators because they were the first people that had to meet persons and get the contacts and so on. They were very secretive. Not confidential. They were very secretive about contacts. Which is good. But over time we had to tell them 'It's not a secret, its confidentiality.' I did lectures with CAST [College of Arts Science and Technology] and UTech [University of Technology] who trained public health inspectors and nurses and so on and every time, any kind of lecture you gave, that always came up. [I would get comments like] 'They are some health care workers who know those who are HIV-positive and they don't let us know! And that's unfair because we are being put at risk!' And I had to throw it back on them and say 'Well, many times we don't know. We have to take universal precautions.' Even to this day there is still a little bit of that, but much less so. But there was a time when other staff wanted to know who is [HIV-positive] and when they did, it was sometimes to the detriment of the patient. There was a reason to be secretive at the time" (author interview with Dr. Tina Hilton Kong, July 4, 2018).

62. *XNews*, "Lesbian Lover May Have AIDS," December 5, 1996, 27; *Jamaica Herald*, "Worry over AIDS in Women's Prisons," August 31, 1997, 1A.

63. A. Brathwaite, STD *Control Programme.*

64. In an article about the first case of HIV/AIDS in Jamaica, the journalist for the *Gleaner* writes, "While AIDS is said to be most prevalent among homosexuals, sources close to the [first] case here said that this case was not related to homosexuality" (*Daily Gleaner*, "AIDS Is Here").

65. "For the first time, those with the disease [HIV/AIDS] are women indicating that the disease is being spread through heterosexual contact" (*Daily Gleaner*, "24 Die Here from AIDS," November 24, 1987, 1).

66. Though a woman, Terri-Ann was the first person to publicly "come out" as HIV-positive in Jamaica, on the television program Tuesday Forum in 1994, she

reported that she contracted the virus from her boyfriend. *Daily Gleaner*, "Terri-Ann Speaks."

67. *XNews*, "Why I Am a Lesbian," June 17, 1993, 11; *Jamaica Star*, "Tell Me Pastor: I Have Bisexual Feelings," June 9, 1993, 6; *XNews*, "Lesbian DJ Beats Lover," May 7, 1997, 1.

68. *XNews*, "Lesbians Giving Males Stiff Competition," March 19, 1997, 3; *XNews*, "Man Loses Wife to Lesbian," July 2, 1997, 3; *XNews*, "Dr. Flex: Wants Lesbian Lover," April 2, 1997, 28.

69. Silvera, "Man Royals and Sodomites." This observation that the "low profile" granted to lesbians does not exempt them from the violence perpetrated against gay men is also noted in the *Star*'s article ventriloquizing bar talk on the topic of homosexuality. "A woman wi' get 'way wid lesbianism, but dem naw 'low a man wid 'omosexuality. No sah!" Bald Head said. "Dem angle di sodomite dem same way like di b…man dem" (*Jamaica Star*, "Bar Talk: Homo Strippers," June 11, 1993, 7).

70. It was not until 1987 that the Jamaican state began requiring HIV tests for migrant farmworkers *returning* to Jamaica. Figueroa et al., "HIV/AIDS Epidemic in Jamaica." Trevor Rhone's film *Safe Travel* was created in collaboration with the Ministry of Health to be used as an educational tool for World AIDS Day in 1991 to educate Jamaicans across the island about HIV/AIDS. The film documents the life of a rural family that grapples with safe sex, STI's, and HIV because the husband engages in sex with other women while employed as a farmworker in Belle Glades, Florida. Interviews with several of Jamaica's contact investigators working in the 1990s confirmed that the film was well received when it was shown across the island through the outreach efforts of the Jamaican Information Service.

71. Figueroa et al., "HIV/AIDS Epidemic in Jamaica."

72. Figueroa and Brathwaite, "Under-Reporting."

73. Jillson-Boostrom, *AIDS in Jamaica*, 4.

74. *XNews*, "Homos Attack *XNews*," August 1, 1996, 4.

75. *XNews*, "Jealous Homo Shoots Lover Eight Times," September 1, 1998, 3.

76. *XNews*, "They're Calling Him Homo," July 2, 1997, 27; *XNews*, "Oral Sex Scandal at Up Park Camp," October 1, 1997, 3.

77. *XNews*, "*XNews* Is Fastest Growing Newspaper," January 19, 1995, 3.

78. *XNews*, "Gays Attack Shabba," February 25, 1993, 3.

79. Harriott, "Changing Social Organization."

80. Harriott, "Changing Social Organization."

81. Warders who were implicated in the condom riots were not exempt from economic struggles. In his report on social life in prisons after the condom riots, Morgan Pearson writes, "Underpaid and unmotivated, sometimes the warders present a desperate portrait to inmates. It is not unusual for an inmate to be greeted by a warder in this manner: 'Beg you a lunch money nuh?'" (Morgan Pearson, "Scarce Ganja, Mad Prisoners," *Daily Gleaner*, September 21, 1997, 2A).

82. Mervyn Morris notes that the play was modified with "a tactful eye for adaptability here in Jamaica" (Morris, "Teaching AIDS," *Jamaica Observer*, June 13,

1993, 49). See also Jenni Campbell, "'One of Our Sons' Brings Quality Theatre to Life," *Jamaica Herald*, June 4, 1993, 7B.

83. Sealy, *One of Our Sons*, 140.

84. *XNews*, "Homos Caught Red Handed in Pajero," October 24, 1996, 3; *XNews*, "Homos Caught in the Act," June 24, 1998, 6; *XNews*, "Boom Bye Bye: Cops Surprise Homos while in the Act," November 14, 1996, 3.

85. *XNews*, "Gays Dominate City's Love Spots," October 20, 1994, 3. During her fieldwork on the island in the 1980s, Lisa Douglas became aware of elite white married men's liaisons with other men, but she did not investigate them specifically. Nevertheless, in outlining the "rules about how one may carry out an affair," she identified discretion as a key mandate for elite married men, regardless of who their partner(s) may be. Douglas, *The Power of Sentiment*, 170.

86. *XNews*, "Homo Pastor Gets Slammed," November 4, 1998, 3; *XNews*, "Homo Seek," March 21, 1995, 2.

87. Royes, *Jamaican Men*, 11.

88. *XNews*, "Pastor Sexually Assaults Young Boy," August 21, 1998, 3; *Jamaica Star*, "Designer on Buggery Charges," May 25, 1994, 1; Sheila Watson-Thomas, "Homeless Boys Are Rape Victims," *Jamaica Herald*, June 15, 1993, 1.

89. Cliff, *No Telephone to Heaven*, 129.

90. *XNews*, "More Teenage Boys Are Becoming Homosexuals," December 3, 1997, 2; *XNews*, "How to Stop Your Little Boy from Growing Up Gay," April 8, 1998, 7.

91. Moore and Johnson, "'Fallen Sisters'?"; Henriques, *Prostitution and Society*.

92. Murphy et al., "Human Immunodeficiency Virus."

93. Author interview with Ian McKnight, July 28, 2018.

94. *Jamaica Star*, "Gays Invade Hookers' Beat," July 21, 1989, 1; *XNews*, "Male Hookers 'Full Up' Park," March 12, 1997, 1.

95. *XNews*, "Hardcore Homos on the Loose," July 27, 1997, 3.

96. *XNews*, "Gays Sexing in Barbican," December 14, 1995, 3; *XNews*, "Gay Business a Big Business Inna Jamaica," October 22, 1997, 3.

97. *XNews*, "Bisexual Bares His Soul," November 7, 1996, 3; *XNews*, "Jealous Homo Shoots Lover"; *XNews*, "Homos Locked in Dispute," June 13, 1996, 3.

98. *Jamaica Star*, "Brutal Killings among Homos," June 4, 1993, 1.

99. *Jamaica Star*, "Are Cops Probing Homosexual Killings?," May 13, 1994, 9.

Chapter Four. Performance

1. Nettleford, "National Identity and Attitudes," 60.

2. Reid, "Cultural Revolution in Jamaica," 145.

3. Wynter, "We Must Learn."

4. Fanon, *Wretched of the Earth*; Césaire, *Discourse on Colonialism*.

5. Glissant, *Caribbean Discourse*, 5.

6. Richard Schechner (*Between Theater and Anthropology*) refers to this as "restored behavior" or "twice behaved behavior." See also V. Turner, *The Anthropology of Performance*.

7. D. Taylor, *Archive and the Repertoire*, 19–20.

8. T. Robinson, "The Properties of Citizens."

9. Anthony Bogues ("Rex Nettleford"), for instance, suggests that NDTC's main intervention lay in centering the Black body as a site of decolonization.

10. *Daily Gleaner*, "'Roots and Rhythms' Opens August 1," July 30, 1962, 7.

11. NDTC, "Memorandum of Association," Kingston, NDTC, 1963.

12. Baxter, "The Dance Renaissance."

13. Caribbean dance also took shape in London with the establishment of Les Ballet Nègres by Jamaican Berto Pasuka in 1946, and Boscoe Holder and His Caribbean Dancers by Trinidadian Boscoe Holder in 1950. See Barnes, "Presenting Berto Pasuka"; McLean, *Boscoe Holder*.

14. G. White, "Rudie, Oh Rudie!"

15. Ryman, "Jamaican Heritage in Dance."

16. Baxter, "The Dance Renaissance."

17. Department of Extramural Studies, *Summer School in Dance*, Kingston, University College of the West Indies, 1961.

18. NDTC, "Tenth Anniversary," Kingston, NDTC, 1972.

19. "Interview with Rex Nettleford," *Dance and Dancers*, November 20–23, 1965.

20. *Daily Gleaner*, "Merry-Go-Round," August 17, 1970, 6.

21. Rex Nettleford, "NDTC and the Seventies," *NDTC Newsletter* 10 (1970), 2–3.

22. Scott and Nettleford, "'To Be Liberated,'" 107.

23. Author interview with the late Barry Moncrieffe, August 2, 2017.

24. Author interview with Bridget Spaulding (née Casserly), June 20, 2019. Such close affective relationship was not characteristic of subsequent generations of NDTC members. D. A. Thomas, "Democratizing Dance."

25. Author interview with Marjorie Whylie, June 26, 2019.

26. *NDTC Newsletter*, "Dance in Education," 9 (1969), 30.

27. *Daily Gleaner*, "National Dance Company Formed," September 19, 1962, 7.

28. *NDTC Newsletter*, "Dance in Cabaret," 9 (1969), 30.

29. Edna Manley, letter to Dr. Miller, April 4, 1961.

30. Heather Royes, letter to Rex Nettleford, May 8, 1969.

31. Jean Smith, letter to Rex Nettleford, July 30, 1969.

32. Heather Royes, letter to Jean Smith, May 9, 1969.

33. Rex Nettleford, letter to Edward Seaga, September 10, 1963.

34. Alek Zybine, letter to Eddy Thomas, October 10, 1964.

35. Oliver Miller, letter to Rex Nettleford, May 1, 1967; Everard Llewellyn, letter to Eddy Thomas, May 12, 1967; Monica Procope, letter to Rex Nettleford, October 17, 1967.

36. Jamaica was the only country at the festival to have sold out all of its performances. Greta Lyons, "Jamaican Dancers—Good Enough for Anywhere,"

Daily Gleaner, October 19, 1965, 12. John Furness, officer of the Music and Arts Program at the BBC, noted in his letter (November 8, 1965) to Nettleford, "I am sure you will be delighted to know that people here thought your company's contribution was quite outstanding and very charming, and it looked lovely on the screen."

37. Hugh Nash, "Jamaica Highly Rated," *Daily Gleaner*, October 20, 1965, 6.

38. Edward Seaga, letter to Rex Nettleford, July 30, 1963.

39. Linda Christmas, "On the Black Beat," *Guardian*, September 8, 1972, 5.

40. Rex Nettleford, letter to NDTC company members, "Re: Tour to Carifesta Expo 1969," April 11, 1969.

41. Seaga, "Cults in Jamaica."

42. Seaga was actively involved in NDTC's creative process. He took company members to Salt Lane in West Kingston to observe Pukumina ceremonies and attended NDTC rehearsals to provide feedback on appropriate bodily comportment of the dances inspired by the revival cult. His insistence on technical and formal accuracy proved to be quite effective, as a few of the members who danced in NDTC's *Pocomania* became so immersed in the performance that they would enter into the cult's ritual trance (author interview with the late Bert Rose, May 31, 2019).

43. Through research trips around the island, company members would learn of many rituals and recreational dance forms that would inform their choreography, including kumina, bruckin party, gerreh, maypole, jonkonnu, and dinkimini (Nettleford, *Dance Jamaica*).

44. Rex Nettleford, letter to Edward Seaga, September 10, 1963.

45. *Daily Gleaner*, "Merry-Go-Round."

46. NDTC *Newsletter*, "Is the NDTC Doing What It Ought to Be Doing?," (1969), 8. The class leanings of the company were reflected in NDTC's location, which seminar participants described as "the snug suburbia of Tom Redcam Drive." And while the company did not privilege ballet, the fact that most of its members upon joining the company were experienced in this dance form indicated a particular kind of class standing, given ballet's elite connotations in Jamaica. These critiques mirror Deborah Thomas's subsequent evaluation of the company. She notes that "revalorizing of rural Afro-Jamaican cultural practices neither tended to appreciably alter the structural position of rural Afro-Jamaicans nor to significantly reinvent the ideological systems through which modern progress had been measured" (D. A. Thomas, *Modern Blackness*, 5).

47. Wynter, "One Love?," 70.

48. D. A. Thomas, *Modern Blackness*, 55.

49. Thame, "Racial Hierarchy."

50. Herma Diaz, "Civilization and Dance," *Jamaica Enquirer*, Summer 1969, 48.

51. *Daily Gleaner*, "Letter to the Editor," July 17, 1967, 12.

52. The Jamaican state used an incident that occurred in Coral Gardens to mount a violent campaign in Western Jamaica, rounding up, jailing, and torturing

hundreds of Rastafarians (D. A. Thomas, Jackson, and Wedderburn, *Bad Friday*). Several years later, riots occurred when the radical Afro-Guyanese historian Walter Rodney, who was working in Jamaica as a lecturer at the University of the West Indies, was denied entry into Jamaica after attending a Black Power conference in Montreal (Payne, "The Rodney Riots in Jamaica").

53. Sheila Barnett, "Comments Heard and Overheard on the 1970 Season," *NDTC Newsletter* 11 (1970), 53

54. Barnett, "Comments Heard and Overheard," 50.

55. Maynier-Burke, "Rex Nettleford Choreographer," 4.

56. Scott and Nettleford, "'To Be Liberated'"; Nettleford, Smith, and Augier, *Report on the Rastafari Movement*; Nettleford, *Mirror, Mirror*.

57. *Daily Gleaner*, "NDTC Opening: Metaphysics in Dance," July 28, 1970, 34.

58. Donette Francis (*Fictions of Feminine Citizenship*) might consider this piece to be an articulation of Caribbean anti-romance.

59. Dennis Scott, "Dance and This Society," *NDTC Newsletter* 11 (1970), 15.

60. *NDTC Newsletter*, "Films and Filming," 10 (1970), 20. Recording accessed at the National Library of Jamaica.

61. Author interview with Judith Wedderburn, May 26, 2019.

62. Nettleford, *Dance Jamaica*, 129.

63. Wynter, "One Love," 94. Wynter especially takes issue with how Nettleford characterizes poor and working-class family practices in *Mirror, Mirror*. She maintains that his arguments about the material basis for these kinship patterns fail to implicate middle- and upper-class Jamaicans who participate in the economic disenfranchisement of the island's Black masses.

64. Bourbonnais, *Birth Control*.

65. Jamaica National Family Planning Board, *Annual Report*.

66. Jacobs and Jacobs, *The Family*, 22.

67. T. Robinson, "The Properties of Citizens."

68. *Daily Gleaner*, "Kumina's Royal Night," August 10, 1971, 22.

69. Owen Minott, "Reflections on the NDTC from a Five Shilling Seat," *NDTC Newsletter* 10 (1970), 8.

70. Mervyn Morris, "Dialogue for Three," *NDTC Newsletter* 6 (1969), 17.

71. Author interview with the late Bert Rose, May 31, 2019. Rose indicated that customers of the Kingston store, The Times, were known to ask clerks for the record "Dialogue for Three."

72. *NDTC Newsletter*, "The Making of a Dance—Film and Filming," 6 (1969), 5.

73. Muñoz, "Ephemera as Evidence"; Muñoz, *Cruising Utopia*.

74. For a critique of *Dialogue*, see Richard Buckle, "Putting on the Style," *Sunday Times* (London), September 9, 1972, 5. On the image of NDTC on the cover of *Dance and Dancers*, see *Daily Gleaner*, "NDTC Featured on Cover," September 20, 1972, 26. On Nettleford's claims about the popularity of *Dialogue for Three*, see Linda Christmas, "On the Black Beat," *Guardian*, September 8, 1972, 5.

75. For the English critic's comments, see John Percival, "Jamaican National Dance Theatre," *Times* (London), September 6, 1972, 12. For the Miami review, see John Meyer, "Jamaicans' Colorful Show Marred by Talky Audience," *Miami Herald*, May 4, 1972, 5c.

76. Ricardo Mungarro, "Ballet Nacional de Jamaica—Un Brillante Espectaculo," *La Prensa*, August 19, 1969, 56. Author translation.

77. *NDTC Newsletter*, "Carifest Expo Tour," 7 (1969), 4; *Daily Gleaner*, "Bravos from Puerto Rican Audience," August 30, 1971, 18.

78. Author interview with the late Barbara Requa, July 13, 2019.

79. Stella, "Partyline," *Jamaica Star*, August 30, 1969, 10.

80. Henriques, *Family and Colour*.

81. According to Henriques (*Family and Colour*), Chinese and East Indian men also took mistresses from lower-class backgrounds, but they tended to marry among themselves (as opposed to seeking lighter-complexioned wives); Syrians generally did not take mistresses (98).

82. Yvonne DaCosta, "A View from the Wings," *NDTC Newsletter* 9 (1969), 20.

83. Thame, "Racial Hierarchy."

84. Black nationalist opposition to such interracial intimacies was related to the fact that the categories "mistress" and "servant" (or "slave," for that matter) are not mutually exclusive, because spheres of sexuality and labor overlap in Plantation America (Henriques, *Prostitution and Society*). On patriarchal nationalism, see T. Robinson, "The Properties of Citizens."

85. Mair notes, "White women viewed them [brown women] as serpents that exercised sinister authority over susceptible white men" (Mair, *A Historical Study*, 293).

86. Tinsley, *Thiefing Sugar*, 193.

87. Tinsley, *Thiefing Sugar*, 196.

88. Mervyn Morris, "NDTC, Su-Su and Truth," *Sunday Sun*, August 15, 1982, 20.

89. Rex Nettleford, letter to artist, August 1965; Rex Nettleford, letter to doctor, October 14, 1968. Names intentionally withheld.

90. Rex Nettleford, letter to artistic director, October 3, 1968. Name intentionally withheld.

91. Here I follow the lead of Nadia Ellis ("Out and Bad"), who in her discussion of a male dancehall artist, states, "I make absolutely no claims as to the sexual identity of this dancer. To refer to his queer dancing body is to make a claim for the way his mobile physicality breaks out of certain Jamaican masculine norms" (15). My approach is different from that of Thomas Glave, who notes "the late great Rex Nettleford, who was—as most people knew—really and truly gay . . . I used to say that I thought it sad that someone as powerful as Rex couldn't (wouldn't) come out, although now I'm wondering about that sentiment" (K. Campbell, "Thomas Glave," 53).

92. See Sedgwick, *Epistemology of the Closet*; Abdur-Rahman, *Against the Closet*.

93. L. White, *Speaking with Vampires*, 82.

94. As indicated earlier, some of the women who led these groups were Ivy Baxter, Madame Soohih, Faye Simpson, Barbara Fonseca, and Punky and Betty Rowe.

95. Author interview with Marjorie Whylie, June 26, 2019.

96. On the gendered politics of Jonkunno, see Ryman, "Jonkonnu." On the gendered politics of ska, see G. White, "Rudie, Oh Rudie!"

97. *Daily Gleaner*, "Ballet: Male Dancers," December 22, 1943, 6; *Daily Gleaner*, "Ballet Dancing," December 15, 1943, 6.

98. Joyce MacDonald, "Ballet—and What It Takes," *Daily Gleaner*, April 12, 1959, 14. NDTC recognized the difficulty of attracting and retaining male dancers. The company's newsletter noted, "The shortage of male dancers continues to be a problem so the boy's class begins on January 31 and Company members are asked to recommend this to their brothers, friends of friends and anyone with genuine interest" (NDTC, "The News between Seasons," NDTC *Newsletter* 2 [1967], 3). This sentiment about the inappropriateness of (certain kinds of) dance for men just did not exist in Jamaica. A Bahamian noted, "Go in a lot of places over the hill late at night and you'll see kids spending every penny they've got playing a juke box, on buying a drink, and dancing. Often just dancing by themselves. It's not really the drink they need, it's dancing. It's something instinctive, something necessary. And yet, if you see some kid who is a really good dancer, and ask him if he has ever tried learning to dance on stage, he will look at you with a cut eye and say 'Man, that's cissy stuff! I like dancing but I ain't no cissy!'" (John Lambert, "'Mafundi Bahamia' Aim Is to Open Window of the Mind," *The Tribune*, January 29, 1970, 8.

99. Author interview with the late Barry Moncrieffe, August 2, 2017.

Chapter Five. Politics

1. Sidney Mintz ("The Caribbean") notes, "The plantation system was not only an agricultural device; it also became the basis for an entire societal design. This design involved the perpetuation of societies sharply divided at the outset into two segments, one large and unfree, the other small and free, with a monopoly of power in the hands of the latter" (27).

2. Henriques, *Jamaica*; Henriques, *Family and Colour*.

3. Best, "Independent Thought," 7.

4. Jefferson, "Some Aspects."

5. Rex Nettleford (*Caribbean Cultural Identity*) describes these imperatives in terms of a dual process of decolonization and creolization.

6. Senior, *The Message Is Change*.

7. See, for instance, H. Levy, "Social Action Center Story"; Bogues, "Black Power"; Ford-Smith, "Sistren-Woman's Theatre."

8. Stephens and Stephens, *Democratic Socialism in Jamaica*.

9. The ArQuives possess GFM materials because GFM and the Canadian publication *The Body Politic* exchanged subscriptions of their newsletters. When the ArQuives inherited *The Body Politic*'s archive, it also inherited its GFM materials (author interview with Laurence Chang, June 12, 2017).

10. The Caribbean International Resource Network (IRN) compiled and digitized some of the GFM materials it located in Jamaica in 2009. These digital materials are available on the Digital Library of the Caribbean (DLOC) (King, "Building a Digital Archive"). These materials were then donated to the Schomburg Center for Research on Black Culture. The IHLIA LGBT Heritage Archives came to possess GFM materials when it inherited the archives of two organizations that were GFM interlocutors, the Spartacus International Gay Guide and the International Lesbian and Gay Association (IHLIA LGBT Heritage, email message to author, November 3, 2022).

11. In partnership with the Caribbean IRN, I donated digitized versions of these materials to the existing GFM archive on DLOC. I also coordinated an online event that brought together former GFM members to discuss their work in this group. The corpus of GFM digital materials and a link to the video of this event are available at DLOC, https://dloc.com/collections/icirngfm.

12. Mohammed, "Women's and Feminist Activism"; Antrobus, *The Rise and Fall*; Paravisini-Gebert, "Decolonizing Feminism."

13. Following Jacqui Alexander, I use the term "erotic autonomy" to describe the means by which to unsettle the workings of neocolonial heteropatriarchal state power and the way in which sexual agency carries the potential for individual and collective self-determination. See Alexander, *Pedagogies of Crossing*. For more on GFM's work, see Batra, "'Our Own Gayful Rest'"; M. Chin, "Tracing Gay Liberation"; M. Chin, "Constructing 'Gaydren.'"

14. Author interview with Dennis (pseudonym), January 27, 2019.

15. For example, L. B. Wellington, "Homosexuals," *Daily Gleaner*, February 29, 1980, 6.

16. Jennifer Ffrench, "Our Sick Attitude towards Sex," *Jamaica Daily News*, February 28, 1978, 7.

17. JGN, "Homophobic Attack," 36 (1979), 1; JGN, "Ursola Attacked," 56 (1980), 7; JGN, "Gays Attacked," 67 (1980), 1; Mampala Morgan, "Suss-Uration," JGN 74 (1981), 5; M'Lady, "Girl Talk," JGN 47 (1979), 6; Tony Long, "Gay Club Syndrome," JGN 61 (1980), 1; JGN, "Gay Debate Takes Place," 60 (1980), 2.

18. JGN, "Editorial," 53 (1979), 3.

19. Elsie, "The Future of the Closet," JGN 1 (1977), 2.

20. "John Harriet" is a pseudonym. Two members ceased to be active after the committee's original task. Of the remaining four members, I was able to interview only two, as one had died and I was unable to locate the other.

21. Author interview with Laurence Chang, June 12, 2017.

22. Author interview with John Harriet, July 28, 2017.

23. Laurence Chang, "Homosexuals," *Daily Gleaner*, January 28, 1978, 8.

24. For example, Laurence Chang, "Gay vs Bigotry," *Jamaica Daily News*, March 11, 1978, 7; Chang, "Gays Answer Detractors," *Jamaica Star*, January 10, 1980, 7.

25. For example, letter to GFM from F. R. received September 21, 1979. Jamaica Gay Freedom Movement Records, Sc MG 902, box 1, folder 4, Schomburg Center.

26. For example, letter to GFM from J. T. received December 3, 1978. Jamaica Gay Freedom Movement Records, Sc MG 902, box 1, folder 3, Schomburg Center.

27. Letter from Laurence Chang to L. T. dated November 5, 1978, Chang personal records.

28. Author interview with Donna Smith, August 18, 2017.

29. Bernal, "IMF and Class Struggle."

30. "Winston Smalls" is a pseudonym.

31. Letter from Winston Smalls (pseudonym) to Laurence Chang dated January 8, 1980, Chang personal archive.

32. US Department of State, *Country Reports*, 534.

33. Laurence Chang, "Gays in Jamaica," in *Third Annual Conference of the International Gay Association*, 1981, accessed February 25, 2023, https://ufdc.ufl.edu/AA00001485/00001.

34. Andromeda I, "A Time for Us," *JGN* 2 (1977), 2.

35. Letter from Bernice Bell (pseudonym) to Gay Freedom Movement, September 22, 1979, Jamaica Gay Freedom Movement Records, Sc MG 902, box 1, folder 4, Schomburg Center.

36. Letter from Paulette Baker (pseudonym) to Gay Freedom Movement, March 28, 1980, Jamaica Gay Freedom Movement Records, Sc MG 902, box 1, folder 5, Schomburg Center.

37. Letter from Laurence Chang to Paulette Baker, April 2, 1980, Jamaica Gay Freedom Movement Records, Sc MG 902, box 1, folder 5, Schomburg Center.

38. "Frances Camden" is a pseudonym.

39. Ford-Smith, *Lionheart Gal*.

40. Silvera, "Man Royals and Sodomites," 524. See also Richardson, "I Was Born," 74.

41. See *JGN*, "Homophobic Attack"; *JGN*, "Ursola Attacked"; *JGN*, "Gays Attacked."

42. French, "Organizing Women," 3; see also Ford-Smith, "Sistren-Woman's Theatre."

43. Reddock, "Women's Organizations and Movements."

44. H. Levy, "Social Action Center Story"; Phillips, "Democratic Socialism."

45. Bolland, "Labor Protests."

46. Bogues, "Black Power"; Payne, "The Rodney Riots in Jamaica"; R. Lewis, "Walter Rodney."

47. *JGN*, "Editorial," 24 (1978), 3.

48. Coore-Hall, *Feminist Advocacy and Activism*.

49. Ford-Smith, *Lionheart Gal*.

50. Such an approach aligns with the predominant Women in Development framework that guided women's efforts for change within the Caribbean in this period. See Reddock, "Women's Organizations and Movements."

51. Ford-Smith, *Lionheart Gal.*

52. Antrobus, *The Rise and Fall*, 6.

53. Letter to Gay Freedom Movement from Revolutionary Marxist League dated March 18, 1982, Jamaica Gay Freedom Movement Records, Sc MG 902, box 1, folder 4, Schomburg Center.

54. *JGN*, "VD Clinic Reopened," 38 (1978), 1; *JGN*, "GFM Is Alive and Well," 49 (1979), 1. Volunteer health workers staffed the VD clinic and utilized the infrastructure and medical supplies from their workplaces to provide confidential testing services to same-gender-desiring Jamaicans.

55. *JGN*, "No Club after All," 66 (1980), 2; *JGN*, "Maddams Reopens," 59 (1980), 1.

56. "Lena Knight" is a pseudonym.

57. Author interview with Lena Knight, July 18, 2017.

58. *JGN*, "GFM Goes through Changes," 48 (1979), 1; Gay Freedom Movement, "Report of Gay Freedom Movement Workshop," August 26, 1979, https://dloc .com/AA00001412/00001?search=workshop+=gfm.

59. *JGN*, "Youth Group Proposed," 29 (1978), 1.

60. *JGN*, "Prison Outreach," 16 (1978), 2; undated handwritten notes, Jamaica Gay Freedom Movement Records, Sc MG 902, box 1, folder 1, Schomburg Center.

61. *JGN*, "Letter to the Gay Queens," 24 (1978), 7.

62. *JGN*, "Gay Pen Pal Club," 13 (1978), 8.

63. "John Trenton" is a pseudonym. Letter from John Trenton to Laurence Chang dated October 18, 1978, Chang personal archive.

64. *JGN*, "Gay Friends," 30 (1978), 8.

65. Letter to Laurence Chang from John Trenton dated December 9, 1978, Jamaica Gay Freedom Movement Records, Sc MG 902, box 1, folder 3, Schomburg Center.

66. Warner, "Publics and Counterpublics."

67. M. Chin, "Queering Chinese Crossings."

68. Aquarius, "Personally Speaking," *JGN* 44 (1979), 7.

69. Letter to *JGN* editor from Lamar Brown (pseudonym) dated February 5, 1978, Jamaica Gay Freedom Movement Records, Sc MG 902, box 1, folder 3, Schomburg Center.

70. *JGN*, "Editorial Policy," 1980, accessed February 25, 2023, https://ufdc.ufl .edu/AA00002989/00001.

71. "Garret Elliot Murray" is a pseudonym.

72. Author interview with Garret Elliot Murray, June 23, 2017. "Frances Camden" is a pseudonym.

73. *JGN*, "GFM Goes Public," 55 (1979), 2.

74. *Jamaica Daily News*, "First Open Homosexual Talks," December 11, 1979, 12; *Jamaica Star*, "Discussion on Homosexuality," December 7, 1979, 19.

75. *JGN*, "GFM/JPA Meet Again," 70 (1980), 1.

76. *JGN*, "GFM Meets Guidance Counsellors," 64 (1980), 2; *JGN*, "GFM/Nurses Talk," 77 (1984), 2.

77. "Keisha" is a pseudonym. Author interview with Garrett Elliot Murray, June 23, 2017.

78. Dorothy Austin, "Gays in Lecture," *Daily Gleaner*, January 31, 1982, 7.

79. Laurence Chang, "Gay Protest," *Jamaica Daily News*, March 18, 1980, 7.

80. Sympathetic news coverage included Vernon Witter, "Let the Locals Promote Their Gay-Ness," *Jamaica Star*, December 10, 1979, 5; Vincent Tulloch, "Examining Homosexuality," *Daily Gleaner*, February 4, 1978, 8; Ken Jones, "A Funny Thing Is Happening," *Jamaica Star*, December 11, 1979, 3. Hostile news coverage included Everton Hannon, "Homosexual Upsurge," *Jamaica Daily News*, April 7, 1982, 5; Keith Parker, "Homosexuality," *Daily Gleaner*, March 14, 1978, 8; Byron Balfour, "More on Gays," *Jamaica Star*, February 9, 1980, 12.

81. For the original correspondence, see Phyllis Thomas, "Those Aggressive Gays," *Jamaica Star*, February 9, 1980, 12. For Fuller's response, see Eve Fuller, "Gay Answers Detractor," *Jamaica Star*, June 6, 1980, 13. Capitalization in original.

82. *JGN*, "Gay Storm Rages in Press," 12 (1978), 1.

83. The series began on January 10, 1982, in the *Daily Gleaner*, which published an additional weekly installment of the series for the next month.

84. Donovan Campbell, "Homosexuality," *Jamaica Star*, March 8, 1980, 7; Hugh Porter, "Help Them," *Jamaica Daily News*, March 31, 1980, 7.

85. DeB, "Take My Word," *Daily Gleaner*, September 2, 1978, 3.

86. For Gordon's views, see Rev. Ernle Gordon, "Homosexuals Yearn for Loyalty and Tenderness," *Daily Gleaner*, January 31, 1982, 10. For Dunn's views, see Rev. B. V. Dunn, "The Growth of Sodomy," *Jamaica Daily News*, March 25, 1982, 5. Capitalization in original.

87. *Jamaica Star*, "KSAC Committee Resolution Says—Stamp Out Homosexual Activities in the Society," January 28, 1982, 5.

88. Vernon Witter, "KSAC and Gays," *Jamaica Star*, February 1, 1982, 3.

89. Glendon Cooper, "Homosexuality," *Jamaica Daily News*, February 3, 1982, 5.

90. News release, Chang personal archive. The exhibit consisted of twenty-four paintings in gouache on panels and blocks of wood.

91. Archie Lindo, "Nothing Vulgar about Chang's Work," *Jamaica Star*, November 7, 1980, 3; *Daily Gleaner*, "Exhibition," October 20, 1980, 12; *Daily Gleaner*, "Bolivar," November 2, 1982, 6; *Daily Gleaner*, "Art Show Extended," November 10, 1980, 12.

92. *JGN*, "Press Bars GFM Ad," 74 (1981), 1.

93. *JGN*, "JBC Bars Gay TV Programme," 18 (1978), 1.

94. Byron Balfour, "Gays Now in Kingston," *Jamaica Star*, December 20, 1979, 14; Vincent Tulloch, "Examining Homosexuality," *Daily Gleaner*, February 4, 1978, 8.

95. Stephens and Stephens, *Democratic Socialism in Jamaica*.

96. Bloom, "We Are All Part of One Another"; Drucker, "'In the Tropics'"; LaViolette and Whitworth, "No Safe Haven."

97. Bacchetta, "Rescaling Transnational 'Queerdom.'"

98. *JGN*, "Editorial," 73 (1981), 7.

99. *JGN*, "*Gaily News* Subscriptions," 13 (1978), 8.

100. *JGN*, "Befriend a Gay Friend," 15 (1978), 8.

101. *JGN*, "Gay Friend," 24 (1978), 8.

102. Letter to GFM from Remy (pseudonym) dated January 7, 1980; letter to GFM from Yuda (pseudonym) received December 14, 1979, Chang personal archive.

103. Letter to Laurence Chang from Daniel Jones (pseudonym) dated October 22, 1978, Jamaica Gay Freedom Movement Records, Sc MG 902, box 1, folder 3, Schomburg Center. (Letter typed in all caps.)

104. Even though the letter does not directly state his racial positioning, Jones's access to the resources necessary for such extensive travel from apartheid South Africa would suggest that he was not racialized as Black. His error in situating Jamaica in the "far east" would seem to indicate that he was also not of Asian heritage. It is possible that Jones was categorized as "white" or perhaps "coloured" in the context of South Africa's legal system of racial classification.

105. Roberts, *The Population of Jamaica*; Kuper, *Changing Jamaica*; D. W. Cooper, "Migration from Jamaica."

106. Thomas-Hope and Nutter, "Occupation and Status"; Soto, "West Indian Child Fostering"; Rubenstein, "Remittances and Rural Underdevelopment."

107. Letter to Laurence Chang from Patricia Campbell (pseudonym) dated February 18, 1980, Jamaica Gay Freedom Movement Records, Sc MG 902, box 1, folder 5, Schomburg Center.

108. *JGN*, "Looking In," 64 (1980), 8.

109. *JGN*, "Salsa Soul Sisters," 12 (1978), 2.

110. For work that discusses contemporary gender and sexual minority activism across the Anglophone Caribbean region in ways that unsettle North Atlantic human rights discourses, see Nikoli Attai's recent *Defiant Bodies*.

111. Tony Long, "A Continuing Series on Being Gay III: Self Acceptance," *JGN* 8 (1978), 4.

112. Tony Long, "A Continuing Series on Being Gay V: Coming Out," *JGN* 11 (1978), 4.

113. Tony Long, "A Continuing Series on Being Gay VI: Activism," *JGN* 12 (1978), 4.

114. Sedgwick, *Epistemology of the Closet*, 71.

115. G. Turner, "Catching the Wave"; Jackson and Persky, *Flaunting It!*

116. *JGN*, "Toronto Mention," 36 (1979), 2; *JGN*, "We're Going Places," 37 (1979), 6; *JGN*, "Italian and Colombian Contact," 42 (1979), 2.

117. *JGN*, "GFM for U.K. Gay Conference," 18 (1978), 1.

118. *JGN*, "Costa Rican Gays," 48 (1979), 4.

119. *JGN*, "Amnesty International Contacts GFM," 57 (1980), 1.

120. *JGN*, "SHRG & GFM to Twin?," 71 (1980), 1

121. Unfortunately, this secretariat did not become active.

122. *JGN*, "International Gay Association to Discuss Third World Gays," 48 (1979), 4; *JGN*, "US Group Conducts Human Rights Survey," 71 (1980), 2.

123. Stamford, *Spartacus: International Gay Guide*.

124. *JGN*, "Blackheart Seeks Material," 81 (1984), 1; *JGN*, "Local Input for US Groups," 79 (1984), 1.

125. M'Lady, "Girl Talk," *JGN* 56 (1980), 5.

126. E. Dantes, "Gaypercussions," *JGN* 64 (1980), 5; Clinton Bright, "Gay Parents," *JGN* 78 (1984), 4; Mampala Morgan, "Suss-Uration," *JGN* 74 (1981), 5.

127. *JGN*, "Editorial," 73 (1981), 7; *JGN*, "Gay Pride Week . . . Recap," 47 (1979), 1; Aquarius, "Personally Speaking," *JGN* 53 (1979), 4.

128. *JGN*, "Editorial," 51 (1979), 2.

129. *JGN*, "Editorial," 22 (1978), 3.

130. *JGN*, "Report on the 3rd Annual IGA Conference," 73 (1981), 2.

Epilogue

1. Baucom, *Specters of the Atlantic*.

2. Keeling, *Queer Times, Black Futures*, 32.

3. Muñoz, *Cruising Utopia*, 1.

4. Brodber, *Nothing's Mat*, 36.

5. Chanca, "Segundo Viage," 204.

6. Wynter, "Unsettling the Coloniality."

7. Chanca, "Segundo Viage," 205, my translation.

8. Hulme, *Colonial Encounters*.

9. See Andil Gosine (*Nature's Wild*) on how Caribbean sexuality becomes central to discussions about the relationship between humanity and animality.

Bibliography

Archives

ArQuives, Toronto
Digital Library of the Caribbean
Epidemiological Research and Training Unit Library, Kingston
Hope Enterprises Library, Kingston
IHLIA LGBT Heritage Archives, Amsterdam
Jamaica AIDS Support Library, Kingston
Jamaica Ministry of Health Library, Kingston
Jamaica National Dance Theatre Company Archives, Kingston
Jamaica National Family Planning Board Library, Kingston
Jamaica National Library, Kingston
Jamaica Red Cross, National Headquarters Library, Central Village
Kingston and St. Andrew Public Library, Kingston
New York Library of the Performing Arts, New York
Public Broadcasting Corporation of Jamaica, Kingston
Schomburg Center for Research on Black Culture, New York
Toronto Reference Library, Toronto
University of West Indies, Mona, Kingston

Newspapers

Jamaica Daily Express
Jamaica Daily Gleaner
Jamaica Daily News
Jamaica Herald
Jamaica Observer
Jamaica Star
Jamaica Times
Jamaica X News

Secondary Works

Abdur-Rahman, Aliyyah. *Against the Closet: Black Political Longing and the Erotics of Race*. Durham, NC: Duke University Press, 2012.

Afroz, Sultana. "The Manifestation of Tawhid: The Muslim Heritage of the Maroons in Jamaica." *Caribbean Quarterly* 45, no. 1 (1999): 27–40.

Agard-Jones, Vanessa. "What the Sands Remember." GLQ: *A Journal of Lesbian and Gay Studies* 18, no. 2–3 (2012): 325–46.

Alexander, M. Jacqui. *Pedagogies of Crossing: Meditations on Feminism, Sexual Politics, Memory, and the Sacred*. Durham, NC: Duke University Press, 2005.

Allen, Jafari. "Friendship as a Mode of Survival." In ¡*Venceremos? Erotics of Black Self Making in Cuba*, 129–56. Durham, NC: Duke University Press, 2011.

Amin, Kadji. "Genealogies of Queer Theory." In *The Cambridge Companion to Queer Studies*, edited by Siobhan Somerville, 17–29. Cambridge: Cambridge University Press, 2020.

Anderson, Moji, and Erin C. MacLeod, eds. *Beyond Homophobia: Centring LGBTQ Experiences in the Anglophone Caribbean*. Kingston: University of the West Indies Press, 2020.

Antrobus, Peggy. "Crisis, Challenge and the Experiences of Caribbean Women." *Caribbean Quarterly* 35, no. 1/2 (1989): 17–28.

Antrobus, Peggy. *The Rise and Fall of Feminist Politics in the Caribbean Women's Movement, 1975–1995*. Kingston: Centre for Gender and Development Studies, University of the West Indies, 2000.

Appadurai, Arjun. "Number in the Colonial Imagination." In *Orientalism and the Postcolonial Predicament: Perspectives on South Asia*, edited by Carol A. Breckenridge and Peter van der Veer, 314–39. Philadelphia: University of Pennsylvania Press, 1993.

Apter, Andrew. "M. G. Smith on the Isle of Lesbos: Kinship and Sexuality in Carriacou." *New West Indian Guide/Nieuwe West-Indische Gids* 87, no. 3–4 (2013): 273–93.

Arondekar, Anjali. *For the Record: On Sexuality and the Colonial Archive in India*. Durham, NC: Duke University Press, 2009.

Arondekar, Anjali. "The Sex of History, or Object/Matters." In *History Workshop Journal* 89 (2020): 207–13.

Arondekar, Anjali, and Geeta Patel. "Area Impossible: Notes toward an Introduction." GLQ: *A Journal of Lesbian and Gay Studies* 22, no. 2 (2016): 151–71.

Atkinson, Lesley-Gail. *The Earliest Inhabitants: The Dynamics of the Jamaican Taino*. Kingston: University of the West Indies Press, 2006.

Attai, Nikoli A. *Defiant Bodies: Making Queer Community in the Anglophone Caribbean*. New Brunswick: Rutgers University Press, 2023.

Austin-Broos, Diane J. "Gay Nights and Kingston Town: Representations of Kingston, Jamaica." In *Postmodern Cities and Spaces*, edited by Sophie Watson and Katherine Gibson, 149–64. London: Blackwell Oxford, 1995.

Bacchetta, Paola. "Rescaling Transnational 'Queerdom': Lesbian and 'Lesbian' Identitary-Positionalities in Delhi in the 1980s." *Antipode* 34, no. 5 (November 1, 2002): 947–73.

Bair, Barbara. "True Women, Real Men: Gender, Ideology, and Social Roles in the Garvey Movement." In *Gendered Domains: Rethinking Public and Private in Women's History*, edited by Dorothy O. Helly and Susan M. Reverby, 154–66. Ithaca, NY: Cornell University Press, 1992.

Bandopadhyay, Amrita. "Romancing Jamaica: Chinese-Jamaican Women and Nationalist Aesthetics." *Caribbean Review of Gender Studies* 12 (2018): 245–68.

Barnes, Thea. "Presenting Berto Pasuka." In *British Dance: Black Routes*, edited by Christy Adair and Ramsay Burt, 29–48. Abingdon: Routledge, 2016.

Barrow, Christine. *Family in the Caribbean: Themes and Perspectives*. Princeton, NJ: Markus Wiener, 1996.

Barrow, Christine. "Mating and Sexuality in Carriacou: Social Logic and Surplus Women." In *M. G. Smith: Social Theory and Anthropology in the Caribbean and Beyond*, edited by Brian Meeks, 148–64. Kingston: Ian Randle, 2011.

Bashford, Alison, and Philippa Levine, eds. *The Oxford Handbook of the History of Eugenics*. New York: Oxford University Press, 2010.

Batra, Kanika. "'Our Own Gayful Rest': A Postcolonial Archive." *Small Axe: A Caribbean Journal of Criticism* 14, no. 1 (2010): 46–59.

Baucom, Ian. *Specters of the Atlantic: Finance Capital, Slavery, and the Philosophy of History*. Durham, NC: Duke University Press, 2005.

Baxter, Ivy. "The Dance Renaissance." In *The Arts of an Island*, 287–317. Metuchen, NJ: Scarecrow Press, 1970.

Bean, Dalea. "'A Dangerous Class of Woman': Prostitution and the Perceived Threat to Military Efficiency in Jamaica during World Wars I and II." *Jamaican Historical Review* 24 (2009): 42–50.

Bean, Dalea. *Jamaican Women and the World Wars: On the Front Lines of Change*. London: Springer, 2017.

Beckles, Hilary. *Britain's Black Debt: Reparations for Caribbean Slavery and Native Genocide*. Kingston: University of the West Indies Press, 2013.

Benítez-Rojo, Antonio. *The Repeating Island: The Caribbean and the Postmodern Perspective*. Durham, NC: Duke University Press, 1996.

Bernal, Richard L. "The IMF and Class Struggle in Jamaica, 1977–1980." *Latin American Perspectives* 11, no. 3 (1984): 53–82.

Besson, Jean. "Reputation and Respectability Reconsidered: A New Perspective on Afro Caribbean Peasant Women." In *Women and Change in the Caribbean*, edited by Janet Momsen, 15–37. Bloomington: Indiana University Press, 1993.

Besson, Jean, and Barry Chevannes. "The Continuity-Creativity Debate: The Case of Revival." *NWIG: New West Indian Guide/Nieuwe West-Indische Gids* 70, no. 3–4 (1996): 209–28.

Best, Lloyd. "Independent Thought and Caribbean Freedom." In *Readings in the Political Economy of the Caribbean*, edited by Norman Girvan and Owen Jefferson, 7–28. Kingston: New World Group, 1971.

Black, Edwin. IBM *and the Holocaust: The Strategic Alliance between Nazi Germany and America's Most Powerful Corporation*. Washington, DC: Dialog Press, 2012.

Black, Edwin. *War against the Weak: Eugenics and America's Campaign to Create a Master Race*. Washington, DC: Dialog Press, 2012.

Blake, Judith. *Family Structure in Jamaica: The Social Context of Reproduction*. Glencoe, IL: Free Press, 1961.

Bloom, Lisa. "We Are All Part of One Another: Sodomy Laws and Morality on Both Sides of the Atlantic." *New York University Review of Law & Social Change* 14 (1986).

Bogues, Anthony. "Black Power, Decolonization, and Caribbean Politics: Walter Rodney and the Politics of The Groundings with My Brothers." *Boundary 2* 36, no. 1 (2009): 127–47.

Bogues, Anthony. "Rex Nettleford: The Canepiece, Labour, Education and the Caribbean Intellectual." *Caribbean Quarterly* 57, no. 3–4 (2011): 20–32.

Bolland, O. Nigel. "Creolisation and Creole Societies: A Cultural Nationalist View of Caribbean Social History." *Caribbean Quarterly* 44, no. 1/2 (1998): 1–32.

Bolland, O. Nigel. "Labor Protests, Rebellion and the Rise of Nationalism during Depression and War." In *The Caribbean: A History of the Region and Its People*, edited by Stephan Palmie and Francisco Scarano, 459–74. Chicago: University of Chicago Press, 2011.

Bolles, A. Lynn. "Kitchens Hit by Priorities: Employed Working-Class Jamaican Women Confront the IMF." In *Women, Men, and the International Division of Labor*, edited by June C. Nash and Maria P. Fernandez-Kelly, 138–60. Albany: SUNY Press, 1983.

Bost, Darius. "Traumatizing Black Masculinities: Bearing Witness to Male Rape in the African Diaspora." *Journal of West Indian Literature* 21, no. 1/2 (2012): 83–104.

Bourbonnais, Nicole. *Birth Control in the Decolonizing Caribbean: Reproductive Politics and Practice on Four Islands, 1930–1970*. New York: Cambridge University Press, 2016.

Bourbonnais, Nicole. "Class, Colour and Contraception: The Politics of Birth Control in Jamaica, 1938–1967." *Social and Economic Studies* 61, no. 3 (2012): 7–37.

Bourbonnais, Nicole. "'Dangerously Large': The 1938 Labor Rebellion and the Debate over Birth Control in Jamaica." *New West Indian Guide/Nieuwe West-Indische Gids* 83, no. 1/2 (2009): 39–69.

Brathwaite, Alfred. *Contact Investigation in an Integrated FP/MCH/STI/HIV Program*. Kingston: Ministry of Health, 2004.

Brathwaite, Alfred. *Some Facts about V.D.* Kingston: Ministry of Health, 1974.

Brathwaite, Alfred. *STD Control Programme Annual Report*. Kingston: Ministry of Health, 1987.

Brathwaite, Edward Kamau. "Caliban, Ariel, and Unprospero in the Conflict of Creolization: A Study of the Slave Revolt in Jamaica in 1831–32." *Annals of the New York Academy of the Sciences* 292, no. 1 (1977): 41–62.

Brathwaite, Edward Kamau. "Caribbean Man in Space and Time." *Savacou* 11, no. 12 (1975): 1–11.

Brathwaite, Edward Kamau. *Contradictory Omens: Cultural Diversity and Integration in the Caribbean*. Kingston: Savacou, 1974.

Brathwaite, Edward Kamau. *The Development of Creole Society in Jamaica, 1770–1820*. Oxford: Oxford University Press, 1971.

Brathwaite, Edward Kamau. "The Unborn Body of the Life of Fiction: Roger Mais' Aesthetics with Special Reference to 'Black Lightning.'" *Journal of West Indian Literature* 2, no. 1 (1987): 11–36.

Brereton, Bridget. "Family Strategies, Gender, and the Shift to Wage Labor in the British Caribbean." In *Gender and Slave Emancipation in the Atlantic World*, edited by Pamela Scully and Diana Paton, 143–61. Durham, NC: Duke University Press, 2005.

Briggs, Jill. "'As Fool-Proof as Possible': Overpopulation, Colonial Demography, and the Jamaica Birth Control League." *Global South* 4, no. 2 (2010): 157–77.

Briggs, Laura. *Reproducing Empire: Race, Sex, Science, and US Imperialism in Puerto Rico*. Berkeley: University of California Press, 2003.

Brodber, Erna. *Nothing's Mat: A Novel*. Kingston: University of the West Indies Press, 2014.

Brotherton, Pierre Sean. "Contagious Bodies: Multiple Narratives from a Jamaican HIV/AIDS Hospice." Master's thesis, York University, 1998.

Brown, Khytie K. "Mermaids and Journeymen: Revival Zion and Africana Religious Futures." *Black Theology* 19, no. 3 (2021): 229–39.

Bryan, Patrick. "The Creolisation of the Chinese Community in Jamaica." In *Ethnic Minorities in the Caribbean*, edited by Rhoda Reddock, 173–271. Kingston: University of the West Indies Press, 1996.

Burg, Barry Richard. *Sodomy and the Pirate Tradition: English Sea Rovers in the Seventeenth-Century Caribbean*. New York: NYU Press, 1995.

Bush, Barbara. "Colonial Research and the Social Sciences at the End of Empire: The West Indian Social Survey, 1944–57." *Journal of Imperial and Commonwealth History* 41, no. 3 (2013): 451–74.

Bush, Barbara. *Slave Women in Caribbean Society, 1650–1838*. Bloomington: Indiana University Press, 1990.

Butler, Judith. *Bodies That Matter: On the Discursive Limits of Sex*. New York: Routledge, 1993.

Campbell, Kofi Omoniyi Sylvanus, ed. "Patricia Powell." In *The Queer Caribbean Speaks: Interviews with Writers Artists and Activists*, 101–8. London: Palgrave Macmillan, 2014.

Campbell, Kofi Omoniyi Sylvanus, ed. "Thomas Glave." In *The Queer Caribbean Speaks: Interviews with Writers Artists and Activists*, 33–60. New York: Palgrave Macmillan, 2014.

Campbell, Mavis Christine. *The Dynamics of Change in a Slave Society: A Sociopolitical History of the Free Coloreds of Jamaica, 1800–1865*. Rutherford, NJ: Fairleigh Dickinson University Press, 1976.

Campbell, Shirley, Althea Perkins, and Patricia Mohammed. "'Come to Jamaica and Feel All Right': Tourism and the Sex Trade." In *Sun, Sex, and Gold: Tourism and Sex Work in the Caribbean*, edited by Kamala Kempadoo, 125–56. Lanham, MD: Rowman and Littlefield, 1999.

Canny, Nicholas. *Kingdom and Colony: Ireland in the Atlantic World, 1560–1800*. Baltimore: Johns Hopkins University Press, 1988.

Carby, Hazel V. *Imperial Intimacies*. London: Verso, 2019.

Carnegie, Charles V. "The Fate of Ethnography: Native Social Science in the English-Speaking Caribbean." NWIG: *New West Indian Guide/Nieuwe West-Indische Gids* 66, no. 1/2 (1992): 5–25.

Carr, Bill. "Roger Mais: Design from a Legend." *Caribbean Quarterly* 13, no. 1 (1967): 3–28.

Castello, June. "Where Have All the Feminists Gone: Learning the Lessons of a Long Time Passed in the Women's Movement in the Caribbean." *Caribbean Quarterly* 52, no. 2–3 (2006): 1–13.

Central Bureau of Statistics. *Population Census of Jamaica 1960*. Kingston: Government Printer, 1960.

Césaire, Aimé. *Discourse on Colonialism*. New York: Monthly Review Press, 1972.

Chanca, Diego Álvarez. "Segundo Viage de Cristobal Colon." In *Coleccion de Los Viajes y Descubrimients Que Hicieron Por Mar Los Espanoles Desde Fines Del Siglo XV*, vol. 1, edited by Martin Fernandez de Navarrete, 198–224. Madrid: Impresa Nacional, 1853.

Chevannes, Barry. "Healing the Nation: Rastafari Exorcism of the Ideology of Racism in Jamaica." *Caribbean Quarterly* 36, no. 1/2 (1990): 59–84.

Chevannes, Barry. *Learning to Be a Man: Culture, Socialization and Gender Identity in Five Caribbean Communities*. Kingston: University of the West Indies Press, 2001.

Chevannes, Barry. *Sexual Practices and Behavior in Jamaica: A Review of the Literature*. Washington, DC: AIDSCOM, 1992.

Chin, Matthew. "Antihomosexuality and Nationalist Critique in Late Colonial Jamaica: Revisiting the 1951 Police Enquiry." *Small Axe* 24, no. 3 (63) (2020): 81–96.

Chin, Matthew. "Constructing 'Gaydren': The Transnational Politics of Same-Sex Desire in 1970s and 1980s Jamaica." *Small Axe* 23, no. 2 (2019): 17–33.

Chin, Matthew. "Queering Chinese Crossings in Late Twentieth Century Jamaica: Larry Chang and the Gay Freedom Movement." *Interventions* 24, no. 8 (2022): 1309–27.

Chin, Matthew. "Tracing Gay Liberation through Post Independence Jamaica." *Public Culture* 31, no. 2 (2019): 323–42.

Chin, Timothy. "'Bullers' and 'Battymen': Contesting Homophobia in Black Popular Culture and Contemporary Caribbean Literature." *Callaloo* 20, no. 1 (1997): 127–41.

Clarke, Edith. *My Mother Who Fathered Me: A Study of the Family in Three Selected Communities in Jamaica.* Kingston: University of the West Indies, 1957.

Cliff, Michelle. *No Telephone to Heaven.* New York: Dutton, 1987.

Cobham, Rhonda. "Jekyll and Claude: The Erotics of Patronage in Claude McKay's Banana Bottom." *Caribbean Quarterly* 38, no. 1 (1992): 55–78.

Conner, Randy P., and David Hatfield Sparks. *Queering Creole Spiritual Traditions: Lesbian, Gay, Bisexual, and Transgender Participation in African-Inspired Traditions in the Americas.* New York: Routledge, 2013.

Cook, Matt. *Queer Domesticities: Homosexuality and Home Life in Twentieth-Century London.* London: Palgrave Macmillan, 2014.

Cooper, Carolyn. "Slackness Hiding from Culture: Erotic Play in the Dancehall." In *Noises in the Blood*, 136–73. Durham, NC: Duke University Press, 1995.

Cooper, Carolyn. *Sound Clash: Jamaican Dancehall Culture at Large.* New York: Palgrave Macmillan, 2004.

Cooper, Dereck W. "Migration from Jamaica in the 1970s: Political Protest or Economic Pull?" *International Migration Review* 19, no. 4 (1985): 728–45.

Coore-Hall, Jacqueline A. *Feminist Advocacy and Activism in State Institutions: Investigating the Representation of Women's Issues and Concerns in the Jamaican Legislature.* London: Springer, 2020.

Crenshaw, Kimberle. "Demarginalizing the Intersection of Race and Sex: A Black Feminist Critique of Antidiscrimination Doctrine, Feminist Theory and Antiracist Politics." *University of Chicago Legal Forum* 1 (1989): 139–67.

Cummings, Ronald. "Jamaican Female Masculinities: Nanny of the Maroons and the Genealogy of the Man-Royal." *Journal of West Indian Literature* 21, no. 1/2 (2012): 129–54.

Curtin, Philip D. *Two Jamaicas: The Role of Ideas in a Tropical Colony, 1830–1865.* Cambridge, MA: Harvard University Press, 1955.

Dalby, Jonathan R. "'Such a Mass of Disgusting and Revolting Cases': Moral Panic and the 'Discovery' of Sexual Deviance in Post-emancipation Jamaica (1835–1855)." *Slavery & Abolition* 36, no. 1 (2015): 136–59.

Davenport, Charles B. "Race Crossing in Jamaica." *Scientific Monthly* 27, no. 3 (1928): 225–38.

Davenport, Charles B., and Morris Steggerda. *Race Crossing in Jamaica.* Washington, DC: Carnegie Institution of Washington, 1929.

De Barros, Juanita. "'Race' and Culture in the Writings of J. J. Thomas." *Journal of Caribbean History* 27, no. 1 (1993): 36–53.

De Barros, Juanita. *Reproducing the British Caribbean: Sex, Gender, and Population Politics after Slavery.* Chapel Hill: University of North Carolina Press, 2014.

DeCaires Narain, Denise. "Naming Same-Sex Desire in Caribbean Women's Texts: Toward a Creolizing Hermeneutics." *Contemporary Women's Writing* 6, no. 3 (2012): 194–212.

Decena, Carlos Ulises. *Circuits of the Sacred: A Faggotology in the Black Latinx Caribbean*. Durham, NC: Duke University Press, 2023.

Deleuze, Gilles. *Difference and Repetition*. New York: Columbia University Press, 1994.

D'Emilio, John. "Capitalism and Gay Identity." In *Powers of Desire: The Politics of Sexuality*, edited by Ann Snitow, Christine Stansell, and Sharon Thompson, 110–13. New York: Monthly Review Press, 1983.

Dikötter, Frank. "Race Culture: Recent Perspectives on the History of Eugenics." *American Historical Review* 103, no. 2 (1998): 467–78.

Douglas, Lisa. *The Power of Sentiment: Love, Hierarchy, and the Jamaican Family Elite*. Boulder, CO: Westview Press, 1992.

Drucker, Peter. "'In the Tropics There Is No Sin': Sexuality and Gay-Lesbian Movements in the Third World." *New Left Review*, July/August 1996, 75–101.

Eagleton, Terry. *Literary Theory: An Introduction*. Oxford: Oxford University Press, 1983.

Edmondson, Belinda. *Caribbean Middlebrow: Leisure Culture and the Middle Class*. Ithaca, NY: Cornell University Press, 2009.

Edmondson, Belinda. *Making Men: Gender, Literary Authority, and Women's Writing in Caribbean Narrative*. Durham, NC: Duke University Press, 1999.

Eglash, Ron. *African Fractals: Modern Computing and Indigenous Design*. New Brunswick, NJ: Rutgers University Press, 1999.

Ellis, Nadia. "Between Windrush and Wolfden: Class Crossings and Queer Desire in Andrew Salkey's Postwar London." In *Beyond Windrush: Rethinking Postwar Anglophone Caribbean Literature*, edited by J. Dillon Brown and Leah Reade Rosenberg, 60–78. Jackson: University Press of Mississippi, 2015.

Ellis, Nadia. "Black Migrants, White Queers and the Archive of Inclusion in Postwar London." *Interventions* 17, no. 6 (2015): 893–915.

Ellis, Nadia. "Out and Bad: Toward a Queer Performance Hermeneutic in Jamaican Dancehall." *Small Axe* 15, no. 2 (2011): 7–23.

Eng, David, and Jasbir Puar. "Introduction: Left of Queer." *Social Text* 38, no. 4 (2020): 1–23.

Epidemiological Research and Training Unit. *Role of the Contact Investigator in the Control of Sexually Transmitted Diseases*. Kingston: Epidemiological Research and Training Unit, 1986.

Faber, Tom. "Welcome to Jamaica—No Longer 'the Most Homophobic Place on Earth.'" *Guardian*, December 6, 2018. https://www.theguardian.com/global -development/2018/dec/06/jamaica-lgbt-rights-activists-pride-two-decades -of-progress-j-flag.

Fabian, Johannes. *Time and the Other: How Anthropology Makes Its Object*. New York: Colombia University Press, 1983.

Fanon, Franz. *The Wretched of the Earth.* New York: Grove Press, 1963.

Ferguson, Roderick. *Aberrations in Black: Towards a Queer of Color Critique.* Minneapolis: University of Minnesota Press, 2003.

Ferreira da Silva, Denise. "Fractal Thinking." *Accessions* 2 (2016). Accessed February 22, 2023. https://accessions.org/article2/fractal-thinking/.

Figueroa, Peter, and Alfred Brathwaite. "Is Under-Reporting of AIDS a Problem in Jamaica?" *West Indian Medical Journal* 44, no. 2 (1995): 51–54.

Figueroa, Peter, Alfred Brathwaite, Maxine Wedderburn, Elizabeth Ward, K. Lewis-Bell, Joseph Amon, Yasmin Williams, and Evadne Williams. "Is HIV/STD Control in Jamaica Making a Difference?" *AIDS (London, England)* 12 (1998): S89–98.

Figueroa, Peter, Alfred Brathwaite, Elizabeth Ward, Marion DuCasse, Inge Tscharf, O. Nembhard, and Evadne Williams. "The HIV/AIDS Epidemic in Jamaica." *AIDS (London, England)* 9, no. 7 (1995): 761–68.

Flores-Villalobos, Joan. "'Freak Letters' Tracing Gender, Race, and Diaspora in the Panama Canal Archive." *Small Axe* 23, no. 2 (2019): 34–56.

Ford-Smith, Honor. *Lionheart Gal: Life Stories of Jamaican Women.* Toronto: Sister Vision Press, 1987.

Ford-Smith, Honor. "Sistren-Woman's Theatre: A Model for Consciousness-Raising." *Jamaica Journal* 19 (1981): 2–12.

Ford-Smith, Honor. "Unruly Virtues of the Spectacular: Performing Engendered Nationalisms in the UNIA in Jamaica." *Interventions* 6, no. 1 (2004): 18–44.

Foster, Thomas A. *Rethinking Rufus: Sexual Violations of Enslaved Men.* Athens: University of Georgia Press, 2019.

Foucault, Michel. *The Archaeology of Knowledge.* London: Tavistock, 1972.

Foucault, Michel. *The History of Sexuality*, vol. 1: *An Introduction.* New York: Random House, 1978.

Francis, Donette. *Fictions of Feminine Citizenship: Sexuality and the Nation in Contemporary Caribbean Literature.* London: Springer, 2010.

Frazier, Edward Franklin. *The Negro Family in the United States.* Chicago: University of Chicago Press, 1939.

Freccero, Carla. "Queer Times." *South Atlantic Quarterly* 106, no. 3 (2007): 485–94.

Freeman, Elizabeth. *Time Binds: Queer Temporalities, Queer Histories.* Durham, NC: Duke University Press, 2010.

Freidlob, Alan, and Robert Emerson. *Evaluation of the Sexual Transmitted Diseases (STD) Contact Investigation Program in Jamaica.* Kingston: Ministry of Health, 1996.

French, Joan. "Colonial Policy towards Women after the 1938 Uprising: The Case of Jamaica." *Caribbean Quarterly* 34, no. 3–4 (1988): 38–61.

French, Joan. "Organizing Women through Drama in Rural Jamaica." *FAO Ideas and Action*, 163 (1985): 3–7.

French, Joan, and Honor Ford-Smith. *Women and Organization in Jamaica, 1900–1944.* Kingston: Sistren, 1986.

Gallagher, Catherine, and Stephen Greenblatt. "Counterhistory and the Anecdote." In *Practicing New Historicism*, 49–74. Chicago: University of Chicago Press, 2000.

Gebru, Timnit. "Race and Gender." In *The Oxford Handbook of Ethics of AI*, edited by Markus Dubber, Frank Pasquale, and Sunit Das, 251–69. Oxford: Oxford University Press, 2020.

Ghisyawan, Krystal Nandini. *Erotic Cartographies: Decolonization and the Queer Caribbean Imagination*. New Brunswick, NJ: Rutgers University Press, 2022.

Gill, Lyndon K. "Chatting Back an Epidemic: Caribbean Gay Men, HIV/AIDS, and the Uses of Erotic Subjectivity." *GLQ: A Journal of Lesbian and Gay Studies* 18, no. 2–3 (2012): 277–95.

Gill, Lyndon K. *Erotic Islands: Art and Activism in the Queer Caribbean*. Durham, NC: Duke University Press, 2018.

Glissant, Édouard. *Caribbean Discourse: Selected Essays*. Charlottesville: University of Virginia Press, 1989.

Glissant, Édouard. "Creolization in the Making of the Americas." *Caribbean Quarterly* 54, no. 1/2 (2008): 81–89.

Glissant, Édouard. *Poetics of Relation*. Ann Arbor: University of Michigan Press, 1990.

Goldberg, Jonathan. "Sodomy in the New World: Anthropologies Old and New." *Social Text* 29 (1991): 46–56.

Goldberg, Jonathan, and Madhavi Menon. "Queering History." *PMLA* 120, no. 5 (2005): 1608–17.

Goldthree, Reena N. "'Vive La France!' British Caribbean Soldiers and Interracial Intimacies on the Western Front." *Journal of Colonialism and Colonial History* 17, no. 3 (2016). https://muse.jhu.edu/pub/1/article/639506.

Goldthree, Reena N. "Writing New Histories of War and Women's Activism in Jamaica: An Interview with Dalea Bean." *Caribbean Review of Gender Studies* 12 (2018): 345–62.

Gosine, Andil. *Nature's Wild: Love, Sex, and Law in the Caribbean*. Durham, NC: Duke University Press, 2021.

Government of Jamaica. *Report of the Commission of Enquiry into the Police Force*. Kingston: Government Printing Office, 1951.

Gray, Obika. *Radicalism and Social Change in Jamaica, 1960–1972*. Knoxville: University of Tennessee Press, 1991.

Gregory, Joy. "The Fading History of Trevor Owen: A Figure of Jamaica's Independence Fashion Industry." *Textile* 16, no. 2 (2018): 146–65.

Gupta, Akhil, and James Ferguson. "Beyond 'Culture': Space, Identity, and the Politics of Difference." *Cultural Anthropology* 7, no. 1 (1992): 6–23.

Gutzmore, Cecil. "Casting the First Stone! Policing of Homo/Sexuality in Jamaican Popular Culture." *Interventions* 6, no. 1 (2004): 118–34.

Halberstam, Jack. "Female Masculinity." In *Female Masculinity*. Durham, NC: Duke University Press, 1998.

Hall, Catherine. "Gender Politics and Imperial Politics: Rethinking the Politics of Empire." In *Engendering History: Caribbean Women in Historical Perspective*, edited by Verene Shepherd, Bridget Brereton, and Barbara Bailey, 48–59. Kingston: Ian Randle, 1995.

Hall, Douglas. *In Miserable Slavery: Thomas Thistlewood in Jamaica, 1750–86*. Kingston: University of the West Indies Press, 1989.

Hall, Stuart. "Cultural Identity and Diaspora." In *Identity: Community, Culture, Difference*, edited by Jonathan Rutherford, 222–37. London: Lawrence and Wishart, 1993.

Hall, Stuart. "Minimal Selves." In *The Real Me: Post Modernism and the Question of Identity*, edited by Lisa Appignanesi and Homi Bhabha, 44–46. London: Institute of the Contemporary Arts, 1987.

Hammonds, Evelynn. "Black (W)holes and the Geometry of Black Female Sexuality." *Differences: A Journal of Feminist Cultural Studies* 6, no. 2–3 (1994): 126–46.

Harriott, Anthony. "The Changing Social Organization of Crime and Criminals in Jamaica." *Caribbean Quarterly* 42, no. 2–3 (1996): 54–71.

Harrison, Faye V. "The Gendered Politics and Violence of Structural Adjustment: A View from Jamaica." In *Situated Lives: Gender and Culture in Everyday Life*, edited by Louise Lamphere, Helena Ragone, and Patricia Zavella, 451–68. London: Taylor and Francis, 1997.

Harrison, Faye V. "Jamaica and the International Drug Economy." *TransAfrica Forum* 7, no. 3 (1990): 49–57.

Hartman, Saidiya. *Lose Your Mother: A Journey along the Atlantic Slave Route*. New York: Farrar, Straus and Giroux, 2008.

Hawthorne, Evelyn J. *The Writer in Transition: Roger Mais and the Decolonization of Caribbean Culture*. New York: Peter Lang, 1989.

Henriques, Fernando. *Family and Colour in Jamaica*. London: MacGibbon and Kee, 1953.

Henriques, Fernando. *Jamaica, Land of Wood and Water*. London: McGibbon and Kee, 1957.

Henriques, Fernando. *Prostitution and Society*. London: Panther, 1965.

Henry-Wilson, Maxine. "The Status of the Jamaican Woman, 1962 to the Present." In *Jamaica in Independence: Essays on the Early Years*, edited by Rex Nettleford, 229–56. Kingston: Heinemann Caribbean, 1989.

Heuman, Gad J. *Between Black and White: Race, Politics, and the Free Coloreds in Jamaica, 1792–1865*. Westport, CT: Greenwood Press, 1981.

Higman, Barry W. "The Development of Historical Disciplines in the Caribbean." In *General History of the Caribbean*, vol. 6: *Methodology and Historiography of the Caribbean*, edited by Barry W. Higman, 3–18. London: UNESCO, 1999.

Higman, Barry W. *Slave Population and Economy in Jamaica, 1807–1834*. Cambridge: Cambridge University Press, 1976.

Higman, Barry W. *Writing West Indian Histories*. London: Macmillan, 1999.

Holt, Thomas C. "The Essence of the Contract: The Articulation of Race, Gender, and Political Economy in British Emancipation Policy, 1838–1866." In *Beyond Slavery: Explorations of Race, Labor, and Citizenship in Postemancipation Societies*, edited by Frederick Cooper, Thomas C. Scott, and Rebecca J. Scott, 33–59. Chapel Hill: University of North Carolina Press, 2000.

Hong, Grace Kyungwon. *The Ruptures of American Capital: Women of Color Feminism and the Culture of Immigrant Labor*. Minneapolis: University of Minnesota Press, 2006.

Hope Enterprises. *Evaluation of AIDS Messages in Jamaica: A Report of Focus Group Findings*. Kingston: Hope Enterprises, 1988.

Hope Enterprises. *Report on Pretest of STD/AIDS Public Service Announcement*. Kingston: Hope Enterprises, 1995.

Hoppit, Julian. "Political Arithmetic in Eighteenth-Century England." *Economic History Review* 49, no. 3 (1996): 516–40.

Hopwood, Jennifer. "A Study of Gender Relationships and Their Association with the Practice of Safe Sex by Women Who Call into the National HIV/STD Helpline." Master's thesis. University of the West Indies, Mona, 1994.

Hulme, Peter. *Colonial Encounters: Europe and the Native Caribbean, 1492–1797*. London: Methuen, 1986.

Human Rights Watch. *Not Safe at Home: Violence and Discrimination against LGBT People in Jamaica*. New York: Human Rights Watch, 2014.

Hurwitz, Samuel J., and Edith F. Hurwitz. "A Token of Freedom: Private Bill Legislation for Free Negroes in Eighteenth-Century Jamaica." *William and Mary Quarterly* 24, no. 3 (1967): 423–31.

Ilmonen, Kaisa. "Creolizing the Queer: Close Encounters of Race and Sexuality in the Novels of Michelle Cliff." In *Close Encounters of Another Kind: New Perspectives on Race, Ethnicity and American Studies*, edited by Tumas Huttunen, Kaisa Ilmonen, Janne Korkka, and Elina Valovitra, 180–95. Tyne: Cambridge Scholars, 2005.

Inter-American Commission on Human Rights. "Discrimination Based on Sexual Orientation and Gender Identity." In *Report on the Situation of Human Rights in Jamaica*. Washington, DC: Inter-American Commission on Human Rights, 2015. Accessed February 25, 2023. http://www.oas.org/en/iachr/docs/pdf/Jamaica2012eng.pdf.

Isenia, Wigbertson Julian. "Looking for Kambrada." *Tijdschrift Voor Genderstudies* 22, no. 2 (2019): 125–43.

Jackson, Angeline. "Is 'the Most Homophobic Place on Earth' Turning Around?" *Time*, June 1, 2015. https://time.com/3900934/most-homophobic-place-on-earth-turning-around/.

Jackson, Edward, and Stan Persky. *Flaunting It! A Decade of Gay Journalism from the Body Politic: An Anthology*. Vancouver: New Star Books, 1982.

Jackson, Shona N. *Creole Indigeneity: Between Myth and Nation in the Caribbean*. Minneapolis: University of Minnesota Press, 2012.

Jacobs, Len, and Beth Jacobs. *The Family and Family Planning in the West Indies.* London: Allen and Unwin, 1967.

Jamaica Medical Department. *Report of the Medical Services of Jamaica and Its Dependencies.* Kingston: Jamaica Medical Department, 1948.

Jamaica Ministry of Health. *AIDS Control and Prevention Project: Mid-Term Evaluation Status Report.* Kingston: Jamaica Ministry of Health, 1994.

Jamaica Ministry of Health. *National Plan for AIDS.* Kingston: Jamaica Ministry of Health, 1987.

Jamaica National Family Planning Board. *Annual Report for Years 1st April, 1976– 31st March, 1981.* Kingston: Jamaica National Family Planning Board, 1981.

Jefferson, Owen. "Some Aspects of Post-war Economic Development in Jamaica." In *Readings in the Political Economy of the Caribbean,* edited by Norman Girvan and Owen Jefferson, 109–20. Kingston: New World Group, 1971.

J-FLAG. *Annual Country Status Update.* Kingston: J-FLAG, 2018. Accessed February 20, 2023. http://jflag.org/wp-content/%0Auploads/2018/09/Annual -Country-Status-Update.pdf.

J-FLAG. *Human Rights Violations.* Kingston: J-FLAG, 2019.

Jillson-Boostrom, Irene. *AIDS in Jamaica: Present Realities and Future Possibilities.* Kingston: USAID Jamaica, 1987.

Johnson, David K. "America's Cold War Empire: Exporting the Lavender Scare." In *Global Homophobia: States, Movements, and the Politics of Oppression,* edited by Meredith L. Weiss and Michael J. Bosia, 55–76. Urbana: University of Illinois Press, 2013.

Johnson, David K. *The Lavender Scare: The Cold War Persecution of Gays and Lesbians in the Federal Government.* Chicago: University of Chicago Press, 2004.

Johnson, Howard. "The Anti-Chinese Riots of 1918 in Jamaica." *Caribbean Quarterly* 28, no. 3 (1982): 19–32.

Johnson, Jessica Marie. "Markup Bodies: Black [Life] Studies and Slavery [Death] Studies at the Digital Crossroads." *Social Text* 36, no. 4 (2018): 57–79.

Jordan, Winthrop D. "American Chiaroscuro: The Status and Definition of Mulattoes in the British Colonies." *William and Mary Quarterly* 19, no. 2 (1962): 183–200.

Kamugisha, Aaron. *Beyond Coloniality: Citizenship and Freedom in the Caribbean Intellectual Tradition.* Bloomington: Indiana University Press, 2019.

Kauanui, J. Kehaulani. *Hawaiian Blood: Colonialism and the Politics of Sovereignty and Indigeneity.* Durham, NC: Duke University Press, 2008.

Keeling, Kara. "Looking for M—Queer Temporality, Black Political Possibility, and Poetry from the Future." *GLQ: A Journal of Lesbian and Gay Studies* 15, no. 4 (2009): 565–82.

Keeling, Kara. *Queer Times, Black Futures.* New York: NYU Press, 2019.

Kempadoo, Kamala. *Sexing the Caribbean: Gender, Race, and Sexual Labor.* New York: Routledge, 2004.

Kerr, Madeline. *Personality and Conflict in Jamaica*. Liverpool: University Press, 1951.

Khan, Aisha. "Journey to the Center of the Earth: The Caribbean as Master Symbol." *Cultural Anthropology* 16, no. 3 (2001): 271–302.

Khan, Aliyah. "Voyages across Indenture: From Ship Sister to Mannish Woman." GLQ: *A Journal of Lesbian and Gay Studies* 22, no. 2 (2016): 249–80.

King, Rosamond S. "Building a Digital Archive." *SX Salon* 6 (2011). Accessed February 25, 2023. http://smallaxe.net/sxsalon/discussions/building-digital -archive.

King, Rosamond S. "New Citizens, New Sexualities: Nineteenth-Century Jamettes." In *Sex and the Citizen: Interrogating the Caribbean*, edited by Faith Smith, 214–23. Charlottesville: University of Virginia Press, 2011.

Kopytoff, Barbara K. "The Early Political Development of Jamaican Maroon Societies." *William and Mary Quarterly* 35, no. 2 (1978): 287–307.

Kuper, Adam. *Changing Jamaica*. London: Routledge, 1976.

LaFont, Suzanne, and Deborah Pruitt. "The Colonial Legacy: Gendered Laws in Jamaica." In *Daughters of Caliban: Caribbean Women in the Twentieth Century*, edited by Consuelo Lopez-Springfield, 215–28. Bloomington: Indiana University Press, 1997.

La Fountain-Stokes, Lawrence. "1898 and the History of a Queer Puerto Rican Century: Imperialism, Diaspora and Transformation." In *Chicano/Latino Homoerotic Identities*, edited by David William Foster, 197–215. New York: Garland, 1999.

Lakoff, George, and Mark Johnson. *Metaphors We Live By*. Chicago: University of Chicago Press, 2003.

Lara, Ana-Maurine. *Queer Freedom: Black Sovereignty*. Albany: State University of New York Press, 2020.

Lauretis, Teresa de. "Queer Theory: Lesbian and Gay Sexualities, an Introduction." *Differences: A Journal of Feminist Cultural Studies* 3, no. 2 (1991): iii–xviii.

LaViolette, Nicole, and Sandra Whitworth. "No Safe Haven: Sexuality as a Universal Human Right and Gay and Lesbian Activism in International Politics." *Millennium* 23, no. 3 (1994): 563–88.

Lawrence, O'Neil. "Through Archie Lindo's Lens: Uncovering the Queer Subtext in Nationalist Jamaican Art." *Small Axe: A Caribbean Journal of Criticism* 24, no. 3 (2020): 143–63.

Leap, William. *Word's Out: Gay Men's English*. Minneapolis: University of Minnesota Press, 1996.

Lee, Easton. *The Chinese in Jamaica—A Personal Account*. Unpublished manuscript, 1984.

Lee-Loy, Anne-Marie. *Searching for Mr. Chin: Constructions of Nation and the Chinese in West Indian Literature*. Philadelphia: Temple University Press, 2010.

LeFranc, Elsie, ed. *Consequences of Structural Adjustment: A Review of the Jamaican Experience*. Kingston: University of the West Indies Press, 1994.

Levine, Philippa. "Orientalist Sociology and the Creation of Colonial Sexualities." *Feminist Review* 65, no. 1 (2000): 5–21.

Levine, Philippa. *Prostitution, Race and Politics: Policing Venereal Disease in the British Empire*. New York: Routledge, 2003.

Levy, Horace. "The Social Action Center Story, 1958–1998." In *Spitting in the Wind: Lessons in Empowerment from the Caribbean*, edited by Suzanne Francis Brown, 99–148. Kingston: Ian Randle, 2000.

Levy, Jacqueline. "The Economic Role of the Chinese in Jamaica: The Grocery Retail Trade." *Jamaican Historical Review* 15 (1986): 31.

Lewis, Jovan Scott. *Scammer's Yard: The Crime of Black Repair in Jamaica*. Minneapolis: University of Minnesota Press, 2020.

Lewis, Rupert. "J. J. Thomas and Political Thought in the Caribbean." *Caribbean Quarterly* 36, no. 1/2 (1990): 46–58.

Lewis, Rupert. "Walter Rodney: 1968 Revisited." *Social and Economic Studies* 34, no. 3 (1994): 7–56.

Lind, Andrew W. "Adjustment Patterns among the Jamaican Chinese." *Social and Economic Studies* 7, no. 2 (1958): 144–64.

Lokaisingh-Meighoo, Sean. "Jahaji Bhai: Notes on the Masculine Subject and Homoerotic Subtext of Indo-Caribbean Identity." *Small Axe* 7, no. 1 (2000): 77–92.

Look Lai, Walton. *Indentured Labor, Caribbean Sugar: Chinese and Indian Migrants to the British West Indies, 1838–1918*. Baltimore: Johns Hopkins University Press, 1993.

Love, Heather. *Feeling Backward: Loss and the Politics of Queer History*. Cambridge, MA: Harvard University Press, 2007.

Lowe, Lisa. *Intimacy of Four Continents*. Durham, NC: Duke University Press, 2015.

Lubar, Steven. "'Do Not Fold, Spindle or Mutilate': A Cultural History of the Punch Card." *Journal of American Culture* 15, no. 4 (1992): 43–55.

Macharia, Keguro. *Frottage: Frictions of Intimacy across the Black Diaspora*. New York: NYU Press, 2019.

Mair, Lucille Mathurin. *A Historical Study of Women in Jamaica from 1655 to 1844*. Edited by Hilary M. Beckles and Verene A. Shepard. Kingston: University of the West Indies Press, 2006.

Mais, Roger. *Black Lightning*. London: Jonathan Cape, 1955.

Mandelbrot, Benoit. *The Fractal Geometry of Nature*. New York: W. H. Freeman, 1982.

Mandelbrot, Benoit. *The Fractalist: Memoir of a Scientific Maverick*. New York: Vintage, 2012.

Marquis of Landsdowne, ed. *The Petty Papers: Some Unpublished Writings of Sir William Petty*. London: Constable and Co., 1927.

Maynier-Burke, Shirley. "Rex Nettleford Choreographer on NDTC's 'The Crossing.'" *Jamaica Journal* 43 (1979): 2–11.

McAfee, Kathy. *Storm Signals: Structural Adjustment and Development Alterna-tives in the Caribbean*. London: Zed Books, 1991.

McKittrick, Katherine. "Mathematics Black Life." *Black Scholar* 44, no. 2 (2014): 16–28.

McLean, Geoffrey. *Boscoe Holder*. Port of Spain: MacLean, 1994.

McPherson, Tara. "Why Are the Digital Humanities So White? Or Thinking the Histories of Race and Computation." In *Debates in the Digital Humanities*, edited by Matthew Gold, 139–60. Minneapolis: University of Minnesota Press, 2012.

Mintz, Sidney W. "The Caribbean as a Socio-Cultural Area." *Cahiers d'Histoire Mondiale* 9, no. 1 (1965): 912–37.

Mintz, Sidney W. *Caribbean Transformations*. New York: Columbia University Press, 1989.

Mintz, Sidney W. "Enduring Substances, Trying Theories: The Caribbean Region as Oikoumene." *Journal of the Royal Anthropological Institute* 2, no. 2 (1996): 289–311.

Mitchell, Timothy. "The Stage of Modernity." In *The Question of Modernity*, edited by Timothy Mitchell, 1–34. Minneapolis: University of Minnesota Press, 2000.

Mitra, Durba. *Indian Sex Life: Sexuality and the Colonial Origins of Modern Social Thought*. Princeton, NJ: Princeton University Press, 2020.

Mohammed, Patricia. "Women's and Feminist Activism in the Caribbean." In *The Wiley Blackwell Encyclopedia of Gender and Sexuality Studies*, ed-ited by Nancy Naples, Renee Hoogland, Maithree Wickramasinghe, and Wai Chung Angela Wong, 2480–85. Wiley Online Library, 2016. https://onlinelibrary.wiley.com/doi/abs/10.1002/9781118663219.wbegss412.

Moore, Brian L., and Michele A. Johnson. "'Fallen Sisters'? Attitudes to Female Prostitution in Jamaica at the Turn of the Twentieth Century." *Journal of Caribbean History* 34, no. 1/2 (2000): 46–70.

Moore, Brian L., and Michele A. Johnson. "'We Are Heathen': Asian Cultures in the Culture War." In *"They Do as They Please": The Jamaican Struggle for Cultural Freedom after Morant Bay*, 360–404. Kingston: University of the West Indies Press, 2011.

Morgan, Jennifer L. *Reckoning with Slavery: Gender, Kinship, and Capitalism in the Early Black Atlantic*. Durham, NC: Duke University Press, 2021.

Morgan, Kenneth. "Slave Women and Reproduction in Jamaica, c. 1776–1834." *History* 91, no. 2 (2006): 231–53.

Morgensen, Scott Lauria. "Settler Homonationalism: Theorizing Settler Colonial-ism within Queer Modernities." *GLQ: A Journal of Lesbian and Gay Studies* 16, no. 1/2 (2010): 105–31.

Moussawi, Ghassan. *Disruptive Situations: Fractal Orientalism and Queer Strate-gies in Beirut*. Philadelphia: Temple University Press. 2020.

Mullings, Beverley. "Globalization, Tourism, and the International Sex Trade."
    In *Sun, Sex and Gold: Tourism and Sex Work in the Caribbean*, edited by
    Kamala Kempadoo, 55–81. Oxford: Rowman and Littlefield, 1999.

Muñoz, José Esteban. *Cruising Utopia: The Then and There of Queer Futurity*. New
    York: NYU Press, 2009.

Muñoz, José Esteban. "Ephemera as Evidence: Introductory Notes to Queer Acts."
    Women & Performance: A Journal of Feminist Theory 8 (1996): 5–16.

Munroe, Trevor. *The Politics of Constitutional Decolonization: Jamaica, 1944–62.*
    Kingston: Institute of Social and Economic Research, University of the West
    Indies, 1972.

Murphy, E. L., W. N. Gibbs, J. P. Figueroa, B. Bain, L. LaGrenade, B. Cranston,
    and W. A. Blattner. "Human Immunodeficiency Virus and Human
    T-Lymphotropic Virus Type I Infection among Homosexual Men in
    Kingston, Jamaica." *Journal of Acquired Immune Deficiency Syndromes* 1,
    no. 2 (1988): 143–49.

Nettleford, Rex. *Caribbean Cultural Identity: The Case of Jamaica*. Kingston:
    Institute of Jamaica, 1978.

Nettleford, Rex. *Dance Jamaica: Cultural Definition and Artistic Discovery—The
    National Dance Theatre Company of Jamaica, 1962–1983*. New York: Grove
    Press, 1985.

Nettleford, Rex. "Introduction: The Fledgling Years." In *Jamaica in Independence:
    Essays on the Early Years*, edited by Rex Nettleford, 1–18. Kingston: Heine-
    mann Caribbean, 1989.

Nettleford, Rex. *Mirror, Mirror: Identity, Race, and Protest in Jamaica*. Kingston:
    W. Collins and Sangster, 1970.

Nettleford, Rex. "National Identity and Attitudes to Race in Jamaica." *Race* 7, no. 1
    (1965): 59–72.

Nettleford, Rex, M. G. Smith, and Roy Augier. *Report on the Rastafari Movement
    in Kingston, Jamaica*. Kingston: University of the West Indies Press, 1960.

Nixon, Angelique V. *Resisting Paradise: Tourism, Diaspora, and Sexuality in
    Caribbean Culture*. Jackson: University Press of Mississippi, 2015.

Noxolo, Patricia. "Caribbean In/Securities: An Introduction." *Small Axe* 22, no. 3
    (2018): 37–46.

Nugent, Lady Maria. *Lady Nugent's Journal of Her Residence in Jamaica from 1801
    to 1805*. Edited by Philip Wright. Kingston: University of the West Indies
    Press, 2002.

Padgett, Tim. "The Most Homophobic Place on Earth." *Time*, April 12, 2006.
    https://content.time.com/time/world/article/0,8599,1182991,00.html.

Palmié, Stephan. "Creolization and Its Discontents." *Annual Review of Anthropol-
    ogy* 35 (2006): 433–56.

Paravisini-Gebert, Lizabeth. "Decolonizing Feminism: The Homegrown Roots of
    Caribbean Women's Feminism." In *Daughters of Caliban: Caribbean Women*

in the Twentieth Century, edited by Consuelo Lopez Springfield, 3–17.
Bloomington: Indiana University Press, 1997.

Parker, Jeffrey. "Empire's Angst: The Politics of Race, Migration and Sex Work in
Panama, 1903–1945." PhD diss., University of Texas at Austin, 2013.

Parker, Matthew. *Goldeneye: Where Bond Was Born—Ian Fleming's Jamaica*. New
York: Random House, 2014.

Payne, Anthony. "The Rodney Riots in Jamaica: The Background and Significance
of the Events of October 1968." *Journal of Commonwealth & Comparative
Politics* 21, no. 2 (1983): 158–74.

Petty, William. *The Political Anatomy of Ireland*. London: D. Brown and W. Rog-
ers., 1691.

Petty, William. *Political Arithmetick*. London: R. Clavel and H. Mortlock, 1690.

Phillips, James. "Democratic Socialism, the New International Economic Order,
and Globalization: Jamaica's Sugar Cooperatives in the Post-colonial Transition." *Global South* 4, no. 2 (2010): 178–96.

Poovey, Mary. *A History of the Modern Fact: Problems of Knowledge in the Sciences of Wealth and Society*. Chicago: University of Chicago Press, 1998.

Porter, Theodore M. *Trust in Numbers: The Pursuit of Objectivity in Science and
Public Life*. Princeton, NJ: Princeton University Press, 1995.

Powell, Patricia. *A Small Gathering of Bones*. Boston: Beacon Press, 1994.

Price, Richard. "Introduction: Maroons and Their Communities." In *Maroon
Societies: Rebel Slave Communities in the Americas*, edited by Richard Price,
1–32. Baltimore: Johns Hopkins University Press, 1996.

Pruitt, Deborah, and Suzanne LaFont. "For Love and Money: Romance Tourism
in Jamaica." *Annals of Tourism Research* 22, no. 2 (1995): 422–40.

Pugh, Emerson W. *Building IBM: Shaping an Industry and Its Technology*. Cambridge, MA: MIT Press, 1995.

Putnam, Lara. *The Company They Kept: Migrants and the Politics of Gender in
Caribbean Costa Rica, 1870–1960*. Chapel Hill: University of North Carolina
Press, 2002.

Rao, Rahul. *Out of Time: The Queer Politics of Postcoloniality*. Oxford: Oxford
University Press, 2020.

Reddock, Rhoda. "Women's Organizations and Movements in the Commonwealth Caribbean: The Response to Global Economic Crisis in the 1980s."
Feminist Review 59 (1998): 57–73.

Reddock, Rhoda, and Dorothy Roberts. "Introduction." In *Sex, Power and Taboo:
Gender and HIV in the Caribbean and Beyond*, edited by Dorothy Roberts,
ix–xxx. Kingston: Ian Randle, 2009.

Reid, Victor Stafford. "The Cultural Revolution in Jamaica after 1938." In *The
Routledge Reader in Caribbean Literature*, edited by Alison Donnell and
Sara Lawson Welsh, 144–47. London: Routledge, 1996.

Richards, Eric. "Scotland and the Uses of the Atlantic Empire." In *Strangers within
the Realm: Cultural Margins of the First British Empire*, edited by Bernard

Bailyn and Philip D. Morgan, 67–114. Chapel Hill: University of North Carolina Press, 1991.

Richardson, Angela. "I Was Born the Day I Came Out." In *Tongues on Fire: Caribbean Lesbian Lives and Stories*, edited by Rosamund Elwin, 73–79. Toronto: Women's Press, 1997.

Roberts, George W. *The Population of Jamaica*. Cambridge: Cambridge University Press, 1957.

Robinson, Cedric J. *Black Marxism: The Making of the Black Radical Tradition*. London: Zed Books, 1983.

Robinson, Tracy. "Mass Weddings in Jamaica and the Production of Academic Folk Knowledge." *Small Axe* 24, no. 3 (2020): 65–80.

Robinson, Tracy. "The Properties of Citizens: A Caribbean Grammar of Conjugal Categories." *Du Bois Review: Social Science Research on Race* 10, no. 2 (2013): 425–46.

Rohlehr, Gordon. "History as Absurdity: A Literary Critic's Approach to *From Columbus to Castro* and Other Miscellaneous Writings of Dr. Eric Williams." In *Is Massa Day Dead? Black Moods in the Caribbean*, edited by Orde Coombs, 69–98. New York: Anchor Books, 1974.

Romain, Gemma. *Race, Sexuality and Identity in Britain and Jamaica: The Biography of Patrick Nelson*. New York: Bloomsbury Academic, 2017.

Rosenberg, Leah. "The New Woman and 'the Dusky Strand': The Place of Feminism and Women's Literature in Early Jamaican Nationalism." *Feminist Review* 95, no. 1 (2010): 45–63.

Ross-Frankson, Joan. *The Economic Crisis and Prostitution in Jamaica: A Preliminary Study*. Kingston: Sistren, 1987.

Rotman, Brian. "Toward a Semiotics of Mathematics." *Semiotica* 72, no. 1/2 (1988): 1–36.

Royes, Heather H. *Jamaican Men and Same-Sex Activities: Implications for HIV/STD Prevention*. Washington, DC: AIDSCOM, 1993.

Rubenstein, Hymie. "Remittances and Rural Underdevelopment in the English-Speaking Caribbean." *Human Organization* 42, no. 4 (1983): 295–306.

Ryman, Cheryl. "The Jamaican Heritage in Dance." *Jamaica Journal* 44, no. 4 (1980): 2–14.

Ryman, Cheryl. "Jonkonnu: A Neo-African Form." *Jamaica Journal* 17, no. 1 (1984): 13–23.

Santos-Febres, Mayra. "The Fractal Caribbean." YouTube, 2019. Accessed February 20, 2023. https://www.youtube.com/watch?v=8tFlLkUSr84&list =LL.

Saunders, Patricia J. "Is Not Everything Good to Eat, Good to Talk: Sexual Economy and Dancehall Music in the Global Marketplace." *Small Axe* 7, no. 1 (2003): 95–115.

Sayers, William. "The Etymology of Queer." *Quarterly Journal of Short Articles, Notes and Reviews* 18, no. 2 (2005): 17–19.

Schechner, Richard. *Between Theater and Anthropology.* Philadelphia: University of Pennsylvania Press, 1985.

Scott, David. *Conscripts of Modernity: The Tragedy of Colonial Enlightenment.* Durham, NC: Duke University Press, 2004.

Scott, David. *Omens of Adversity: Tragedy, Time, Memory, Justice.* Durham, NC: Duke University Press, 2013.

Scott, David. "The Tragic Vision in Postcolonial Time." *PMLA* 129, no. 4 (2014): 799–808.

Scott, David, and Rex Nettleford. "'To Be Liberated from the Obscurity of Themselves': An Interview with Rex Nettleford." *Small Axe* 10, no. 2 (2006): 97–246.

Seaga, Edward. "Cults in Jamaica." *Jamaica Journal* 3, no. 2 (1969): 3–13.

Sealy, Godfrey. *One of Our Sons Is Missing.* In *You Can Lead a Horse to Water and Other Plays*, edited by Judy Stone, 105–61. Oxford: Macmillan Caribbean, 2005.

Sedgwick, Eve Kosofsky. *Epistemology of the Closet.* Berkeley: University of California Press, 1990.

Sedgwick, Eve Kosofsky. "Paranoid Reading and Reparative Reading, or, You're So Paranoid, You Probably Think This Essay Is about You." In *Touching Feeling: Affect, Pedagogy and Performativity*, 123–51. Durham, NC: Duke University Press, 2003.

Sedgwick, Eve Kosofsky. *Tendencies.* Durham, NC: Duke University Press, 1993.

Senior, Olive. "The Colon People." *Jamaica Journal* 11, no. 3/4 (1978): 62–71.

Senior, Olive. "The Colon People, Part 2." *Jamaica Journal* 42 (1979): 87–103.

Senior, Olive. *The Message Is Change: A Perspective on the 1972 General Elections.* Kingston: Kingston Publishers, 1972.

Sheller, Mimi. "Acting as Free Men: Subaltern Masculinities and Citizenship in Postslavery Jamaica." In *Gender and Slave Emancipation in the Atlantic World*, edited by Diana Paton, 79–98. Durham, NC: Duke University Press, 2005.

Sheller, Mimi. *Citizenship from Below: Erotic Agency and Caribbean Freedom.* Durham, NC: Duke University Press, 2012.

Sheller, Mimi. *Consuming the Caribbean: From Arawaks to Zombies.* London: Psychology Press, 2003.

Sheller, Mimi. "Quasheba, Mother, Queen: Black Women's Public Leadership and Political Protest in Post-emancipation Jamaica, 1834–65." *Slavery and Abolition* 19, no. 3 (1998): 90–117.

Shepherd, Verene A. "Past Imperfect, Future Perfect? Reparations, Rehabilitation, Reconciliation." *Journal of African American History* 103, no. 12 (2018): 19–43.

Shepherd, Verene A. *Transients to Settlers: The Experience of Indians in Jamaica, 1845–1950.* London: Peepal Tree Press, 1994.

Silvera, Makeda. "Man Royals and Sodomites: Some Thoughts on the Invisibility of Afro-Caribbean Lesbians." *Feminist Studies* 18, no. 3 (1992): 521–32.

Simpson, Audra. *Mohawk Interruptus: Political Life across the Borders of Settler States*. Durham, NC: Duke University Press, 2014.

Simpson, George Eaton. "Jamaican Revivalist Cults." *Social and Economic Studies* 5, no. 4 (1956): 321–442.

Skelton, Tracey. "Boom, Bye, Bye: Jamaican Ragga and Gay Resistance." In *Mapping Desire: Geographies of Sexualities*, edited by David Bell and Gill Valentine, 264–83. London: Routledge, 1995.

Smith, Christen A. "Counting Frequency: Un/Gendering Anti-Black Police Terror." *Social Text* 39, no. 2 (2021): 25–49.

Smith, Faith. *Creole Recitations: John Jacob Thomas and Colonial Formation in the Late Nineteenth-Century Caribbean*. Charlottesville: University of Virginia Press, 2002.

Smith, Faith. "Sexing the Citizen." In *Sex and the Citizen: Interrogating the Caribbean*, edited by Faith Smith, 1–20. Charlottesville: University of Virginia Press, 2011.

Smith, Faith. "The Soundings with My Sisters: Sovereignty, Intimacy, Disappointment." *Small Axe* 21, no. 3 (2017): 124–37.

Smith, Len, Janet McCalman, Ian Anderson, Sandra Smith, Joanne Evans, Gavan McCarthy, and Jane Beer. "Fractional Identities: The Political Arithmetic of Aboriginal Victorians." *Journal of Interdisciplinary History* 38, no. 4 (2008): 533–51.

Smith, Michael G. *A Framework for Caribbean Studies*. Kingston: University College of the West Indies, Extra-Mural Department, 1955.

Smith, Michael G. *Kinship and Community in Carriacou*. New Haven, CT: Yale University Press, 1962.

Smith, Michael G. *West Indian Family Structure*. Seattle: University of Washington Press, 1962.

Smith, Richard. *Jamaican Volunteers in the First World War: Race, Masculinity and the Development of National Consciousness*. Manchester: Manchester University Press, 2004.

Smith, Susan J., and John G. Stover. *AIDS and Sexually Transmitted Diseases in Jamaica: Highlights of a Nationwide Survey and Focus Group Series Assessing Current Knowledge, Attitudes and Practices*. Glastonbury, CT: SOMARC/The Futures Group, 1989.

Smith, Susan J., and John G. Stover. *Impact of the 1988–89 National AIDS Communications Campaign on AIDS-Related Attitudes and Behaviors in Jamaica*. Glastonbury, CT: SOMARC/The Futures Group, 1990.

Sobo, Elisa Janine. *One Blood: The Jamaican Body*. Albany: SUNY Press, 1993.

Somerville, Siobhan B. "Queer." In *Keywords for American Cultural Studies*, edited by Bruce Burgett and Glenn Hendler, 203–7. New York: NYU Press, 2014.

Soto, Isa. "West Indian Child Fostering: Its Role in Migrant Exchanges." *Center for Migration Studies Special Issues* 7, no. 1 (1989): 121–37.

Speed, Shannon. *Incarcerated Stories: Indigenous Women Migrants and Violence in the Settler-Capitalist State*. Chapel Hill: University of North Carolina Press, 2019.

Spillers, Hortense J. "Mama's Baby, Papa's Maybe: An American Grammar Book." *Diacritics* 17, no. 2 (1987): 65–81.

Spivak, Gayatri. "Can the Subaltern Speak?" In *Marxism and the Interpretation of Culture*, edited by Cary Nelson and Lawrence Grossberg, 271–313. Urbana: University of Illinois Press, 1972.

Stamford, John, ed. *Spartacus: International Gay Guide*. Amsterdam: Spartacus, 1979.

Stephens, Evelyne H., and John D. Stephens, eds. *Democratic Socialism in Jamaica*. Princeton, NJ: Princeton University Press, 1986.

Stevens, Nikki, Anna Lauren Hoffmann, and Sarah Florini. "The Unremarked Optimum: Whiteness, Optimization, and Control in the Database Revolution." *Review of Communication* 21, no. 2 (2021): 113–28.

Stocking, George. *Race, Culture and Evolution: Essays in the History of Anthropology*. New York: Free Press, 1968.

Stoler, Ann L. *Race and the Education of Desire: Foucault's History of Sexuality and the Colonial Order of Things*. Durham, NC: Duke University Press, 1995.

Stolzoff, Norman C. *Wake the Town and Tell the People: Dancehall Culture in Jamaica*. Durham, NC: Duke University Press, 2000.

Stone, Rosemarie. *No Stone Unturned: The Carl and Rosie Story*. Kingston: Ian Randle, 2007.

Strasser, Max. "Top Twelve Most Homophobic Nations." *Newsweek*, February 27, 2014. http://www.newsweek.com/top-twelve-most-homophobic-nations-230348.

Suffee, Réshad. "Homosexuality and the Law: The Construction of Wolfenden Homonormativity in 1950s England." *Journal of Homosexuality* 63, no. 2 (2016): 250–77.

Swingen, Abigail L. *Competing Visions of Empire: Labor, Slavery, and the Origins of the British Atlantic Empire*. New Haven, CT: Yale University Press, 2015.

Tambe, Ashwini. *Codes of Misconduct: Regulating Prostitution in Late Colonial Bombay*. Minneapolis: University of Minnesota Press, 2009.

Taylor, Diana. *The Archive and the Repertoire: Performing Cultural Memory in the Americas*. Durham, NC: Duke University Press, 2003.

Taylor, Frank F. *To Hell with Paradise: A History of the Jamaican Tourist Industry*. Philadelphia: University of Pittsburgh Press, 2003.

Thame, Maziki. "Racial Hierarchy and the Elevation of Brownness in Creole Nationalism." *Small Axe* 21, no. 3 (2017): 111–23.

Thames, Carol. "Two Happy People in the World." In *Tongues on Fire: Caribbean Lesbian Lives and Stories*, edited by Rosamund Elwin, 27–40. Toronto: Women's Press, 1997.

Thomas, Adam. "'Outcasts from the World': Same-Sex Sexuality, Authority, and Belonging in Post-emancipation Jamaica." *Slavery & Abolition* 40, no. 3 (2019): 423–47.

Thomas, Deborah A. "Democratizing Dance: Institutional Transformation and Hegemonic Re-Ordering in Postcolonial Jamaica." *Cultural Anthropology* 17, no. 4 (2002): 512–50.

Thomas, Deborah A. *Exceptional Violence: Embodied Citizenship in Transnational Jamaica.* Durham, NC: Duke University Press, 2011.

Thomas, Deborah A. *Modern Blackness: Nationalism, Globalization, and the Politics of Culture in Jamaica.* Durham, NC: Duke University Press, 2004.

Thomas, Deborah A. *Political Life in the Wake of the Plantation: Sovereignty, Witnessing, Repair.* Durham, NC: Duke University Press, 2019.

Thomas, Deborah A., John Jackson, and Junior Gabu Wedderburn. *Bad Friday: Rastafari after Coral Gardens.* New York: Third World Newsreel, 2011.

Thomas, John Jacob. *Froudacity; West Indian Fables.* London: T. Fisher Unwin, 1889.

Thomas-Hope, Elizabeth M. "The Establishment of a Migration Tradition: British West Indian Movements to the Hispanic Caribbean in the Century after Emancipation." In *Caribbean Social Relations*, edited by Colin G. Clarke, 66–81. Liverpool: University of Liverpool, Center for Latin American Studies, 1978.

Thomas-Hope, Elizabeth M., and R. D. Nutter. "Occupation and Status in the Ideology of Caribbean Return Migration." In *The Impact of International Migration on Developing Countries*, edited by Reginald T. Appleyard, 287–300. Paris: Development Centre of the OECD, 1989.

Thompson, Alvin O. "Gender and Marronage in the Caribbean." *Journal of Caribbean History* 39, no. 2 (2005): 262–89

Tinsley, Omise'eke N. "Black Atlantic, Queer Atlantic: Queer Imaginings of the Middle Passage." GLQ: *A Journal of Lesbian and Gay Studies* 14, no. 2/3 (2008): 191–215.

Tinsley, Omise'eke N. *Ezili's Mirrors: Imagining Black Queer Genders.* Durham, NC: Duke University Press, 2018.

Tinsley, Omise'eke N. *Thiefing Sugar: Eroticism between Women in Caribbean Literature.* Durham, NC: Duke University Press, 2010.

Torpey, John. *Making Whole What Has Been Smashed: On Reparations Politics.* Cambridge, MA: Harvard University Press, 2006.

Traub, Valerie. "The new unhistoricism in queer studies." PMLA 128, no. 1 (2013): 21–39.

Trexler, Richard C. *Sex and Conquest: Gendered Violence, Political Order, and the European Conquest of the Americas.* Ithaca, NY: Cornell University Press, 1995.

Trouillot, Michel-Rolph. "North Atlantic Universals: Analytical Fictions, 1492–1945." *South Atlantic Quarterly* 101, no. 4 (2002): 839–58.

Turner, Georgina. "Catching the Wave: Britain's Lesbian Publishing Goes Commercial." *Journalism Studies* 10, no. 6 (2009): 769–88.

Turner, Sasha. *Contested Bodies: Pregnancy, Childrearing, and Slavery in Jamaica.*
Philadelphia: University of Pennsylvania Press, 2017.

Turner, Victor. *The Anthropology of Performance.* New York: PAJ Publications,
1986.

Ulysse, Gina. "Uptown Ladies and Downtown Women: Female Representations of Class and Color in Jamaica." In *Representations of Blackness and
the Performance of Identities*, edited by Jean Rahier, 147–72. Westport, CT:
Greenwood Press, 1999.

US Department of State. *Country Reports on Human Rights Practices for 1987.*
Washington, DC: US Government Printing Office, 1988.

Vassell, Linnette. "The Movement for the Vote for Women, 1918–1919." *Jamaican
Historical Review* 18 (1993): 40.

Veer, Henrietta De. "Sex Roles and Social Stratification in a Rapidly Growing Urban
Area—May Pen, Jamaica." PhD diss., University of Chicago, 1979.

Vendryes, Margaret R. *Barthé: A Life in Sculpture.* Jackson: University Press of
Mississippi, 2008.

Walcott, Rinaldo. "Queer Returns: Human Rights, the Anglo-Caribbean and
Diaspora Politics." *Caribbean Review of Gender Studies* 3 (2009): 1–19.

Walker, Christine. *Jamaica Ladies: Female Slaveholders and the Creation of Britain's
Atlantic Empire.* Chapel Hill: University of North Carolina Press, 2020.

Warner, Michael. "Introduction: Fear of a Queer Planet." *Social Text* 29 (1991): 3–17.

Warner, Michael. "Publics and Counterpublics." *Public Culture* 14, no. 1 (2002):
49–90.

Wedenoja, William. "The Quest for Justice in Revival, a Creole Religion in
Jamaica." In *The Wiley-Blackwell Companion to Religion and Social Justice*,
edited by Michael D. Palmer and Stanley M. Burgess, 224–40. Oxford:
Wiley-Blackwell, 2012.

Wekker, Gloria. *The Politics of Passion: Women's Sexual Culture in the Afro-
Surinamese Diaspora.* New York: Columbia University Press, 2006.

White, Garth. "Rudie, Oh Rudie!" *Caribbean Quarterly* 13, no. 3 (1967): 39–44.

White, Hayden. *Metahistory: The Historical Imagination in Nineteenth-Century
Europe.* Baltimore: Johns Hopkins University Press, 1973.

White, Luise. *Speaking with Vampires: Rumor and History in Colonial Africa.*
Berkeley: University of California Press, 2000.

Whitehead, Tony. "Men, Family and Family Planning: Male Role Perception and
Performance in a Jamaican Sugartown." PhD diss., University of Pittsburgh,
1976.

Williams, Eric. *Capitalism and Slavery.* Chapel Hill: University of North Carolina
Press, 1944.

Williams, Lawson. "Homophobia and Gay Rights Activism in Jamaica." *Small Axe*
7, no. 1 (2000): 106–11.

Wilson, Peter J. "Reputation and Respectability: A Suggestion for Caribbean Ethnology." *Man* 4, no. 1 (1969): 70–84.

Women's Empowerment for Change. *The Health Seeking Behavior of LGBTQ Women in Jamaica: Sexual and Reproductive Health*. Kingston: Women's Empowerment for Change, 2019.

Woodard, Vincent. *The Delectable Negro: Human Consumption and Homoeroticism within US Slave Culture*. New York: NYU Press, 2014.

World Population Review. "Most Homophobic Countries 2023." Accessed February 20, 2023. https://worldpopulationreview.com/country-rankings/most -homophobic-countries.

Wynter, Sylvia. *The Hills of Hebron: A Jamaican Novel*. New York: Simon and Schuster, 1962.

Wynter, Sylvia. "Novel and History, Plot and Plantation." *Savacou* 5 (1971): 95–102.

Wynter, Sylvia. "One Love—Rhetoric or Reality?—Aspects of Afro-Jamaicanism." *Caribbean Studies* 12, no. 3 (1972): 64–97.

Wynter, Sylvia. "Unsettling the Coloniality of Being/Power/Truth/Freedom: Towards the Human, after Man, Its Overrepresentation—an Argument." *CR: The New Centennial Review* 3, no. 3 (2003): 257–337.

Wynter, Sylvia. "We Must Learn to Sit Down Together and Talk about a Little Culture." *Jamaica Journal* 2, no. 4 (1968): 23–32.

Young, Robert. *Colonial Desire: Hybridity in Theory, Culture, and Race*. London: Routledge, 1995.

Index

Hawthorne, Evelyn, 57

Henriques, Fernando, 41, 45–46, 52, 57, 61, 175n5

Henry, Patricia, 71–73, 79

Higman, Barry, 14

Hills of Hebron, The (Wynter), 41, 44–45, 49

Hills Were Joyful Together, The (Mais), 57

history making, 3–20, 153–54, 163n32, 163n34

HIV/AIDS, 18–19, 35, 63–89, 151, 154, 179n8, 180nn18–20, 180n23, 183n64, 185n70. *See also* contact investigators (CI's)

homophobia, 36, 43–44, 159n4, 181n27

homosexuality, 11, 19, 42–49, 55, 62–73, 79–85, 114–15, 128–50, 174n111

Hong, Grace, 22

Hotels Aid Law (1944), 47

Humphrey, Laud, 147

Hyde, Eugene, 107

Immigrant Marriage Divorce and Succession Law (1896), 27

Indigenous/Native people, v, 4, 10, 15–23, 39–42, 60, 82, 96, 101–6, 156–57

International Gay Association (IGA), 149–51

interracial unions, 25, 29

intimacy, 81, 86, 106–10, 113–15, 153–54, 173n94

Isaacs, Will O., 42–44, 61

Jacobs, Beth, 110

Jacobs, Len, 110

Jamaica: and Asians, 29–30; and Blackness, 26, 30, 60, 105; and class, 31–32, 35, 55–58, 61; and colonialism, 8, 25, 30, 60; and family, 33, 41, 60; history of, 9–13, 121; homophobia in, 11–12, 159n4; and homosexuality, 11, 64–66, 79, 85, 128, 132, 135–36, 145; and migration, 28, 170n50; post-independence, 113–14, 129; and queerness, 1–5, 9, 11–12, 17–18, 21–36, 52–55, 58, 155, 159n4; queer violence in, 2, 8, 11–12, 122, 153, 154, 165n63; sex work in, 34, 182n45; and women, 24, 29, 33, 53, 131, 170n50

Jamaica, Land of Wood and Water (Henriques), 41, 46

Jamaica AIDS Support (JAS), 70–71, 79, 82, 179n13

Jamaica Gaily News (JGN), 120–24, 128, 132–36, 140, 143, 150. *See also* Gay Freedom Movement (GFM)

Jamaica Labor Party (JLP), 34

Jamaica Psychological Association (JPA), 137–38

Jamaica's Birth Control League, 32

Jamaica's Family Planning Association, 32

Jamaica's Forum for All-Sexuals Lesbians and Gays (J-FLAG/Equality JA), 1, 36, 64, 179n8

Jamaica's National HIV/STD Helpline, 71–76, 79, 110

Jamaica's Sex Disqualification (Removal) Law of 1944, 30

Jamaica's Status of Children's Act (1976), 130

Jamaica Star (publication), 84, 87–88

Jay, Karla, 147

Jekyll, Walter, 171n75

Johnson, Hazel, 96, 117

Johnson, Mark, 160n10

Keeling, Kara, 78

Kempadoo, Kamala, 22, 64

Kerr, Madeline, 41, 51–52

Kingston and St. Andrew Corporation (KSAC), 140

kinship, 39–41, 49, 110–11, 114, 175n5. *See also* family

Kinship and Community in Carriacou (Smith), 41

Knight, Lena, 131

labor, 28, 151, 169n35

Lai, Walton Look, 169n40

Lakoff, George, 160n10

"Lavender Scare," 44

Lee, Easton, 108

lesbians, 45, 54, 111

Love in Action (Henriques), 41